D1474054

Tiggie

The Lure and Lore of Commercial Fishing in New England

by
Charles "Tiggie" Peluso
and
Sandy Macfarlane

iUniverse Star
New York Bloomington

Tiggie

The Lure and Lore of Commercial Fishing in New England

iUniverse Star
an iUniverse, Inc. imprint

iUniverse books may be ordered through booksellers or by contacting:

iUniverse
1663 Liberty Drive
Bloomington, IN 47403
www.iuniverse.com
1-800-Authors (1-800-288-4677)

First published by Rooftop Publishing 06/06/2007

Publisher: Kevin King
Senior Editor: Lesley Bolton
Cover Design: April Mostek
Book Design: Jessica Sheese
Production Manager: Brad Collins
Senior Publicist: Nick Obradovich

All images throughout the book, unless otherwise noted, are courtesy of Tiggie Peluso and family.

ISBN: 978-1-4401-0164-9 (pbk)
ISBN: 978-1-4401-1011-5 (ebk)

Library of Congress Control Number: 2007928457

Printed in the United States of America

Table of Contents

PART IV – INSHORE FISHING

PART V – FRESHWATER FISHING

Acknowledgments

Several people interviewed in the course of writing this book helped greatly in corroborating Tiggie's stories. Among them, I am grateful to Bill Amaru, Mike Anderson, Fred Bennett, Jay Lanzillo, Bob Luce, Gerry Quigley, Sherrill Smith, and Otto Zavatone. Other fishermen, including Will Case, Mark Palmer, Craig Poosikian, and Rolfe Scofield, added colorful anecdotes throughout the process, and I am grateful to them all. Paul Caruso from the Massachusetts Division of Marine Fisheries provided insights into the striped-bass fishery. I thank the late Henry Scammell for his technical expertise, keen eye, flair with words, and, along with Dwight Ritter, encouragement. My thanks also go to Gregg Rivara for his critical review of the manuscript. I also value key suggestions made during the writing process by Dinty Moore, Nancy Eichorn, Jeff McLaughlin, Robin Treese, and Brenda and Tony Halter. I am very grateful to Charlotte Noerdlinger for her editing skills and Rigmor Plesner for her proofreading and additional editing. To Tiggie's daughter, Louise, I offer my gratitude for suggestions throughout this process and for helping with logistics concerning her father. Finally, I am indebted to the waitresses at the Hole-in-One restaurant in Orleans, who had to put up with Tiggie and me for lengthy breakfast meetings.

Sandy Macfarlane

Dedications

This is for all of the fishermen who made fishing such an enjoyable experience—Al Hanson, Jackie Our, Red Moran, Fred Bennet, Bob Luce, Sten Carlson, John Christiansen, Bob Our, Gerry Quigley, and Cassabooboo, you live in my memories and my heart—and for my daughters, Louise and Elaine; my nephew, Charlie; my sons-in-law, Tom and Bill; my grandchildren, Brock, Patrick, Tim, Hannah, and Willy; and all of my friends...whom I love as much as I loved fishing all those years.

Tiggie Peluso

This book is for all the fishermen—offshore, inshore, shellfish, and freshwater fish—past, present, and hopefully future, who have helped shape the culture of a land surrounded by water. Their independent spirit, resilience, dedication to hard work, bravery, and Yankee ingenuity make them an impressive group. We are better for having them in our midst, and I am especially grateful to them for their insights about a difficult way of life and their chosen profession.

Sandy Macfarlane

Preface

Tiggie Peluso moved to Cape Cod after World War II to start a life as a fisherman. He had fished freshwater lakes and rivers with his father, who was a "gambler and gangster," as Tiggie said, when they lived in Chelsea, just outside Boston. Tiggie grew up in that world, but he chose to leave it for a very different life, one filled with hard work, uncertain income, danger, monotony, and the sea.

He began by fishing offshore for sea scallops and switched to longlining for cod, haddock, and halibut. Eventually, he moved inshore and fished for bay scallops and quahogs and finally for striped bass. Throughout his life, whenever he got a chance, he continued to fish the freshwater ponds as well. Anyone who knows Tiggie comments on his expert ability at all the types of fishing he has done, and most folks talk with a bit more than just a tinge of envy in their voices.

Fishermen are notoriously wary of people outside their industry. Trust among them comes hard and must be earned. They rarely speak to outsiders about what actually goes on aboard the boats.

Tiggie was different. While becoming expert in four separate types of fishing is unusual, he did something even more uncommon. He wanted to write down stories of his fishing experiences, but Tiggie had only an eighth-grade education. His spelling was lousy, and he couldn't get the stories on paper by himself. He met a woman, though, who said she was a secretary and who wanted to learn to snorkel. So he taught her to snorkel, and she listened to him recount stories of his first twenty years fishing commercially, which she transcribed into a rather large document. The deal seemed a bit lopsided, and if there were any other "services" traded, he remained coy about them. When asked why he wanted to write about this, he said he had met quite a few characters and whenever he had told some of the stories, people seemed interested. He thought it would be a good idea to write them down. He had no other explanation.

Tiggie kept the papers for forty years, never finding the right circumstances to do anything with them. Then, in 2003, when he was eighty years of age and thinking about his legacy, he had a chance meeting with me. I sat next to him at the local coffee shop and listened to stories of his exploits at sea. We had known each other for three decades, but I did not know he had fished offshore. I knew him as an inshore fisherman. After several breakfasts together, he asked me if I would help him write his stories, and I agreed.

I found Tiggie's stories to be fascinating and compelling on many levels. They were certainly well-spun yarns, full of colorful characters and difficult-to-believe events. On a deeper level, though, they provided a glimpse into the hearts and souls of men working in a world with which I had no personal experience. I had never fished commercially, and even though I lived and worked among commercial fishermen in the community, knew many fishermen personally, and had gone out fishing many times, I had not experienced the day-to-day life of trying to make a living at fishing. Tiggie's stories conjured images of the difficult business of fishing, but more importantly, they wove a tapestry of the Cape and her people and shed light on an important era when the fishing industry changed dramatically.

Cape Cod is a very different place now than it was in the middle of the twentieth century. Surrounded by water, Cape people were tied to the water around them more than they are today. These were traditional fishing and farming communities where the people understood the natural forces that shape the land. The population was far smaller, and poorer; making ends meet was a constant struggle. For working people today, that much has not changed—it is increasingly difficult to make a living on the Cape. The fishermen lived by a creed that the waters would provide as they always had; all you needed was the stamina to reap the bounty provided by the sea. That creed may no longer be true either.

Tiggie brought the people and the times he fished into focus as he described a culture of the Cape that is long gone. He did it his way and in his own words; in the process, he allowed us into his world and the world of those with whom he shared his love of fishing. It is his story and that of Cape Cod's fishing communities. Travel to any fishing port and watch the fishermen coming and going, bringing in their catch, and it is clear that parallels and similarities can be found in any New England port. Only the names of the people and places need be changed in order to gain a perspective.

Sandy Macfarlane

PART I – TIGGIE AND SANDY

Chapter One

"Go check Quanset today," Gardy, my boss and the town's shellfish constable, said to me on a clear, blustery December day. "I won't be able to get there until after the boats are in."

God, no, I thought to myself. I wasn't looking forward to that detail. I knew I could count on some ranting and raving from Tiggie and maybe from some of the other fishermen who landed their catch there, too.

Scallop season was in full swing. The season opened on November first and lasted through the winter, if there were enough scallops and if the bay didn't freeze over. It was the third week in December, and there were still about twenty guys fishing. These were the commercial fishermen who made their entire living from fishing, not the people who took a two-week vacation at the beginning of the season to get a little cash ahead.

Apprehensively, I drove my Clambulance to Quanset Pond, a small indentation of Pleasant Bay, the Cape's largest estuary. My nickname for the odd-looking but official town vehicle was emblazoned on the doors. It was a 1968 army-green stretch International Travelall, complete with lights left over from its former life as the town's ambulance. In big white letters, the side read, "Town of Orleans Clambulance," complete with a rendition of a clam instead of the more official town seal. People always smiled when they saw it around town. This day, I was not smiling.

A frigid northwest wind was howling, and the temperature hovered around thirty-six degrees, but the windchill dropped that number to well below freezing. Scalloping was a hard way to make a day's pay in this weather. Luckily for me, Quanset Pond was in the lee of the biting wind.

The first boat to come around the short barrier beach and enter the pond belonged to Tiggie Peluso. "Damn," I said under my breath. I mentally steeled myself for the verbal barrage I knew was coming. Tiggie motored slowly to the ramp, his skiff gliding smoothly until there was no more water under it. His fishing partner jumped out of the boat with an agility that belied the layers of clothing he was wearing, including stiff yellow waterproof foul-weather gear, and he pulled the boat a bit higher on the sandy mud adjacent to the asphalt launching ramp.

"Hi, Tig," I said as he shut the engine off and pulled it up out of the water. "How'd you do today?"

"They're comin' hard," he responded.

"You've been at it since opening day. They're not going to last forever."

"We haven't had a good year in a long time. Just my luck. Them bastards are coming over from Chatham to steal what little we have."

Here it comes, I thought. *He's winding up.* Commercial fishermen from Chatham, the next-door-neighbor town, couldn't legally fish in Orleans waters, even though the two towns shared the bay, because each town managed its own shellfish resources, and a commercial permit holder must be a resident of that town.

"They don't have any goddamn scallops over there, so they're coming over here to take ours at night," he continued.

I didn't answer. "Mind if I look at what you've got?" I asked instead.

"For Christ's sake, I got checked yesterday. Why are you always checking me? Why don't you spend your time getting those goddamn Chatham crooks?" he yelled at me.

"Is that a no?" I asked. Failure to display shellfish to a shellfish officer was an arrestable offense, and I had a police radio in my truck. He knew the rules. I knew he wouldn't refuse.

"Look at any goddamn thing you want to. I don't give a goddamn."

"These don't have a ring. They're seed, Tiggie. What the hell are you doing with all this seed? You know they have to have a raised ring on the shell to be legal," I said.

Gardy and I knew that the number of bona fide legal adult scallops in the bay with a raised ring on the shell was decreasing. We were seeing more and more large scallops with no ring being landed, and Gardy argued with the fishermen constantly about not taking them. The large, no-ring seed scallops were not legal to harvest because they were juveniles that had not spawned in their once-in-a-lifetime opportunity to procreate. Scallops are born in the summer, and after the first winter, just before they spawn, they put on a raised growth ring on the shell. But these juveniles were huge—and without a ring. Preventing the harvest of the large seed would be a hardship for the fishermen who counted on the crop to get them through the winter. Letting them be harvested was bad for future sets of scallops in the bay; if they were not allowed to spawn, there would be fewer new scallops. This was not good.

"Look at the f...ing size to the goddamn things," Tiggie bellowed.

I knew it wouldn't be long before the four-letter words would start.

"Size doesn't matter. You know that."

"What the f... are you talking about? These scallops won't make it all the way to next summer, let alone next November. They're too big. They're all goin' to f...in' die if we don't get them now."

"You don't know that."

"They never live when they're big like this."

"Course they won't live if you take them all first."

"Goddamn it!"

The decibel level was rising, and more boats were coming to the landing. The other fishermen heard what was going on between Tiggie and me. I walked over to another boat to check a batch of scallops. I saw only eight to ten bona fide adult scallops in a full bushel. I looked at another fisherman's catch and saw the same thing. Clearly, the lion's share of adults had already been taken, and the size of the seed was just too much of a temptation. All the fishermen were coming in with seed scallops, born probably very early the previous summer, judging by their size. But they didn't have a ring.

"What the f... are you going to do? Take all my goddamn scallops?" Tiggie screamed at me.

"Not today. You're all coming in with these. We'll be talking to the selectmen about this."

3

"You better not talk to the selectmen without telling us when that meetin's gonna take place. I'm f...ing gonna be there!"

"Guess I'll have something to look forward to then," I said as calmly as I could manage.

"Goddamn it. I should never have gotten you that f...ing job. Biologist, my ass. You don't know anything about this."

"I know these are large seed scallops, and I know if you take them now, they'll never get a chance to spawn." I had been on the job as shellfish biologist for "only" six years, and I had never fished commercially. Those two facts, plus being a woman and a college graduate, meant I knew nothing, according to Tiggie.

"You don't f...ing know any such thing. Prove that they're seed."

"We'll see," I answered. This was going to get ugly.

Twenty-five years later, I found myself sitting with Tiggie in the Hole-in-One, a local coffee shop, listening to him calmly tell stories about fishing and about his life on the water. We had known each other for thirty years, for half of which, Tiggie was a belligerent commercial fisherman, and I was a shellfish biologist and shellfish officer—we were on opposite sides of the law. Yet, there I was, asking him questions about fishing. I had retired from the town, and he had retired from fishing. Now we were equals.

Tiggie claims he got me the job as shellfish biologist, and he is probably right. I had been working at a grocery store where Tiggie came to buy meat, but I wanted to use my college degree in conservation of natural resources and work in that field somehow. I must have told him that. When the fishermen met with the selectmen, in 1974, suggesting that a biologist was needed to find out why one of the bays was no longer filled with quahogs (hard clams), I attended the meeting.

Tiggie piped up and said, "There's a biologist sitting right there in the back of the room. Why don't we hire her?"

The next thing I knew, I was working for the town part-time, a job that led to a full-time position. I'm not sure anyone in the room realized it, but the request that biological principles be added to the traditional methods of shellfish management meant the rules of the shellfish management game were going to change dramatically, and I was going to be a key player in those changes.

I hadn't seen much of Tiggie in more than a decade. Beginning in the spring of 2003, though, I kept running into him at the coffee shop. Both of us knew that our past relationship had not exactly been one of mutual adulation—he ranted at my attempts to enforce shellfish regulations and manage shellfish resources for the good of the town, rather than to line the pockets of commercial shellfishermen exclusively, and my actions curbed his ability to earn money from those resources.

We were both at the Hole-in-One restaurant when someone asked me for a copy of a book I had just published, *Rowing Forward, Looking Back: Shellfish and the Tides of Change at the Elbow of Cape Cod*. It is a book I like to call a clam's-eye view of Mother Nature versus human nature. It describes what happens to shellfish and the bays where shellfish live when a small coastal community is bombarded by development pressure. The book is set in Orleans, Massachusetts, where I worked for over a quarter century, beginning as Massachusetts' first shellfish biologist and later becoming the town's first conservation administrator.

Tiggie sat across the U-shaped counter and from about twenty feet away, said in a voice loud enough for everyone seated at the counter to hear, "What book?"

"My book," I answered.

"You wrote a book?" he growled.

"Yes," I said.

"Am I in it?" he asked.

"No," I said, "and you should be goddamn thankful you're not," a remark that got a laugh from most of the men sitting at the counter.

"Boy, she's got your number, Tig," I heard someone say.

"Are you going to give me a copy?" he asked.

I told him no and said he could buy one. He feigned a hurt expression, and I relented, going out to my car to get a book for him with a proper inscription. He thanked me, but I wondered if he would ever actually read it.

A few days later, I was back at the same coffee shop, and there was nowhere to sit except the empty stool at the counter next to Tiggie. I took a deep breath and said to myself, *Why not?* and sat down. We'd buried whatever hatchet there was between us years ago. Tiggie flashed

5

his mostly toothless grin, seeming pleased that I had sat next to him, and started telling me stories.

When I worked for the Shellfish Department, the only way Tiggie communicated with me was by bellowing at me; at the coffee shop, his age had caught up with him, and he had mellowed, talking civilly to me in tone and word choice. Tiggie told me a few things about fishing offshore, sharing his fascinating stories, and I realized that he was telling me about fishing in an important era in the Northeast fishing industry, when the men fished by the seat of their pants, using skills learned on the water without the benefit of electronic gadgetry so prominent on today's fishing boats.

A reporter friend of mine asked me to write an article about Tiggie for the *Cape Cod Times*, coinciding with his eightieth birthday. When I asked Tiggie's permission to send the article to the newspaper, he said, "I don't give a goddamn what you do." It was a typical Tiggie reaction.

But then, his expression softened, and he asked, "Are they going to give you something for it?"

"Yes," I responded.

"Go ahead then," he said gently.

He was delighted with the article and the attention it garnered. He asked everyone he saw if they had seen the article and if they had, he'd ask, "Wasn't it great?" The owners of the Hole-in-One cut out the picture of him and the headline, framed it, and displayed it prominently on the fireplace mantle in the restaurant.

One day, Tiggie said, "Now, I have a question to ask you." I nodded. "Will you help me write my stories?"

Without any hesitation, I said, "Sure." I knew instinctively from what I had heard already that Tiggie's stories provided a valuable historical record of an era long gone now, most of whose practitioners were gone; time was running short to capture it. When he talked to me, he was describing a way of life that was an integral part of Cape Cod, when people were connected to the sea around them. It was a time before tourists and second-home buyers staked their claim, before grid-locked traffic, before the conversion of nearly every acre of woods to some form of development, and before saltwater fishing became a source of pleasure, not necessarily a source of food, and definitely not a livelihood.

His stories were compelling, and I had not heard of any publication that chronicled the type of fishing that he was describing to me. He told me much later that he was shocked that I had agreed to the project, but he kept his poker face at the time.

He said I made his life miserable when I worked for the town. Now the tables were turned. If I wanted to get his story, I'd have to put up with him, and first thing in the morning, no less. Before long, meeting him for breakfast became a regular occurrence. Tiggie and I sat together, and I knew regulars at the counter were speculating on what was going on between Tiggie and me. A couple of days sitting together was one thing, but this was going on every single day. It was an odd coupling any way you looked at it. But I was hooked. Each day, I left him and rushed home, fired up the computer, and typed in some key words to bring the stories back to my mind.

Finally, John, a coffee-shop friend of Tiggie's, worked up the courage to ask what was going on. It was a comment more than a question, but Tiggie sort of straightened himself up in the chair, puffed up a bit, and said, "She's writing a book about me."

"You are?" John asked somewhat incredulously, looking at me.

"Did you read that article in the paper?" Tiggie asked.

"Yeah. That was pretty good," he answered.

"She wrote that. And she agreed to write my stories."

"I can't wait to read that when it comes out," John responded. "What are you doing about the language?" he asked me.

"He's mellowed from the old days," I responded as if Tiggie weren't sitting right there.

"You're a saint to put up with him every day," John said to me.

"I'm beginning to agree with you," I said smiling.

That was it. The jig was up. Now everyone knew why we were sitting together every day. *Too bad*, I thought. It was more fun to have the speculation and gossip going on, making me chuckle when I imagined the conversations taking place. Tiggie probably felt proud and honored that I'd actually sit with him, and knowing him, he probably felt younger than his age, thinking he still had what it took to snag a much younger woman. I smiled at the thought.

I wondered what it was that had brought us together as collaborators after so many years of butting heads with one another. Based on our history, I considered it an ironically odd twist of fate. I was fascinated to learn that this person I had known for thirty years, I really didn't know at all. I wanted to know more.

Chapter Two
The Treasure Trove

One day, Tiggie surprised me even more. He started the conversation about swimming, but there was much more to this day than swimming.

"I was swimming at Cliff Pond [Nickerson State Park in Brewster] one day, and I felt someone watching me. Did you ever have that feeling?"

"Yeah," I said.

"I swam for a while, and when I came out of the water, I still couldn't see anyone. I came back a few days later and felt the same thing. I finally saw who it was. There was this woman watching me. Finally, she talked to me. She said she loved watching me swim, because it seemed so effortless, and she wanted me to teach her how to snorkel. She wanted more than that, but that's what she said she wanted. She said she was a secretary. This was twenty years after I started fishing [in 1946]. A lot of things happened to me while I was fishing, and I met a lot of characters. I thought it would be interesting to write it all down, but with my lousy spelling, I knew I couldn't do it. So, we made a deal. I'd teach her to snorkel if she'd type stories for me that I dictated to her. I can't even remember her name now. I didn't want to get involved with her since I was living with someone else at the time, but we met at the lake for a long time. I told her stories, and she took it all down in shorthand, and I taught her to snorkel. Then she typed it up for me. I don't know where that is, but I'll look for it. You might find it interesting."

"I hope you find it. I'd like to read it," I said.

A few days later, Tiggie ambled into the Hole (Hole-in-One is much too long a name for the locals, so it gets shortened when we talk about the place) while I was reading the paper and sat down opposite me. There was no preliminary greeting—he just put a manila envelope on the table and said, "These are the stories the woman typed for me. Don't lose it. It's my only copy, and Louise will kill me if I lose this."

"Thank you. I'll make sure to take very good care of it."

I don't know what we talked about that day, but I couldn't wait to get home and take a look at the material Tiggie presented to me. I'm not sure what I was expecting, but he had already told me about his educational background that ended in the eighth grade. The language he used most of the time, and especially on the shore, was loaded with profanity, so I assumed the manuscript would be as well. My conversations with him, though, were not only civilized, but his working vocabulary was much more sophisticated than one might expect. The language he used had been toned down to fairly common usage and was hardly brackish, let alone salty. I wondered which side of this man would show up on the pages—the gruff, profane fisherman I knew on the shore, or the calm, articulate man I was getting to know. I was anxious to get into the manuscript and find out.

I went home and started reading, and what struck me first was the language. The stories didn't sound like a fisherman on the docks telling another fisherman of his exploits, with expletives peppered throughout. These were told just as Tiggie had been telling me stories personally, with an extensive vocabulary and good grammar.

Second were the stories themselves. Told in a chronological and sensible order, they were amazing to me.

By the time I finished reading the manuscript, over 225 pages later, I realized that Tiggie had handed me a treasure trove. The document in my hand was an invaluable glimpse into the world of commercial fishing seldom seen by those not in that world. Fishermen generally don't talk to landlubbers about what goes on offshore. I was privy to a treatise on the methods of fishing: the gear, the boats, and the how-to, but it was much, much more than that.

It was also the story of men interacting with each other and with the natural elements, the camaraderie among men who owed their lives to one another, whose friendships and working relationships were strained by working in close quarters under vexing conditions and under the constant threat of danger. It was the story of how they dealt with one another on a daily basis, how egos and fear played on one another, how quick thinking and quick action could mean the difference between a good trip and tragedy, or really between life and death and how one false move could mean disaster.

It was the story of how these fishermen left port in the middle of the night, reaching the fishing grounds forty or so miles away, arriving by daylight to set the gear. They found those fishing grounds so far from land with merely a compass, a watch, and a lead line. It was the story of the fish, the fishing pressure, and the temptations where the impulse was to harvest at least as much from the common resource as your rival fisherman and hopefully more than he. It was the story of the animosity between the fishermen and the buyers and the fishermen's constant feeling that they were being cheated when they sold their catch. It was the story of less-than-perfect relationships with women, an ever-present theme in thought and action, and it was much, much more.

Tiggie has said a lot of things about fishing, and many things have been said about Tiggie, the fisherman, throughout his life. A local author, Sherrill Smith, wrote, "He lives to fish and fishes to live, and he is no more complicated than that." But Tiggie's own words, "I learned to think like a fish," say it all.

PART II – THE EARLY YEARS

Chapter Three
Families and "Families"

Tiggie hadn't told me much about his early life, and I was curious.

"Where did you grow up?" I asked.

"In Chelsea." Chelsea is a city adjacent to Boston. "Did I ever tell you about my father?"

"No."

"Pa was a gangster and a gambler. He owned a few pool halls in Chelsea and was pretty high up in the pecking order of the 'family.' He didn't do the dirty work himself, though—he got someone else to do it."

"He was a lieutenant, not an enforcer? Is that how it worked?" I asked.

"Yeah, I guess so. I don't think he broke the knee caps or did any killing himself, but he was pretty high up in the business. He didn't talk about it, so I really don't know. Everybody was in it somehow back then. We were living in sort of a Little Italy—Chelsea, Revere, Malden—they were all part of it. Pa told me about one time when one of his pool halls was robbed.

"There was a lot of money there that night—the pool hall was a bookie joint, too, I guess. Anyway, he had a guy working for him who wore a very distinctive—is that a good word?"

"Very good."

"...distinctive ring that he wore on his pinky finger—gold with a big stone. These guys came in all wearing masks over their faces to rob the place. There was a big take that night, and they got away with the money, but Pa noticed the ring on one of the guys, so he knew who it was and told his friends not to worry—he'd get the money back. The next day, the guy came to work acting like nothing had happened. Pa told him about the robbery and said to the guy that he knew it was him. The guy said it wasn't, that he had nothing to do with it, but Pa told him he had seen the ring and that he'd better tell him where the money was. Pa said he'd find out anyway and that he was a dead man. He got the money back, and a couple of days later, the guy disappeared and was never seen again.

"Pa was a good guy in my eyes, though. He was the one who taught me how to fish. We fished for trout and perch up on the North Shore. He used to take me to the Ipswich or Andover Rivers."

"Someone told me once that you did a lot of freshwater fishing, too," I said. "I know you used to get a lot of stuff at the shop." We used to own a small tackle shop in town called MacSquids, no longer in existence, where we sold bait and all sorts of fishing and hunting gear. Tiggie was a regular customer. "What was it like fishing with your father?" I asked. "Did he talk much?"

"No, he didn't talk much on those trips, but I liked going with him anyway. I watched what he did and learned. Pretty soon, I was catching lots of fish, and we needed the fish to eat. Gambling didn't always put food on the table. But I liked going with him, and I knew I liked to fish. Actually, now that I think about it, he really taught me a lot about life in a way."

"What about your mother? What was she like?" I asked.

"She had six kids to raise. I had five sisters. Even though Pa was a gambler, there wasn't much money. Ma had to make do. Ma always wanted us to have balanced meals, including vegetables, and sometimes those included hot dogs and dandelions. God, I hated those things. Can you imagine? Hot dogs and dandelions. Every time I see them, I still want to puke."

"What did you do as a kid?"

"Well, the neighborhood was full of gangs. Everyone belonged to a gang—you sort of had to. The only place that was safe was on the front stoop. There was more or less an unwritten law that no one could touch you if you were on the front stoop. So a lot of things that happened were because of the gangs. But we did other things, too. A bunch of us went fishing for smelt. They were worth fifty cents a pound, so I got to help Ma out by selling them."

"It seems you started fishing commercially pretty young."

"Yeah, I guess I did. I also sold coal."

"How did you do that?" I asked.

"I remember the train went by near the house, too. There were open cars loaded up with coal, and we used to jump on the train and climb up on top of the coal, kicking pieces off. Then we'd go back and pick up the pieces. Some we used ourselves, and some we sold. Every little bit helped.

"Did I tell you that we lived in Chelsea rent-free for a while?" Tiggie continued.

"No. How did you pull that off?" I answered.

"Pa won the rent in a poker game with the guy who owned the building. I think it was for about three years. That was a lot of money back then to win."

"Sounds like it," I said.

"But he won a cottage in Foxboro, too," Tiggie added, "on a lake."

"In a poker game?" I asked flabbergasted.

"Yeah," he answered. "We went there every summer for years. There was a dock out on the lake, and I could just sit there and catch fish for dinner. Fishing a lake was different from fishing the rivers, but I got so I could sit on a dock and catch about thirty catfish (or hornpout) and get them cleaned for dinner. I learned, sitting there on the dock, that there was a knack even to fishing for catfish, and I began to be curious about all types of fish and where they lived. That's also where I learned to swim and dive."

"What do you mean?" I asked.

"I became an expert swimmer and diver. Not underwater dive, platform dive. I'd dive from trees or anything else high. There was a public pool with a high board near the cottage that I used. We all learned to swim there at the lake. One of my sisters went on to swim professionally in…What do they call it when they all do the same thing in the water?"

"Synchronized swimming?"

"Yeah. That's it. They wanted me, too, for diving, but I didn't want to do it. When I was in the service, my sisters had a lottery to see who would get my room if I died over there."

"Nice!"

"My sister Nina won, but my dog wouldn't let her get near my room. Nina left the house and went to New Zealand to join a water follies show. She probably spent a third of her life traveling around New Zealand and Australia. I learned to swim long distances. I also learned to control my breath so that I could stay underwater for a really long time. And I learned how to snorkel so I could watch fish."

Tiggie continued his reverie. "I had rheumatic fever as a boy and had to stay out of school for a long time—a couple of years—and had to stay in bed most of that time."

"Did you have to stay back a year?"

"It may have been more than that—I don't remember. I didn't like school anyway, but staying home put me so far behind that I never really caught up and left school after the eighth grade. I learned to read, but I never could spell worth a damn. I felt like a dummy around other people sometimes, but I read a lot and learned things pretty easily, so I was able to get by."

"By the way, how did you get the name 'Tiggie'?" I asked.

"I've thought about that a lot lately, and I really don't have any idea. I've always been known as Tiggie for as long as I can remember."

"Was it someone in your family who named you that?"

"I guess so. I've always been Tiggie."

"Was your father named Charles, too?"

"Yeah. Maybe that's why they called me something different, but I'll be goddamned if I know where it came from."

Chapter Four
Power Struggles

Tiggie was sitting at the counter when I arrived the next day, and there was an empty seat, so I purposely sat with him, and he continued with the stories.

"Did I tell you about the tomatoes?"

"Tomatoes? No."

"I grew up in a tough 'Little Italy' neighborhood in Chelsea, where gangs were everywhere."

"You told me that yesterday."

"Anyway, to survive, you had to belong to a gang. Each neighborhood had their own group, and they prowled the streets looking for new kids to harass. The only safe place was on the front stoop—there was an unwritten law that no one could touch you if you were on the front stoop.

"I was a rugged but small kid, and people always thought they could take me, but I was smart, too. One day, the local gang leader said to me, 'Tiggie, there's a field nearby where the guy grows tomatoes, big, juicy tomatoes. The farmer said we could go pick them if we did something for him. He wants the big rock in the middle of the field gone. You go get that rock out of there, or I'll make your life miserable.' I really had no choice—I had to remove that huge rock from the field. But how?

"I was about nine or ten at the time, didn't have any friends who could drive, so a truck was out of the question, and for a few days, I couldn't figure out how I was going to move that big rock. It was about ten feet across, and I was just a kid. I sat on the stoop trying to figure it out.

"Finally, an idea came to me. I got a bunch of the younger kids together and told them they had to help me. Since I was older, they had no choice. We all went over to the field, bringing shovels with us. For several days, we worked in that field. Finally, we all got on one side of the rock and pushed with all our might, and the rock moved. We had dug a hole next to the rock big enough for it to fall into, and when we moved it, it rolled into the huge hole. Mission accomplished.

"I guess I passed the 'test,' and as a bonus, we had the most delicious tomatoes all summer long."

"That was pretty clever," I said. "Sounds like the beginning of a very practical mind."

"I figured out a lot of things pretty easily.

"Another time, there was this gang leader, Rocky. Rocky heard what I had done with the rock and knew I had actually done the job, and he started getting nervous that I was a threat to his authority. He had been in 'juvie' reform school many times, and each time he got out, he was meaner than when he went in.

"One day, he found me on a train trestle and threatened me with a knife, saying he was going to get me. I knew he was out to kill me. I tried to keep him talking while my mind was racing, trying to figure out how I was going to get off that train trestle alive. He started to come at me, and I picked up a rock and threw it as hard as I could. My aim was right on target—I had hit him in the head—and he fell into the river, and the river took him down a ways. The tide was going out. I thought I had killed him and figured I could look forward to reform school myself.

"I kept looking down the river and couldn't believe what I saw. The kid was alive. He dragged himself to shore and stumbled a bit, but then he started coming my way again. Now I knew I was a dead duck. If he caught up to me, the rock trick worked once, but I didn't think it would work again. I was shaking but tried to look calm on the outside. But instead of lunging for me, he put his knife away, came up, and put his arm around me and said no one had stood up to him before like I had, and from then on, I was okay and could go anywhere I wanted—I would always be protected—and I was.

"I guess I came by the survival instincts naturally."

"Sounds like they served you well," I said.

"Yeah, I guess they did."

PART III – OFFSHORE

Chapter Five
First Boat

For the remainder of this book, when the stories from Tiggie's manuscript appear, they are in Tiggie's words. They will be in a different typeface to distinguish them from my editorial comments and the breakfast conversations in the restaurant.

MY FIRST BOAT

After coming out of the Army in 1946, I had no idea what I wanted to do for my line of work. I had been a civilian meat cutter, and in the Army, I had been a cook. After cooking for 150 men for three years, I decided there must be something better than this, although I didn't have the foggiest notion of what that might be. It was my sister's husband who would lead me into commercial fishing.

John was a down Mainer, six feet three inches tall with a great big line of bull about the sea. About the most that he knew about fishing was what he had gathered from a few trips he had taken on his father's lobster boat. But he convinced me that I should buy a boat and that we should go fishing together. I had a great love for sport fishing, and the challenge of trying to make a living from fishing intrigued me though it had never entered my mind to consider it as an occupation. Under his direction and advice, we set out to find a boat suitable for my pocketbook, that had the grand sum of $1,700 from Army pay and crap game winnings saved religiously by my mother when I sent them home. That was quite a fortune to amass in three years when you were paid $96 a month. My excitement and anxiety was raised to a fevered pitch anticipating the great boat that we were going to procure, though I could have been sold a garbage scow and wouldn't have known the difference between it and a fishing boat. The next several weeks were spent all around the harbor of Boston looking over the various pieces of junk.

Under John's guidance, I managed to buy a first-class slob called the *Ace*. To me, it looked like the *Queen Mary*, all twenty-eight feet of it. It was lying next to the dock, and the owner started the motor. It sounded good to me, although I did not know much about motors. I was so excited the day I bought the boat that I didn't get any sleep at all that night.

The next day, John said that to go fishing you had to have bait. I said, "That makes sense, but what do we get for bait and where do we get it?" With all his knowledge about fishing, he came up with various suggestions, such as buying it or digging for clams. The digging for clams sounded fine, that is until I found out the rigmarole that it entailed.

After obtaining a special license from the state allowing me to dig clams in a polluted area of Winthrop, there came the rude awakening. My brother-in-law had a very bad back which left all the digging to me. I continued digging clams with my back rebelling at every dig. I began to think that maybe this clam digging for bait wasn't such a hot idea.

That afternoon, John and I took the boat for her maiden voyage out to Graves Light. I was full of excitement and anticipation—until I started to feel the first of the swells and chops as we left the harbor. When I looked into the cabin, I saw various containers and articles floating in about six inches of water. It didn't seem quite right to me, and I promptly called it to John's attention. I can still see the queer look on his face as he said, "I think we're sinking."

We promptly turned the boat around or "about" as I would say now after years on the sea. He handed me a guinea pump the likes of which I had never seen before. I pumped like crazy all the way back to the dock. John suggested that the boat probably wasn't as good as he had thought at first. For most of three days, I slept and ate and pumped aboard that tub to keep it from sinking, but it was apparent that something had to be done very soon as my arms were rapidly losing strength.

One of the guys suggested that I haul the boat out on a railway. Being green about water and nautical matters, I thought he was pulling my leg. The only association I had with railways was trains. What the hell did a boat have to do with railways? I told him I didn't like his ribbing me, but I could see that he was in dead earnest.

He proceeded to explain that when someone talked of railways in a boatyard, it was just a set of tracks that protruded down into the water. It had a type of cradle arrangement that you drove the boat into. The winch would then haul you up high and dry, where the boatyard workers made whatever repairs were required.

John and I set out to find a boatyard that would haul us out. At last, we found the sympathetic ear of a yard foreman in Ellis's boatyard in East Boston. He informed me of what the rates would be for hauling my boat out, and we brought the boat around. The boat was hauled into the cradle and up the railway and put to the side so we could work on it.

I noticed dozens of various types of fishing boats, some that made my boat look pretty insignificant, but one boat in particular caught my eye. It was a big boat about forty-five feet long. There were several people working on it, scraping, painting, etc. One man working on the boat, a short, fat fellow by the name of Dan Ballou, said to us, "Boys, the best thing that you can do with that tub of yours is leave it right where it is, or you'll get drowned in it." He was very friendly; you couldn't help but like him, and we became fast friends. We asked him what kind of fishing he did on the boat he was working on. He told us it was a hand-line boat and that he was the owner and skipper. We said that we wanted to do a little trawling and hand lining ourselves. He said he was sorry that he didn't know it a few days before as he had just hired the last two men that he would need. Then he said, "Hey, fellows, I have a good idea. There are a couple of towns on Cape Cod where they need men for that type of fishing. You might be able to get jobs there and learn a little bit about the business. Perhaps the experience would do you a lot of good."

Chapter Six
Getting to Cape Cod

I'd lived in Massachusetts all my life but had never been on Cape Cod. The idea was intriguing.

Dan Ballou started to tell me of these two ports, Harwichport and Chatham, from which small-boat fishing was conducted. "Point them out to me, Dan," I said. Naturally, like all fishermen, I had several maps and charts that I used to carry with me constantly, rolled up neatly, convincing myself that I could understand them. But before Dan could point out the ports, some wise guy standing behind me reached over my shoulder with a stick and poked two holes through my nice, new, beautiful chart where Chatham and Harwichport were, which got me pretty steamed.

After the dust settled, two quiet fellows, who had been in the background, were left. They walked over and introduced themselves as Benny and Warren O'Neil. They told us that they had overheard some of the conversation and that they would like to go to the Cape with us if we went. They pointed out a boat saying it was theirs. They suggested that we go down in their boat, which was bigger than my little tub, and, if it was feasible, fish with it or get jobs on other boats. We agreed and made plans.

About a week later, I was relaxing on the deck of the O'Neil brothers' boat going through the Cape Cod Canal, feeling very elated and looking forward to our new venture. I had never been through the canal, and it was fascinating watching the swirls of water that formed in the hard current.

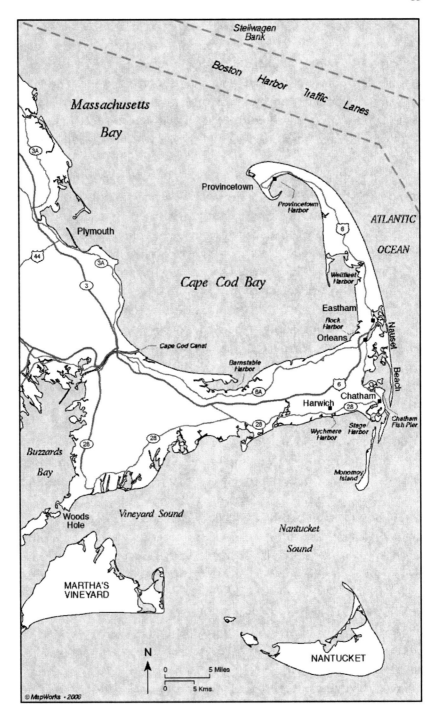

Cape Cod and Fishing Ports

I guess I dozed off for a few minutes, because all at once, I awoke to a very chilling sensation. I looked about me, and I couldn't see a thing. We were in the middle of thick, thick fog; it was my first experience with fog while on a boat. We had proceeded into Buzzards Bay. Buzzards Bay and Nantucket Sound are famous for their fog. John did very well to get us through Buzzards Bay, Woods Hole, and into Nantucket Sound, but I think from then on, it was just dumb luck that we came anywhere near Harwichport.

We arrived in the very beautiful Wychmere Harbor late in the afternoon. At one time, the harbor was a small, land-locked lake, and they dredged an entrance to it from the sea. The first thing you see as you come into the harbor is the famous Snow Inn, a collection of old and new Cape-Cod-type buildings, with white trimming and no paint on the shingles. But the dock was what got my eye. There were eighteen beautiful fishing boats tied up there.

Standing at the head of the dock was one of the largest men I think I had ever seen. He was about six feet four inches, close to four hundred pounds, and attired in pink shorts and an Aussie campaign hat. He bellowed out to us and said that we could tie up at his dock. John swung the boat in there, and we tied up. Then this huge man jumped aboard and introduced himself as Frank Thompson, owner of the dock and the inn. He asked us what our business was there. We gave him a rough synopsis of our plans, and he informed us that he would help us in any way he could. He told us that he wasn't a fish buyer; he just packed the fish in boxes and sold the boxes of fish. He said that a man who would buy fish from us was a guy by the name of Bishop.

All the while, all the boat skippers and crewmen along the dock were giving us close scrutiny, which was a right reserved for experienced fishermen. Looking back on it years later, I can recall doing it myself to all newcomers, wondering how many would make the grade and how many would flop. Actually, if you did make the grade, if you could call it that, the best you could hope to do was $4,000 to $7,000 a year. That was for top fishermen, so you can imagine what the flops made. There's a saying in the fish industry, "You don't make enough to get a good living out of it, but too much to go on relief."

We finally stepped off the boat onto the dock. Most of the men seemed friendly. They didn't look as if they were going to bite, so we kind of mingled and got acquainted. As we shook hands all around, we found out that fishing had been very poor and that there were very few sites available.

The next morning, about nine o'clock, somebody was pounding on the bulkhead and hollering, "Hello, anybody awake there yet?"

John hollered, "Come on down to the forecastle."

A middle-aged, pleasant-looking man appeared and introduced himself as Cal Baker. He informed us that he had heard up at the dock that we were looking for a fishing site. We jumped to our feet assuring him that we were, asking him, "Which boat do you own?"

He said that the big dragger down at the end of the dock was his. One of the O'Neil boys inquired, "What type of fishing do you do in that?"

He said, "She is a sea scalloper."

"What the hell is a sea scalloper? I've never heard of such a thing," I said.

Cal replied, "It's a type of shellfish. Better still, walk down the dock and come aboard the *Flavia*, and I'll give you a rough idea of how this works." We went aboard.

When Tiggie arrived on Cape Cod in 1946, the Cape had very little in the way of active employment. There were some active farms, and there was fishing. Stores servicing the population were often family affairs going back generations. Men who had left the Cape for the war came back at that time, too, and they were all competing for scant employment opportunities. Tourism, as we know it today, had not begun, except for some wealthy families that visited the Cape in the summer. The Cape was a hard and harsh place. But fishing had been a constant since the land had been settled. Sea scalloping seemed as good as anything else since he was a novice commercial fisherman.

Chapter Seven
First Trip

"Did I ever tell you about fishing with Earl Youngren, Al's father?" Tiggie asked one morning. I didn't know the Youngrens personally but had heard stories about both Al and his father, Earl, for years.

"You fished with Earl? For quahogs in Cape Cod Bay?" I asked.

"No. We went sea scalloping out of Harwich."

"That must have been interesting," I said. "I heard that he was not someone you wanted to cross."

"Earl was one tough son of a bitch. It was a hell of an introduction to fishing, and he's the main reason I never stuck with scalloping."

THE FIRST FISHING TRIP

Cal introduced us to the skipper, who was his brother-in-law, Earl Youngren. Earl, who was a short man of approximately five feet six inches and weighed 150 pounds, had about a twenty-two-inch waist and about a forty-inch chest. But his face was the thing that impressed me the most. It was deeply lined; the eyes had deep crow's feet, and his face was burned a leathery brown. He looked as if he hadn't been off a boat or the water for years. We shook hands all around. He had a grip like a vise and dozens of cuts on his fingers. He was about the most rugged man I had encountered in my life.

He asked us if we had we done any fishing or had any sea experience whatsoever. John and Benny O'Neil had been in the Navy, and Warren and I had been in the Army. He said, "I guess that's about as green as anybody can be." He haggled with his brother-in-law for a few minutes and told him he didn't think that it was possible to break in four green men at one time. They argued a little more, and Cal said he would try to talk another experienced scalloper named Coulson into going along.

Most of that first day was spent in final preparations—procuring supplies, taking on ice, water, and numerous other things needed for scalloping. We were going to steam out the next morning at four o'clock. That night, we moved our oil cloths (rain gear—now called oil skins) and miscellaneous gear aboard the *Flavia*. At last, we were off. That was the last we saw of Harwichport for three weeks.

It was about daylight when we got on the fishing grounds. Earl Youngren stopped the boat and took an object from the pilothouse. It was a small tub, or keg, cut in half, that held a long piece of rope that Earl called a sounding line. At various intervals on the line, he had different knots, indicating the depth of the water. On the end of the line was a piece of lead weight of approximately twelve pounds, shaped like an ice-cream cone. The wide part was concave, and in it, he inserted a handful of heavy grease. Naturally, we were all eyes trying to figure out what he was going to do with this odd-looking rig. The grease had us completely baffled. He looked into our inquiring eyes and said, "Just watch, boys." He threw the lead overboard, and the line paid out at a rapid pace, finally coming to a stop at twenty-one fathoms. A fathom is six feet of depth. He said, "The depth is what I'm looking for. I hope the type of bottom is what I want." Then it started to dawn on us what the reason for the grease was—to pick up an impression of the bottom.

This particular time, he was looking for black stones about the size of marbles. One of the boys hauled the line back and handed it to the skipper, who looked at it and said, "Just what I want." There were the black stones.

He said, "Another thing I'm going to tell you fellows, and I'm only going to say it once. If anyone hauls back this sounding lead and looks at it before they hand it to me, they're going overboard."

After Earl set us straight on the formalities of the sounding bit, we got ready to commence fishing. The scallop rakes (drags) on the *Flavia* were approximately eleven feet wide and weighed about three hundred pounds each. The rake was dragged on the bottom and hauled in by a winch, and the contents were dumped on the deck. The next step was called culling. You had wire bushel baskets you put the good scallops in, and all the other stuff was thrown overboard. There was quite an array—skates, stones, goosefish, starfish, various types of sponges, and numerous other plants not known to me at the time.

Earl took a look at the first contents and said, "We are getting a little too much Norwegian gravel."

"What the hell is Norwegian gravel?" I asked. "There isn't a stone smaller than five pounds in the whole lot."

He looked at me with a sly grin on his face and said, "Norwegian gravel is considered any stone that you can pick up with one hand and throw overboard." Then we got into scallops, and they came fast and furious. We were getting approximately ten to fifteen bushels every twenty minutes.

This was all well and fine; there was only one trouble—every one of them had to be shucked. To shuck a scallop, you had a knife you held in the palm of your hand, and you reached in with the knife, cut the muscle that held the two shells together from the top shell, and pried the top shell loose. You threw that overboard, and then you scooped the guts of the scallop out, which you also fired overboard. On the bottom shell, all that was left was the big muscle, or eye of the scallop, which was the only edible part. You cut that loose and threw it into a container and threw the bottom shell overboard. This may sound like a simple task, and it was, if you had only a hundred scallops or so to open. But when you multiplied it by thousands, after eight hours or so, what usually happened was you cut the top shell off and threw it in the container along with the scallop guts while the eye went overboard, and every once in a while, a knife went overboard, too.

The first day, we lost fourteen scallop knives overboard. It was getting so I was afraid to go into the pilothouse asking Earl for another knife. The first two or three times, he looked at me in a rather funny way and asked me if I was eating the goddamned things. He very rarely spoke without swearing, but I found out later that he was not alone there. The last time I asked him for a knife that day, he called me about eight four-letter words in a row.

When I first met Earl, I was a little curious about the slits and cuts on his hands, but when the day was out, I knew what had caused them, and I had about fifty of my own. If you brought your hand up against the shell, it would cut right through the rubber glove. The first time you cut yourself, it was not too bad, but when you cut yourself repeatedly in the same spot, it defied description. We struggled through the day—I thought it would never end.

Earl said, "We'll anchor for the night." Then he said, "Who's a good cook aboard this tub?"

I didn't feel like eating, let alone preparing a meal for everyone else, but the job fell to me. All I wanted to do was hit the bunk.

Earl pointed one of his big paws at me and said, "I guess you're elected, Tiggie."

"What do you want for supper, boys?" I asked.

Earl said, "Don't ask them; ask me. I'm the skipper, and I want fried scallops."

During the day, we had discovered that raw scallops were quite a delicacy, and we had been eating them all day long. The last thing I wanted to eat or cook for supper was fried scallops. But since I was in such disgrace in the eyes of the skipper for losing so many knives overboard, I couldn't argue. While I was getting supper, the boys cleaned the boat up, put the scallop catch on ice in the hold, and anchored the boat for the night. After chow, everybody quickly went to sleep. It seemed that the night was only fifteen minutes long—Earl was hollering for everybody to hit the deck so soon.

In the process of putting on my socks and boots, I noticed that my hands were swollen rather badly. I could just barely stand the pain. I didn't believe it would be possible to get through the day in the shape they were in. I think in the back of my mind, I had realized that this particular type of fishing was not for me.

The day wasn't too long at that, because we lost all the knives including the galley knives and any other utensils that could possibly be used to open scallops. The skipper was wild; four-letter words emanating from him in rapid succession. He said in all his days at sea he had never had to go back to port because he had used up all the scalloping knives—machinery breakdown, low on fuel, bad leaks, but never anything as ridiculous as this. So we sailed into Provincetown. This was my first view of Provincetown. There were lots of fishermen in Provincetown, but after a few days, I discovered there were more fishy men than fishermen there.

After three weeks of scalloping with Earl, I told him that I was going back to Harwichport to try line trawling. Before I went, though, I wanted to know why he was so hard on me, or so it seemed, compared to the way he treated the other fellows. Earl said, "Because the other guys aren't even worth hollering at, and they would never make fishermen anyway. But there was a chance for you."

And so I went back to Harwichport.

As an aside, the sixth man of our crew, Wally Coulson, was an excellent fisherman and knew his job well. A few years after I fished with him, he was out fishing when one of the scallop drags hit him and knocked him overboard, and he was lost at sea. The fisherman who was with him at the time was very upset for quite a while and didn't go fishing for some time. When he finally did make a trip again, on one of the first sets they made, the rake was being hauled out of the water and there was Wally, standing up in it, hair all slicked back, dead as a mackerel. Then the fisherman was really very, very upset for a long time.

"I read the story about sea scalloping. Did that really happen about the guy in the drag?" I asked.

"I didn't see it myself, but I sure heard about it. He came up standing in the drag."

"God, it must have been awful to see that."

"Strange things happen offshore sometimes. It just happens. I lost a lot of friends myself over the years," he said.

"It's a pretty dangerous occupation. Did you think about the danger when you went?" I asked.

"If you thought about the danger, you wouldn't go. All you can do is be careful, but if it's your time, that's the way it is."

"Did you go sea scalloping again?"

"I really didn't like sea scalloping."

"Was it the scalloping or Earl?" I asked.

"Probably a little bit of both. But I couldn't wait to get off that boat. That trip on the *Flavia* was one of the worst trips I ever made. When I switched to long lining, it all seemed to come together."

"Did you know that scallops are being shipped to Europe as the whole animal, guts and all?" I asked.

"I heard that but didn't believe it. Who would eat a scallop with the guts? I always thought that was poisonous."

"Guess that was one of the old wives' tales that's been handed down for generations," I answered. Traditionally, scallops have only been sold as the adductor muscle that holds the two shells together. The rest was always discarded. By not eating the viscera, scallops could be harvested from water with more questionable water quality than other shellfish. The new marketing puts a bit of a wrinkle in scallop management.

Chapter Eight
Line Trawling

Back in Harwichport, I had to find a place to live. I found a room at Mrs. Nickerson's on Main Street and told her that I would be there probably for only a short time. I stayed there for eleven years.

The O'Neil brothers went back to Boston, and we eventually lost touch with each other. My brother-in-law divorced my sister, and I never saw him again.

There were very few sites available among the boats with the exception of the peddlers and drunks. But being inexperienced in line trawling and short of money, I had to take what I could get. The first boat I was on was with Johnnie Barker and Johnnie Costa, both of them excessive drinkers. In fact, it was about two months before I saw Johnnie Barker sober, and at the time, I didn't realize what was wrong with him.

The boat was odd-looking, too. The style was called a Provincetown dory. The stern was very high and wide, the bow very low and pointed. In fact, the bow was lower than the stern. Some of the boys on the dock used to say it was all ass and no forehead.

There are very few fishermen who engage in line trawling along the Atlantic now. Not only is it hard physical labor, but it requires a lot of skill and speed.

First, you have to start at about midnight to cut up two hundred pounds of frozen herring from your freezer plant into approximately one-inch cubes. Two hundred pounds of frozen herring comes to approximately four thousand pieces of bait. These four thousand pieces have to be put on four thousand hooks. Here is where the skill and speed come in.

The gear is coiled in tubs, and each tub consists of ten lines three hundred feet long for a total of three thousand feet. The lines have smaller lines called gangions attached about every six feet with a hook on the end of the gangion line. That means each tub of three thousand feet has approximately five hundred hooks per tub. Most two-man boats fish five tubs per day, but I often fished with just one other person, and we fished eight tubs of gear.

The reason for starting at midnight is that it takes nearly four hours to get to the nearest grounds, and it's usually daylight when you get there. You only have about four hours to bait five to eight tubs of gear or up to four thousand hooks. Getting some shuteye while steaming on the way to the fishing grounds is not an option.

The first tub that I baited took nearly an hour and fifteen minutes. Johnnie Barker said that I should try to get it down to an hour within a week. For some unexplainable reason, I was quite adept at baiting. In fact, inside of a week, I was as good as John Barker but was a long way from catching up with Johnnie Costa. I used to time myself with a watch and try to get twenty baits on a minute. It's not just a case of putting a piece of bait on a hook, though. The gear has to be coiled neatly in the tub so that it doesn't get fouled when the gear is set. By the second week, I was challenging Johnnie Costa. I could see that Johnnie was not the type that was going to let me beat him. Consequently, he was speeding up, so I had to go much faster to catch him.

One night, he had a few drinks, and I was getting quite a bit ahead of him. He looked at me with his dark face, looked at John B., and then said, "This goddamned Tiggie is not only a fast baiter and a good baiter, he's turning into a master baiter." It required several minutes for that to sink in, but it got me really mad, but then I laughed. I started to beat him regularly from then on. I got so I could bait 550 hooks in twenty to twenty-five minutes.

This first trip we made together was very exciting as it was something new, and I was very enthusiastic about it. It seemed that we'd never get there, although it was a clear, calm, beautiful night. Finally, at the crack of dawn, we got there. As this was my first trip, I wasn't able to give Johnnie Costa too much help in getting ready to put the gear overboard. He told me to watch and keep my eyes open and that I would get on to the knack of it.

In the meantime, Johnnie Barker threw the sounding line several times to find the depth of water and type of bottom he preferred for cod and haddock, as that was what we were after that day. Finally, he found the particular spot he preferred and told Johnnie Costa and me to prepare to set out.

You set with the tide. The tide might be running at about two miles per hour, and the boat is traveling at about four miles per hour, so the baited hooks pay out in a nice line behind the boat. You have a bamboo pole about fifteen feet long with a flag on it. About fifteen feet away, you have a keg or small wooden barrel of five-gallon capacity, then comes three hundred feet of buoy line with an anchor but no hooks. After the anchor comes the trawl tied to the buoy line, which lies on the bottom. The end of the trawl line is tied to another buoy line with another anchor, keg, and flag. You usually make three or four sets. A set is a minimum of two tubs of gear tied together—twenty lines or six hundred feet of gear. The flags are your visual sightings, so that you will not set on one of your own strings, or another boat doesn't set on top of yours. There were thirty other boats also fishing in the general area, so at any given time, there were as many as thirty to ninety flags in the water. And believe me, you run back to the wrong flag quite often.

All the lines, buoy lines and trawl, are heaved off the stern of the boat by a short stick. The boat goes ahead about four miles per hour, and you heave the trawl and baited hooks out of the tub trying to keep the lines straight and not have them get fouled.

When the tide runs hard, you have to be very careful as the hooks are flying out that you don't get stuck. If you get a hook stuck in you, you have only a split second to decide whether to pull it out yourself or jump. This very first day, Johnnie Costa got one stuck in the bottom of his nose. He gave it a yank; blood was running all over his face. It really looked worse than it was. I realized that this was quite a serious thing if you didn't pay attention.

"You gave a good description of line trawling, but I'm still a bit fuzzy," I said.

"What don't you understand?"

"How many hooks in a tub of trawl?"

"About five hundred. Each tub had ten strings of about three hundred feet each. They were tied together, so there were about three thousand feet of line in each tub or over a half mile of gear. Every six feet, there was a gangion tied on. You've heard of those?"

"Yeah. They are the smaller lines tied to the main line, and each gangion has a hook at the end. How long is a gangion?"

"About two feet. They're all the same length, so that when you bait the hook, you can coil the main line and then the gangion with all the hooks lined up."

"Why do you line them all up? For aesthetics?" I asked.

"No. When the line is paying out…"

"Paying?"

"Yeah, that's the term for the line going out over the stern. Anyway, you don't want to have to hunt in the tub for the hook—you want to know exactly where it is so you don't get one stuck in you."

"You said you bait four thousand hooks. That's eight tubs of trawl. You had to bait eight tubs every time you went out?"

"It depended on how many were on the boat. I could basically do the work of two men, so lots of times, I only fished with one other person, but most of the time, there were three men on board. Some boats did five tubs, and some the full eight."

"You said something about when a hook got you, you had the choice of pulling it out yourself or 'jumping.' What did you mean by that?"

"The line is being paid out with a hook every six feet. The boat is moving forward, and either you pull the hook out yourself, or the force of the boat moving forward and the tide on the gear will pull it out for you, and you end up with sort of a jump. That's all I meant."

"Neither of those choices sounds very pleasant," I offered.

"That's one of the reasons if the gear is coiled properly and the hooks are all lined up, there's less chance of getting stuck with a hook."

"Were you ever stuck?"

"Sure. But not very often. I had a good sense about the gear and where everything was, and besides, I was usually the one who did the baiting. I had trouble when other people baited the gear and the hooks weren't lined up right. It was a lot worse with a halibut hook," he said.

"Why?" I asked.

"Halibut hooks are so much bigger."

Chapter Nine
New Skills

We finally got three miles of gear set out. It took us about twenty minutes to run to the other end—the first end that we had thrown over. After a bite to eat, it was time to haul.

We steamed up to the flag, picked it up out of the water, untied it from the keg, and untied the keg from the buoy line. Johnnie Costa hauled the first buoy line. When hauling the gear, you have a pair of nippers made out of cotton with slots in them that you hold on the end of your fingers. The line rides in the slots, and you squeeze your fingers to grip the line. As Johnnie was pulling, or hauling as they say in trawling, I could see that it required a lot of strength and tenacity.

Finally, after what seemed like a long time, but actually was not longer than ten minutes, the anchor came to the rail, and I could see the first few hooks with nothing on them. There were no fish on the first line of approximately fifty hooks. But from then on, they started to come, and a beautiful sight it was indeed. We had set right on a school of jumbo haddock.

John B. told me I had better start cleaning them as soon as they came aboard. You don't actually take them off the hooks—you just hold the line in your nippers and snap them off into the box. The man behind the hauler coils the gear into neat bundles and sets all the hooks that have been bent back into shape. As this was my first day and I was completely unskilled in either hauling or coiling, I had to clean fish for the day. And this you do bent over, but I was young and in pretty good shape, so I came through pretty well.

The day's catch was approximately four thousand pounds for which I believe we got eight cents a pound. We had three more days that week equally as good. Friday was the day you got paid, called settling up day. On these small boats, the boat takes a share, and each man takes a share, but this being my first week, Johnnie Barker gave me only a half share, which came to $330, an astronomical sum unbelievable to me at the time. Little did I know that would be the largest amount I was to make in any given week for five years. He paid me in three one-hundred-dollar bills. Till then, I don't believe that I had ever seen a one-hundred-dollar bill before.

I squandered the first big week's pay foolishly, thinking that it would keep on coming, and we made just about nothing for the next three weeks. The two Johnnies stayed drunk for a week. All during the daylight hours, they would be talking about how well we'd do the next day, but after drinking all day, they could never quite make it. Finally, we got started on a trip, both of them drunk, and we ran into Monomoy Point where we ran aground, high and dry. The two Johnnies started a fight—Johnnie C. castigating John B. for running aground and telling him point-blank that he was going to assume command.

At this point in the argument, I was seriously thinking of saying something, that is until Johnnie Barker picked up a gaff, and Johnnie Costa picked up a bait knife. Being a coward, I decided I would try to make the beach, but when I made known my intentions, they promptly stopped fighting. Later, I learned that these fights and arguments meant very little between them, so from then on, I ignored them.

The season progressed into July, and I had heard the boys on the dock on numerous occasions refer to shark time, but I didn't pay much attention to this talk. What a rude awakening awaited me! The day started, or that is, the fishing part of it, like any other day, with the setting of gear, the runs back, and the hauling. This was going to be my first day at hauling. I finally got the buoy line in the boat, and the gear felt very, very light. Then I saw that all that I had was four empty hooks, and the groundline just cut off.

I said to John, "What the hell happened here?"

He held the line in his hand and examined it very closely, then he said, "It's been bitten off by ground sharks."

"What the devil is a ground shark?" I asked.

He said that it was a type of shark that just swam along the bottom.

You never see this type of shark, and when they're really bad, you inevitably lose all your fish, as they follow the trawl along the bottom and bite the fish off as they go. Or, if the fish is wound up close to the ground line, then they bite it off, too. One end is bitten off, and when you go to haul the other end, that too is bitten off, and you have lost all the gear that was in the middle. That's what happened that day.

We lost four tubs of gear plus the fish. A tub of gear costs about $50. On the way in, I did a little figuring, and it seemed to me that we were $200 in the hole not counting the gas and bait.

Then I asked John, "What do you do in a situation like this?"

He told me, "Fishing is one of the few businesses that you can go into and have some days cost you $50 apiece or better just for the privilege of going." This was the first of many, many rude awakenings in this business.

I had learned how to heave the gear and was coming along very nicely with my coiling and other various skills. In fact, Johnnie Costa would even bark a compliment to me once in a while. This particular morning, as I was setting gear, I noticed a lot of big, black birds, about the size of seagulls, sitting on the water in groups of fifty to one hundred. I believe their real name is black shearwaters. Johnnie Barker said to Johnnie Costa, "Them bastard hags are here." I couldn't imagine what they were talking about, then I happened to notice the birds were following the boat and diving into the water, stealing all the bait off the hooks. They took just about every bit of the bait off the hooks, and we got very few fish that day.

Then came the month of August, and the foggy season set in—day after day, nothing but fog. We lay by the side of the dock for about two weeks till finally nobody had any money. All the time, I was hoping that the foggy spell would lift. I heard some of the boys talking about the fact that some of these spells could last for weeks and weeks. Then one day, Johnnie Barker, being half loaded, made the statement that we were going to start fishing in the fog as desperate times were upon us. We did go for the next two weeks, had several collisions, and lost quite a bit of gear.

The fall came, and we had a few brief flurries of fair fishing, and then the weather began to get bad. By the time the winter arrived, I had managed to save exactly nothing, paid none of my back bills, and borrowed about a quarter of my next year's pay potential. In fact, that winter, things were so bad down at the dock that we fishermen were forced to extreme measures to get food (or at least meat).

Frank Thompson had a big Great Dane named Tyrus. One of his men used to feed the dog eight pounds of meat a day, putting the meat in a big bowl on the dock where Tyrus used to like to eat it. That is, he did until Frank found out that most of the fishermen were stealing Tyrus's dinner. From then on, Frank's man would stay until the dog had completely finished his dinner. For the rest of the winter, we ate mostly eels, quahogs, clams, and a few feeds of frozen herring.

"Would you have ever guessed when you were fishing that the sharks you hated so much would become something they fish for purposely now?" I asked.

"Those goddamned things. They ruined more fishing days than I care to remember. No, I can't believe they are fishing for them now, but I see them coming in all the time over at Chatham, and that's what they've got. There's actually a limit on the goddamn things."

Tiggie had described coiling and baiting gear and how important it was to do it correctly, but it wasn't until a chance meeting with an old friend, Otto Zavatone, that I got a clearer picture of the process and the importance of attention to detail. Otto demonstrated the process.

Once the fish are caught and the gear hauled aboard the boat, the gear must be coiled in the tubs for baiting for the next time. Otto explained that a palette with four long lines is placed in the bottom of a shorter tub—more or less a half tub—and the lines are draped over the edge. The end of the string of gear has a loop and leader of a couple of fathoms that is placed in the bottom of the tub and forms the first coil. The line that was used, called Brownell, a trade name, was well suited to the task and coiled nicely. When the first hook was encountered, it was placed at the far side of the tub, and the coils continued. The second hook was placed in line with the first and just below it, and the third hook was placed just below the second so that as the hooks were encountered, they formed a straight line across the entire diameter of the tub in a north-south direction, north being the far side and south closest to the coiler. There was no void space in the center, because that would allow a hook to possibly fall into the center and foul the gear as it was being uncoiled. Once a row of hooks went across the entire tub, the process would begin again with the next hook at the far edge, the fisherman working back and forth until all the hooks were placed neatly in a straight line. The long lines draped over the tub were used to tie the gear into a bundle or a string of gear, three hundred feet long with fifty hooks. This precise placement of the hooks meant fewer mishaps in handling the gear at a later time. Otto's face lit up when talking about a good coiler and the end product being "beautiful." He also said, unbidden, that Tiggie was one of the best.

The gear may not come in without problems, though. There may be a bent hook or a broken gangion. In those cases, the coiler often wore a metal "ring" on his finger, designed to reset the shape of a hook that had been straightened through the fishing, or the "hook set" could be attached to the tub. In any case, if the coiler could do it while coiling, the hook was fixed. If it needed more attention than a moment, or if a gangion were broken, they were placed outside the tub to be fixed on the way home.

To bait the gear, a fisherman would sit with a bundle of gear, a full-sized tub, and the bait. The hook was baited and placed on the first coil at about the midpoint around the edge of the tub, west on a compass if north was the far edge of the tub. The next hook would be placed beside the first (heading east to continue with the analogy), and so on, until about half of the tub's far wall had baited hooks lining it. Then the fisherman would work toward the starting point. The line fell into the tub almost in a coil if it had been done properly in the first step, and so the baiting went very fast. This is where it was critical to know that when you reached for a hook to bait, you knew exactly where it would be in the coiled gear to prevent getting stuck. So when Tiggie talks about trying to get twenty hooks baited in a minute and coiling the gear neatly in the tub, he's talking about blisteringly fast repetitive motion to end up doing 550 hooks in twenty to twenty-five minutes at the beginning of his fishing career.

As we shall see, the process was even more crucial when fishing for halibut to have proper gear because larger hooks were used and baiting was done on the fly as the hooks were heading over the transom.

When heaving the baited hooks over the side, the fisherman took the pole and stuck it under the gear that was flying over the side to make sure the hooks didn't get caught in the transom. But he had to keep an eye on the tub to make sure that when he came to the end of a string, he was able to tie the next string to it to form a continuous line of gear. If he lost his concentration and didn't tie another string on, the gear already set would be tied only to the first anchor buoy where they started to set.

The strings of gear were marked by flag buoys, but it was not like lobster gear where buoys are painted with distinctive color schemes. The anchor line was tied to the flag that was tied to a keg. The keg had the vessel name on it. In later years, big rubber orange or yellow floatation balls were used, but in either case, it's easy to see how finding the right gear in fog or stormy seas could be challenging when there were thirty to ninety flags in the water as Tiggie related.

The guys didn't like working with new gear. The line was coated and needed to be broken in and stretched. To do this, they often tied one end to a tree and the other to their truck and used their truck to stretch the line. This process made it easier to coil.

Chapter Ten
Grounds, Places, and Time

Some of the places we fished had real odd-ball names pertaining to the type of growth or animal life found growing on the bottom. We knew them by names such as the Lemons, the Figs, the Pumpkins, the Mussels, the Claypipes, and a few others. Some grounds are referred to as being a certain distance from a particular point of land, place, or buoy, such as East-Southeast Ridge, Edge of the Ground, Great Hill Ground, South Channel, Shark Ground Channel, Little Round Shoal, Nauset Banks, etc. Most of our fishing was conducted on these various grounds, two to seven hours offshore, which was a considerable distance considering most of our boats were less than fifty feet.

One of the most important grounds that we fished was an area called the Mussels, which was approximately three miles wide and ten miles long, going northeast to southeast, and from thirty-five fathoms at the deepest part to twenty fathoms at the shallowest part. The reason it was called the Mussels was quite obvious, as the bottom was composed mostly of mussels, dead and alive. Among the dead shells on the bottom were millions upon millions of very small, brittle starfish that ate the mussels and were a favorite food of the haddock. Therefore, this particular area was considered our best spot for haddock. Usually, a whole school of haddock came on to the Mussels, and they settled down on the deep end and—this is just a conjecture on my part—I believe that, as they ate the brittle starfish that were lying on the top of the shells, they kept moving into shoal water. This cycle usually required about a week until they disappeared. By then, other brittle starfish that were under the layers of dead shells had crawled around on the top and eventually they induced or attracted another school of haddock onto the grounds.

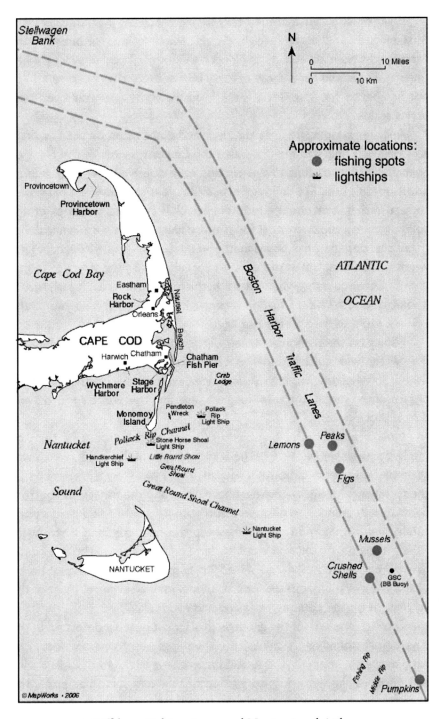

Offshore Fishing Areas and Navigational Aids

Over time, because of the heavy fishing pressures from draggers, the Russian fleet, and other foreign vessels, the time interval between the various schools had been getting longer and longer. In other words, when one day, you could get a catch of forty boxes, three days later, you might not be able to get four. Yet a week from that time, you could get forty boxes again.

Another productive area that is fished quite often by the Chatham and Harwich fleets is an area called the Lemons. Actually, the plant or animal that is prevalent in this locale really doesn't look like a lemon, but it doesn't look like anything else either. It is shaped like a plum or a tomato with a stem about a foot long which is fastened to a rock or any solid object on the bottom. It looks more like a plant than an animal, but if you cut it open, it has blood in it. The outer skin is very tough. In fact, when a hook penetrates the skin, it takes about all your strength to pull it out. Consequently, when you fish this particular area, nearly every hook that doesn't have a fish on gets caught on one of these lemons, and you are liable to have a very bad haul.

Fishing on the Lemons entailed a little good reasoning and judgment. The water was quite shallow in comparison to other places that we fished. So when we had high-course tides, which were controlled by the phases of the moon, the tide was very fast, and this was a spot to avoid during those times.

Most fishing on the Lemons was conducted in spells of calm or moderate weather because of the shallow depth of the water, which was seventeen to twenty fathoms. If you had a very bad storm, it seemed that the turbulence of the water must have disturbed the fish on the bottom because they seemed to disappear. On calm days, you could have a good catch, then a gale wind would come up the next day, and if you went fishing a few days later, you wouldn't have enough to eat. The fish would have completely disappeared. After this happened to you several times, unless you were a complete fool, you would try elsewhere. Most of the fish caught on the Lemons were cod and haddock.

The Figs was one of the grounds that I most heartily detested. In the days before sounding machines, the soundings had to be conducted by hand methods. Some days, it would require several hours of excruciating and discouraging work just to get located. In this particular place, the water is much deeper than on the Lemons or other spots, being forty to fifty-eight fathoms deep. This area gets its name from the growth on the bottom, which very closely resembles a fig. You would catch them on your empty hooks from time to time. The Figs is a very rocky area. The boulders are as big as cars. I can say this now, after seeing what they look like on a modern sounding machine. Years ago, we realized that the bottom was rough, but never quite knew how bad it really is. In fact, it is one of the few places off Cape Cod that the big draggers don't dare to fish. Therefore, when you set there with your trawl, you figured to lose a good portion of your gear. But if the fish were scarce in the other places, you had to take the gamble. Most of the fish on this ground were large codfish up to fifty or sixty pounds. Therefore, it didn't take too many in your count to have a good trip.

Another place of extreme difficulty to find and fish was a place called East-Southeast Ridge. It was a bit deeper than the Figs. If you made a mistake there and set the gear over the edge of the ridge, you came into a mud bottom. Living in this mud bottom was a creature called a slime eel. He would take the bait off your hooks and wind around the ground line, literally tying himself in a knot, creating a big glob of slime, which had to be cut off with a knife, one slime eel at a time. If you did happen to have a few fish on your trawl, the eels would crawl into the fish's mouth and devour him completely from the inside out, leaving only bone and skin. At first glance, when you hauled one of these fish up on the hook, it looked intact, that is, until the water ran out of it. And if you ever set about 1500 hooks on the slime eels, you really had a mess. East-Southeast Ridge was called that because of its direction from the buoy off Chatham.

These various grounds I have discussed were the principle ones we fished. The others were of less value or importance. The Pumpkins, the Pipes, the Big Mussels, and the South Channel were halibut grounds.

Fishermen are a very peculiar breed. They vividly remember just about anything or any important thing that has happened to them pertaining to the sea and fishing and can talk of something that happened thirty years ago or something that happened ten years ago, but if you ask them the year or the date, they probably couldn't tell you. When they are all in a group talking, one will speak up and tell about the time he got so many fish in a certain place, and he can remember it because it was the year that all the mackerel were in the channel, or the time the haddock didn't show up on the Mussels that summer, or the very foggy summer, etc.

It doesn't seem possible that you can do this, but looking back over the years, even though my recollections do run into each other like the colors or paints on a painter's palette, there are so many little, vivid incidents and, yes, even an individual fish or two that I have caught, like a codfish without a tail—the tail had been completely bitten off by a larger fish and had healed over, and the fish was apparently doing well—or the only gold haddock I saw caught, which is very rare. It is called a golden phase, or the time I caught the second biggest haddock off the Cape. And thinking back on these different little trivial things, I can associate them with the various things that happened and have a pretty good idea of when.

Some fishermen keep a complete log of where they have fished on a specific day, the amounts of their catch, and various other data and do fairly well. Then there is the other school, where the fisherman keeps very little record of the spots fished, time of year, and so forth. I was in this category, but I did surprisingly very well. In fact, I had many of the other fishermen ask me if the time was right for such and such a place, which was quite a compliment. Of course, this was not so in the beginning, but after many, many years. For the first few years, they don't think that you know enough to get in out of the rain, so when they start talking to you as an equal, you have it made. I never thought I would get there.

"I'm a bit confused with all the areas you talk about," I said to Tiggie one morning. "Do you have a chart that shows where they are?"

"No, I gave all my charts away," he responded. "I wish I hadn't now, and I don't remember who I gave them to either."

"If I go get a chart, will you put these places on it?" I asked. "I need to know where the Mussels and Lemons and Figs are."

"I could try," he said.

I went to Chatham and got a chart that read, "Fishing areas of Massachusetts," and after looking at it, I thought it would do. I didn't look closely enough, though, because when I gave it to Tiggie the next day, he told me, "That one was no goddamn good. All the depths were in feet. I only had charts in fathoms."

I looked at him quizzically, figuring it wouldn't be that hard to convert to fathoms, but said, "No problem. I'll get another in fathoms." I got him a second one to work with. A couple of weeks went by, and he still had not given me back the chart. I kept telling him I really needed it.

"Remind me to give you back the charts," he said one day. "They're in my truck."

"Did you put the places on it?" I asked.

"Some of them are there," he answered.

"Thanks," I said.

"It wasn't easy. They don't even have the Stonehore or Nantucket Lightships on them. That's how we got our bearings, from the lightships. We started from there on our steams to the grounds. We took the direction and steaming time starting at either of those markers. Without them, I couldn't get started easily."

"I know, they removed the lightships that used to be there for navigation, but can't you estimate where they were located?"

"Not really."

Jumping around from subject to subject was common in our discussions, but we were talking about one of the skills he had honed over years on the water; yet now, he seemed to have great difficulty finding the old fishing places. It made me sad. I asked Bill Amaru to help out, and he gave me the approximate locations of some of the areas. (See map on page 45.)

I had asked him if he knew what the plants or animals were he referred to with the place names, and he had no idea. *Somebody should know what they are*, I thought. I made inquiries starting with the National Marine Fisheries Service in Chatham and Woods Hole and the Cape Cod Commercial Hook Fisherman's Association. The responses indicated that the names given to these areas go back a long time. One person working on the Gulf of Maine cod project sent ship log entries from the mid 1800s where they hauled up "...very large pears, lemons, and strawberries." The entries added that when they found this type of bottom, the fish were plentiful and large. One response referred to the book *Captains Courageous* where these names are used. Several people opined that the "figs" were a type of sponge (*Suberites ficus*) known as "porpoise dung" or "monkey dung" because of the odor. There seems to be agreement on the origin of the lemons being a stalked tunicate or sea squirt (*Boltenia ovifera*) that fits Tiggie's description perfectly. The hunt for the proper nomenclature became a fascinating, if non-definitive, research side trip.

Chapter Eleven
Majestic Fish

"Why was fishing for halibut better than fishing for cod?" I asked Tiggie one day.

"I think everyone liked fishing for them," he answered. "They're such a majestic fish. To see a seven-foot, two-hundred-pound halibut lying on the deck, its white belly up, is really something to see."

"When I was reading about halibut fishing, it reminded me of scallop fever, when everyone gets psyched because they think there might be some scallops in the bay, and they get all revved up. It sounded like there was halibut fever in the spring."

"It's kind of the same thing. It's the anticipation of a good trip and good money. It doesn't happen that often, but when it does, it creates something in your mind that you want again and again even though you know you may have a broker for a trip."

MY FIRST TASTE OF HALIBUT

Spring finally arrived in my first year fishing with Johnnie Barker, and the fishing didn't improve very much, but at least the weather was getting a little more tolerable. Some of the boats were getting ready to go halibut fishing. But Johnnie Barker made no plans to do so as it would entail quite a bit of expense, since you used a different type of gear than you used for cod and haddock fishing.

The halibut gear is broken down into units called skates—a short complement of seven lines, three hundred feet long with a hook hung every eighteen feet, not the six feet of the cod gear. The term "skate" comes from the Canadians. Why they call the gear that, I'm really not sure, but it's kind of odd that they used the same term as the name of an animal in the shark family with "wings" that are also called skates.

Johnnie B told Johnnie Costa and me that he had tried halibuting so many different springs and that it was so erratic that he was unwilling to take the risk, that is, unless the cod and haddock fishing were very poor. Within two or three weeks, several of the boats had made good catches of halibut, and I was beginning to get the fever after seeing the sight of some of these majestic fish. I believe, and so do most commercial fishermen, that a halibut is probably the most beautiful and powerful fish, pound for pound, that swims. It really is quite hard to describe the feeling that comes over you when you first feel one on the trawl and look over the side with the anticipation of a glimpse of it. You get a feeling in the pit of your stomach, and it goes up to your throat and just about engulfs you. It's a feeling, as close as I can remember, akin to the feeling I had the first time I was with a girl.

After much pressure and insistence, Johnnie Costa and I talked Johnnie B into looking around and trying to find some used halibut gear, which we did. After several days' work on the gear, such as shaping hooks, checking to see if there were any bad breaks in the ground line, etc., we were finally ready to make our first try.

When halibuting, you have to use tremendous amounts of bait, usually a thousand pounds or more a trip, and very seldom does your gross weight of halibut exceed the amount of bait you use. The average size of the halibut off Cape Cod is about fifty to one hundred pounds, and once in a while, there is a fish of up to three hundred pounds. These are dressed weights—that would be gutted with the heads and tails cut off.

Our first trip was going to be just a short distance, unlike some of the trips we were to take later. This particular set was east of Great Round Shoal approximately ten miles away, in fifteen fathoms or ninety feet of water. I had never set halibut gear before, so Johnnie Costa had the honors. It is quite tricky and dangerous as you have to bait and set as the boat is going along, unlike cod and haddock gear, which is baited ahead of time. If the weather is snotty, it is not very pleasant work.

Johnnie Costa was very good at it, and I was able to master it without too much difficulty.

After the gear was set, it required a long interval of time before you hauled it back, usually about three hours. Finally, John said, "Let's haul this goddamn gear and make a start." I was very anxious to do so, so John said, "Go ahead and haul, eager beaver." I started to haul and after several minutes, the gear got very, very heavy. I said to myself, *I bet I got a big one on.* But when I saw the first hook, it was just a barn-door skate. I guess anybody that has been around saltwater knows what a skate looks like, so I will forego giving a description. Not only did the first hook have a skate on it, but the next twenty or twenty-five did. The skate's habitat was on the sandy bottom, and it was quite apparent that this section of the gear had drifted onto the sandy bottom. Halibut hooks are very large and unyielding compared to cod and haddock hooks. Consequently, the skates were very difficult to unhook. The more skates I got, the madder and more foolish I got. I banged and pounded them and carried on like a jackass until finally, I had just about spent all my strength. All the while, the two Johnnies were laughing at me. Every time I looked over the side, it seemed like another skate was coming, so I automatically reached down and tried to snap them off. The only trouble was that when I jerked the hook out of the mouth of the next one, it was a halibut of about one hundred pounds. To this day, I can still see it slowly swimming away. I never told the two Johnnies about this—they would have thrown me overboard, I imagine, as that one fish was probably worth $50.

Finally, I finished hauling my skate of gear, and it was Johnnie Costa's turn. In very rapid succession, he hauled in four halibut, which dressed out at 175 pounds apiece. We managed to get six more halibut on the rest of the gear, for a total weight of 1200 pounds, which Johnnie Barker said was a very good trip. Later on, I realized how right he was.

All the way home that afternoon, I kept admiring these beautiful fish. About the easiest way to describe a halibut is to say that it looks like a flounder, a flat fish with dark skin on one side and white on the other. But visualize a flounder up to seven feet long with a head and mouth that could swallow a cod or haddock up to ten pounds with very little effort.

As soon as you got the halibut in the boat, you hit them on the head with a mallet or a bat and turned them on their backs so that the white side was up. If you didn't use this procedure and left them on their bellies, the blood would settle and discolor them which would decrease their value. That afternoon, I was admiring all ten of them, lying there with their bellies up—my first successful halibut trip. The second one wasn't to come for a long time. One trip, we only took one halibut, and a couple of trips were skunks. A skunk means we got nothing at all.

My enthusiasm had been bubbling over after that first big trip, from which I think we shared $150 each. The next five or six trips, I think Johnnie handed me only about $12, but the worst was yet to come.

To go halibuting, you had to buy your bait ahead of time. It usually cost you $30 to $40 per trip, plus the ice to keep it fresh. So you put the bait in the boat, iced it down, then watched it slowly rot and the ice melt after four or five days of bad weather. Then you said to yourself, "I know the weather is going to break." And you did the same thing all over again. I think we dumped five batches of bait and ice in a row, putting us about $300 in the hole.

We did finally make one more trip way down to the South'rd and got quite a few codfish and half a dozen halibut. We paid off our bills and put the halibut gear away for the season, which usually ends around the end of May. After my first complete year of fishing, I realized the tremendous sum of $2900. Now I had a choice of doing one of two things—getting a different site and fishing with somebody else or going back home. But by then, I had grown to love the Cape, or, as they say down here, got sand in my shoes. Yet I realized that I would never be accepted as a Cape Codder, or even come close. Frank Thompson told me one day, "To ever be considered a Cape Codder, you have to live with somebody else's wife for two years and own several cranberry bogs."

Chapter Twelve
Charlie Chase and Al Hanson

I fished for five or six years out of Harwich with two men, Charlie and Al. It was about one of the poorest stretches I encountered, money-wise, that is, in my first twenty years of fishing, but they sure were memorable years.

Most fishermen in Harwichport were of two classes or types. There were the fishermen who lived on the Cape, had families, and were fairly settled. The other type was the group of old fishermen from Boston and Gloucester, who used to sail the old-type schooners and fish from dories such as you would read about in *Captains Courageous*. This latter type of fisherman very rarely ever bathed or shaved and constantly chewed tobacco, which used to dribble down the corners of their mouths. Most of the time, you would try to sit upwind of them.

Charlie Chase was a real old Cape Codder; he was married, a family man. He looked about seventy-five and weighed about ninety-eight pounds soaking wet. I just couldn't visualize him as being able to take this kind of life.

Charlie was carrying sport-fishing parties and said that if he could find a couple of young, rugged fellows, he would like to go back to commercial fishing. So the scene was set.

Among the fishermen was a handsome young fellow about six feet three inches with wavy hair by the name of Al Hanson. He had been stationed in Harwichport and Chatham with the Coast Guard during the war years. He had originally come from Nebraska, but he loved the Cape so much that he never went back. He used to say the only thing they ever used an anchor for in Nebraska was to tie down the outhouses in their famous dust storms.

For many reasons, we became fast friends and were trying to figure out some way that we could be shipmates. Knowing that Charlie was looking for a crew, we went to him with the proposition, and he said he would be glad to have us aboard.

The first trip we took, we caught approximately a thousand pounds of haddock and got six cents a pound for them. Charlie was very pleased and said that we were fast, eager, willing, and handled gear very well. Praise was always appreciated. Of course, it didn't help the financial end of it, because, figuring it roughly in my mind, a thousand pounds at six cents a pound comes to only $60. And $60 split four ways, after expenses, comes to about $10 for eighteen hours work. So it went for the next month—seventeen days of fishing for approximately $72 apiece.

One of these trips will always stand out in my mind. We were hand lining on that day and using open mussels for bait, which were very expensive. We got a thousand pounds of small codfish at four cents a pound. The expenses for that day came out exactly to the dollar the same as our gross stock. In other words, everyone, pertaining to the fishing industry, made money but us. The people who pack the fish, the box-maker, the ice man, the fuel company, and the trackers, plus the commission the fish buyer makes. It didn't take much figuring, even for me, although I had only gone as far as the eighth grade, to know that this was a pretty poor arrangement.

The line Charlie had been feeding us numerous times was, "You have to take the bitter with the sweet."

One day, Al looked up at him after a particularly bad start and said, "I've heard you talk about the bitter and heard you talk about the sweet, and I am trying to figure out where the hell the sweetness comes in."

Sometimes, the sweetness was onshore, not offshore, and some of the best times that the fishermen had were the days spent in the sun working on the gear, watching the pretty girls and the tourists. Fishermen have a saying, "The best part of fishing is the days you don't go."

Chapter Thirteen
The First Big Blow

"Were you out in many storms?" I asked one morning.

"Yeah, but I don't like to think about them too much. The first one was with Al Hanson and Charlie Chase. It was Charlie's boat, and both Al and I were pretty green. The old-timers on the dock always talked about storms, or blows, as they called them."

"How far away were you?"

"I don't remember. What I do remember is the speed that the wind came up. It went from flat-ass calm to twenty-foot seas in a matter of minutes. I didn't know what an ominous sky looked like back then, but I sure do now. After you've been on the water for a few years, you get so you can tell a lot about the weather by looking at the sky. A barometer helps, but if you keep your eye to the sky, you can get a pretty good sense."

"I've tried to learn more about the weather over the years. I remember both Mun [a crusty bear of a man who fished all his life but in his later years worked for the Shellfish Department with Gardy and me] and Harry Hunt [a local fisherman who relied mainly on lobsters for his living] giving me some pointers. Harry said that if the tide goes out and out and out, way more than a tide chart says is correct for the day, there's an easterly storm coming. I've watched that on the shore, and sure enough, each time the tide goes out and I think it's never going to come in again, the next day, the weather turns to crap, and the wind is out of the east, and there is no low tide at all. That has nothing to do with the phases of the moon."

"Offshore, you can't go by that," Tiggie said. "Watching the tide like you're talking about is only good for the inshore areas, the bays and coves."

"How do you tell offshore then?"

"You watch which way the wind is blowing and look from that direction. The wind goes around the compass, so it depends on the season. In the summer, weather coming up the coast is from the sou'west, and that's the major wind but not storms. If it shifts to the southeast, then there might be a blow. In the other seasons, if it's from the southeast, it could very easily veer around to the east or northeast, and then there's trouble. Southeast could mean trouble, too, though. After it's blown by, the wind often changes to howling nor'west."

"That one I knew. That's true offshore, too?"

"Yeah, pretty much."

"One question I've always had—Mun told me about sun dogs and moon dogs, rings around the sun or moon that mean rain is coming within twelve to twenty-four hours. But once it rains, how do you know when it's going to stop? I've heard that certain types of clouds are the key, but if it's still raining, how can you see other types of clouds?"

"You really can't. You can look at the barometer, and if it's rising, the storm should be slowing down. But the best way is to look for the sky to brighten in another direction that will be pushing the storm off."

THE FIRST BIG BLOW

Al was a family man and had four children. I can say that very few men I have known loved the sea or boats as much as he. Like most fishermen, his fondest aspiration was to eventually own his own boat. Most of our idle hours were spent in scheming and plotting how we could eventually have a boat together. In the meantime, though, we realized that we had a lot to learn, and Charlie Chase would be a good teacher.

Up to this time, I had never been caught in a real good blow. Most of the breezes had been fifteen to thirty or thirty-five miles per hour. I had heard the old-timers on the dock talk of this blow or that blow and tell of their narrow escapes and of the various friends and shipmates who had been swept overboard. But it really doesn't strike home until it happens to you.

This day started out like most others, a fairly light breeze from the northwest at approximately ten miles per hour. We had just gotten through setting the gear and had had a bite to eat. Before we started to haul the gear, Charlie said, "Let the sail down." Trawl boats almost always have a small steadying sail in the stern. This is to hold you up into the wind and makes it easier to follow the gear along as you haul. After hauling for fifteen minutes or so, the wind died completely, and the sea became glassy smooth.

Charlie kept scanning the horizon and acting very peculiar. He looked at Al and said we were going to have a very bad blow.

Al said, "What? Are you crazy, you old fool? This looks like the best day we have had in a long time."

Charlie said, "The temperature is dropping rapidly, and the northwest sky is getting very dark. In fact, you boys had better go back and tie up that sail very snug, because when the wind hits, it's going to tear that canvas all to hell."

After several minutes. I came to the conclusion that Charlie was just giving us a long line of baloney, although I did notice it did seem much colder and wasn't a very bright day at that, considering that it was only ten o'clock in the morning. I also noticed a few ripples on the water, and in ten minutes time, we had fifty- to sixty-mile-an-hour gale winds. The sea went from calm to fifteen- to twenty-foot seas in that short time.

Just like Charlie said, the sail was torn to hell, plus several windows were blown out on the pilothouse of the boat. It happened so fast that it was almost unbelievable.

About this time, we noticed it was extremely difficult to haul the gear and keep the boat anywhere near it.

Charlie looked at us and said, "Boys, I haven't done this in quite a few years, but I'm very much afraid that we're going to have to cut the gear loose and leave it."

Al and I spoke in unison, "Never. Like hell!"

There was a fish on every other hook, and prices had gone up a little, so at that particular moment, we didn't feel like cutting loose $300 worth of equipment, plus the time entailed in rigging a new string, plus the fish.

We struggled with it for about fifteen minutes more and then realized the futility of it. We were thirty miles from land and had to make a choice immediately. Finally, reluctantly, Al reached for a knife and cut the gear. It was indeed a sad sight to see all those fish drift away, caught on the trawl, doomed to a slow death and of no benefit to anybody. It seems a sad thing to see fish grow to maturity, considering the hazardous life they have, and have them end up that way.

Charlie swung the boat around into the wind and said, "Boys, this is going to be a rough, rough trip!"

His wooden boat, the *Sally Anne*, which he had named after his daughter, had a low bow and was quite chunky, so it pounded quite badly. He tried it at half throttle and saw that that would be no good as we were pounding ourselves to pieces. So he cut the throttle back down, and I don't think we ever went over three miles an hour for the next seventeen hours.

In the meantime, all the other boats that were fishing in the general vicinity were lost from view. The spray was flying through the broken windows, and the sea was so rough that, coupled with the rain, visibility diminished to nil. I must say something for Charlie—he was really tough. He stayed at the wheel most of the time. In fact, he insisted; it was not so much that he didn't trust us with the wheel, but that it gave him something to hold on to. Al and I were having a difficult time, also.

We finally got to Harwich port at 3:00 a.m. expecting that everyone had given us up. Coming into the channel, Al noticed that there were only seven boats out of the twenty usually tied at the dock. We thought that we had had a bad passage, but after comparing stories and notes with the rest of the boats, which eventually all limped in by daylight, we discovered that we didn't have too bad a time. Several of them had to be towed in by other boats, and a few had very bad leaks or had had the calking pounded out of their seams. All around, it was a very bad trip. Charlie Chase said, "Now you can say that you've been in a breeze."

Chapter Fourteen
Finding Your Way

"A couple of days ago, you were talking about sounding lines. I've heard them called lead lines or sounding leads. Are they all the same thing?" I asked.

"I don't know. I've always known them as sounding lines. You know what they are, don't you?" Tiggie asked.

"I've got the general idea, but I don't think I've ever actually seen one."

"There's a line with knots at different lengths to indicate depth," he explained. "At the end, there's a lead weight that looks like an upside-down ice-cream cone. The fat part of the cone is covered with grease—they put it on pretty thick and then let the line go over the side. Some people used soap instead of grease. I think it was Fels Naptha soap. Anyway, when it hits the bottom, the grease picks up whatever is on the bottom so when it's brought back up again, you know the depth to the bottom and the type of bottom—sand, pebbles, rocks.

"Each type of fish uses a different bottom, so if you want to fish for cod, you look for the type of bottom they like. Same with haddock."

"You didn't have any type of navigation back then, did you?" I asked.

"No. Not like today. Radar was too expensive, and LORAN wasn't available to us."

"So how did you know where you were? It's not like inshore where you can take range markers on the land. You were miles offshore. How did you do it?"

"Depending on where we were heading, we'd generally start our timing from the Stone Horse Lightship at Pollock Rip Channel around the tip of Monomoy [Monomoy Island, a barrier island south of Chatham]. From there, we'd take a compass heading and steam for a certain length of time until we got to where we were heading. Then we'd put the sounding lead over and see where we were."

"See where you were?" I asked.

"Yeah. The bottom changes, so we could really tell where we were by the bottom. I was really good at putting the boat in the right place. I'm not bragging, but I was good. It's something that came naturally to me. I ended up teaching some of the captains how to get where they wanted to go."

"It's amazing to me because you weren't always on the same boat, so the timing would be different, right?"

"Yeah, but you knew how fast you were going and then figured how long it should take. Sometimes, it was hard to get to the right spot. Some of the places we fished were small pieces of bottom, and they were tricky to find. Those who were good at reading the bottom turned out to be the most successful fishermen. I was one of them."

SOUNDING LINES

I had learned from Earl Youngren the importance of the sounding line, and it was just as important to trawling as it was to scalloping. In fact, stories went around the harbors about the value of sounding lines. One I heard came from Nantucket.

There lived a skipper from Nantucket who could virtually find his way around the Atlantic without a compass by just taking bottom samples. The men on his boat were always trying to trick him by taking one of the sounding leads and putting various articles, stones, sand, and pebbles from inland places in them. Then they would hand the skipper this lead, but nobody could fool him. On one trip, one of the crew brought a lead aboard he was sure was going to baffle the skipper. That night, they ran into a violent northeaster; then, the wind backed into the northwest and blew a gale for three days.

The storm abated, the sea calmed, and thick fog set in. The captain called for one of the sounding lines. One of the crew threw it over the side and hauled it back. The captain hollered, "Get that lead in here quick." The crew member, who had brought the phony sounding line aboard, swapped it with the real one and handed it to the captain. The captain looked at it, frowned, scratched his head, then shook it. The crew was beginning to think that they had him stumped. But he looked up at them and said, "Holy Christ! Nantucket is under sixty feet of water, and the lead landed right through the hole in Aunt Margaret's outhouse."

I remembered this story years later when the sounding line was the most important piece of equipment aboard the boat to locate fish, long before the electronic gadgets they have now.

The sounding line figured prominently for us, too. Charlie Chase could be mean and ornery and pull some stupid boners, but he always seemed to come out smelling like a rose. One particular time, he threw the sounding line in forty fathoms of water. He had meant to strike thirty fathoms and was obviously way off course. He told Al to get ready to set gear. Al said he wouldn't set in that spot and told Charlie to proceed to find the Mussels. There was an exchange of several words, and then Charlie said, "Take the goddamned boat and set it where you want." Charlie got mad and sat in a corner sulking. Al ran the boat into the southwest for fifteen minutes and said, "Tiggie, take a sounding." The bottom was solid mussels, and we proceeded to set. We hauled the gear and as luck would have it, set right on top of a school of jumbo haddock and had a catch of forty-five boxes, our biggest catch since we had been fishing together.

When we hit the dock that afternoon, all the boys' eyes were on the fish.

A couple of the skippers asked Charlie, "Where the hell did you get such a fine set like that?"

Charlie looked up at them and said, "My favorite spot on the Mussels, you know, where I always fish, fellows." Al gave me a big wink.

Another time, during the last year Al and I fished with Charlie Chase, the fishing progressively got worse. We weren't getting along at all. Consequently, tempers were very short, and the three of us realized that this situation was bound to terminate fairly soon.

One particular incident happened the last spring that we fished together. We had bought some old halibut gear and were going to give it one more try. This spot we were going to fish was in fairly deep water of about forty fathoms, and we needed longer buoy lines than were customarily used. The day before, Al had been working on some of them on the dock.

The first sounding we took that morning was in thirty fathoms on the Mussels. Now, the Mussels isn't a good place to fish for halibut, as a halibut is big and flat and lies on the bottom, and the Mussels are quite sharp and probably quite uncomfortable.

Charlie said, "We have to run to the north and deeper water, so you had better put the long buoy lines on."

Just about then, Al realized he had forgotten them and left them on the dock. He looked down at Charlie (being as tall as he was, he always looked down at somebody), and said, "I straightened out the buoy lines at the dock, but Tiggie and I forgot to bring them."

I looked at Al and said, "That is quite a play on words."

Charlie was so infuriated he said, "We are going to set the goddamned gear here, and I don't give a damn if we get a goddamned fish."

At this stage of the game, Al and I didn't give a damn either, knowing that it was very unlikely we would even get one fish. But, as I said before, Charlie usually came out smelling like a rose. We got ten big, beautiful halibut. In fact, that was the best trip for about two weeks, amongst the whole fleet.

There was the same old scene on the dock. "Where did you get all the nice halibut, Charlie?"

And Charlie, with that little grin, said, "One of my little ole honey holes."

There was one thing that you didn't do when you got to shore, and that was blab about your skipper or his mistakes, because if you didn't like something that transpired, you took your oil cloths and left the boat. Almost all of the men that fished out of Harwichport and Chatham were constantly changing places on the various boats. It was like a type of musical chairs. You got mad with a skipper, left, fished on another boat for six or eight months, and then came back to the original boat, and so it went around and around. Over the years, I fished, off and on, several times with most of them.

"That was a fascinating comment on why crews change around so much and the etiquette of fishing by not bad-mouthing the skipper at the dock," I said in one of our conversations. "Guess that world is too small, huh?"

"There were a few guys who burned bridges, but most of us just played musical chairs with the boats. You'd fish until something went wrong, and you'd get pissed off and try another boat. Sometimes, it was worse, and you'd try to get back on the original boat. I fished with Charlie Chase and Al Hanson for a few years, and I fished with Red for a few years. God, what a crazy bastard he was."

"You mean Red or Charlie?"

"Red."

"I think he comes on the scene a little later in the book," I said. "When you left a boat, were there hard feelings?"

"Not usually, that I remember. That's just the way it was."

"Was there a problem in finding another site?"

"I didn't have a problem. People knew I could bait gear and was good working with the gear, and I knew where to fish so people came looking for me if they heard I had left another boat. Not everybody could do that, though."

Chapter Fifteen
Pollock in the Rip

Pollock are actually a pretty good fighting fish. We fished about a month for pollock. I don't know offhand how many tons we caught, but it was considerable. For the next three weeks, we managed to average about $470 a week, apiece. This is quite a feat, considering we were only getting two cents a pound for them.

I had a friend named Oscar, who wanted to catch a pollock. Finally, he talked me into letting him come along for a try. When you fish for pollock in the tide rips, the fish don't bite until the tide starts flowing. So this particular day that Oscar was with us, when we rounded Monomoy Point, the tide was still slack, and consequently, the fish were not feeding yet. We milled around for about a half hour without a bite or a sign of the fish. Just then, Oscar said, "This looks like another joyride." Al told Oscar that before the day was over, he'd see all the fish he would ever want to see. And he designated one particular line for Oscar to handle and told him once the fish started to bite, it would be his job to keep on hauling them in.

Oscar had a very strong Swedish accent, and as Al had predicted, as the tide increased, they started to bite. For the next three hours, they came like crazy. I was helping Oscar with his big fish, gaffing them for him and unhooking them. I could see that he was tiring and said, "Oscar, is that enough fish for you?"

He looked at me and in a very Swedish accent, said, "Yesus Christ! Don't they ever stop coming?"

About a week later, my father came down from the city. After hearing so many stories about the pollock, he wanted to try his hand at it. As we came around the Monomoy Point, he took out a beautiful rod case, and I could see him putting a boat rod together. I asked him what he was going to do with that, and he said that was his new boat rod, and he was going to catch a pollock on it. But I told him that he would never land one with it as the boat was steaming along at half speed through rips, and, as the fish run up to thirty pounds, they would make short work of it.

He looked at me and said, "I have to see that to believe it."

The first fish he hooked splintered his rod in several places and bent the ferrule ninety degrees. Finally, the line parted, and he sat there with a stunned look on his face. Of course, this was in the days before the fiberglass or graphite rods.

While he was pondering his first encounter with the pollock, the pollock were surfacing all around the boat by the hundreds. This occasionally happened, and when it did, everyone grabbed a gaff and tried to gaff as many as they could before the fish sound. By the time my father looked around, Al and I had got about forty, and Charlie had got three. His fourth he had by the tail, and he was almost hauled overboard. Al grabbed him by the leg. Before the fish sounded and stopped biting for the day, we had around five hundred pounds of pollock in the boat.

Chapter Sixteen
Crazy Red

I met a man named Red and didn't know at the time that our lives would cross time and time again or that we would fish together for years. Within fifteen minutes after I had met him, I was thoroughly convinced that he was as nutty as a fruit cake, and he probably had the papers to prove it. He became known as Crazy Red.

Physically, we were almost twins—five feet six inches, 170 pounds—the same type of build, but that was where it ended. He had a visored cap, and protruding from the edges of this cap were a few wisps of red hair. When he smiled, you could see that all his top teeth were out, with the exception of the two eyeteeth, giving the appearance of fangs. He had green lenses in his glasses, and when I finally mustered the courage to ask about them, he told me it was because he liked spinach so much, he wanted the whole world to look like it.

He always wore hip boots even when he went to dances, and I saw him dancing with them on. And he was so aggressive that most of the girls agreed to dance with him rather than to get into a row with him. He always carried a knife by his side, too, and he would constantly threaten people with it.

Red was on his own at a very young age, and he lived around Hyannis. He did just about any type of fishing that he could get a job at, just so long as he was near the water and boats—shellfishing, dragging, party boats, etc.

At one period when he was mostly shellfishing, he was constantly harassed and badgered by a big German shepherd every night on his way home. After many close calls, Red thought that it was about time to put an end to this type of foolishness, and he would be damned if he was going to take a different route home every night. As he approached the street, he threw his jacket around his arm, and as the dog approached, he extended it and let the dog bite the jacket. "Now," he said, "you bastard, you get a good grip." And he took out his knife and cut the dog's throat from ear to ear. He was not someone you wanted to pick a fight with.

In spite of all this, we became very close friends, and I had great respect and admiration for his knowledge of fishing and seamanship. He taught me more about fishing than any other single person, making it possible for me to eventually become a skipper.

As we became friendlier, though, I must say we had very little in common except fishing. In fact, Red wasn't the type to bring home to meet Mother, as he'd probably make a pass at her within fifteen minutes. He used to embarrass me constantly, propositioning a girl any place he would encounter her, whether she was young, old, or crippled. He used to have a saying, "If they can't walk, I'll wheel them." After many arguments about this type of carryings on, I asked him how in the hell he had the nerve to do this. He said it wasn't hard and added, "I keep score, and it comes out about fifty percent of the time I get my face slapped, twenty-five percent of the time I don't get an answer, but that last twenty-five percent of the time is worth all of it."

We were playing whist one night, and I had been warned by most of the fishermen that Red had constantly threatened various other fishermen and people with his knife, so I was a little leery of him. As this was running through my mind, he drew out his knife and plunged it into the table and said there had better be no cheating here or else. I kind of gulped a little bit, and I realized that if I didn't do something then and there, this bird was going to pull this crap on me all the time.

If a person has a knife, you never try to grab it away from him, pick it up, or look at it, unless you ask him first, which I did. He gave me a funny look, withdrew it from the table, and handed it to me saying, "Be careful with it, Tiggie; it's sharp and has quite a bite to it." I spent my childhood as a streetwise kid with tough gangs and knew a thing or two about bullies and thugs. I also had had a lot of experience with knives while in the Army, unbeknownst to Red. I casually threw the knife the length of the room at a pretty-girl calendar and hit her between the breasts—it was probably one of the best shots I ever made. Red's eyes bulged out a little, and he gulped. I then walked over to the wall, pulled the knife out, walked back to the table, and slammed it into the wood as far as I could.

I looked at him with my very best tough-guy grin and casually said, "The next time you ever pull a knife on me, remember, Red, that I'm a Wop, and they are quite famous for their ability to use a knife. So while you're pulling out your knife, I'm going to be already cutting with mine."

That was the last time he ever threatened me with his knife, or we ever had an argument that could terminate in violence.

"Red must have been some piece of work. I bet you two were quite a pair, him with his top front teeth out and you with your bottom two out," I said.

"I don't remember him telling me what happened to his teeth—probably got clobbered trying to put the make on someone's wife. I got mine knocked out by my cousin when I was pretty young. But I figured if people didn't like me the way I was, too bad, so I was determined not to let it bother me. I never even got fitted for false teeth—I've been this way for years."

"What was it like fishing with Red?"

"He was crazy, but for some reason, we got along. He knew where the fish were, too. He taught me a lot. It was in his blood, and he never wanted to do anything else. But you didn't want to cross him. I don't remember him ever actually hurting anyone, but he threatened a lot. Most people took the threats seriously. But he really was a crazy bastard. We had a shotgun on board to kill the sharks or hags, and he used to fire it over my head just for the hell of it."

"I bet that broke your rhythm."

"I never had rhythm," he said with a twinkle. I knew he was talking with a double meaning, but I chose to ignore the comment.

"I've noticed that you went into a lot of detail about halibut fishing but not cod and haddock. Why not? Was that just routine?"

"We got a lot of cod and haddock, but I guess I just like fishing for halibut more. More of a challenge to find them, and they were such a magnificent fish. Cod were cod. What's so special about them? You set out eight tubs of trawl gear, and if you're lucky, you get thousands of pounds back, that is, if the hags or sharks didn't get them first. Most of the year, that's what we fished for and I guess why everyone looked forward to spring. After a long winter of little money, we all wanted to get some halibut, but it was probably the cod that paid the bills in the long run."

Chapter Seventeen
Lucky and Unlucky

Another captain named Charlie Mathews, alias Black Magic, was a very good fisherman and caught a lot of fish. Of course, not many of the boys called him Black Magic to his face, that is, with the exception of Al Hanson, Bobby Our, and a few of the other big boys. Most certainly, I did not, as I had just started to get a little friendly with him; I knew he could be a mean son of a bitch, too.

I knew he needed a man, so I worked up enough courage to ask him for a job, and much to my surprise, he said, "Get your gear and come aboard." My stay with him was brief, and Charlie was the only one to ever fire me from any job that I have ever had in my life.

Charlie kept a very neat boat. In fact, I think he was too extreme in this. He would always walk around the deck, under the house in the fo'c's'le, poking off the herring scales with his jackknife, scrubbing at this or that, throwing water here and there. And, unlike most fishermen, he was always scrupulously clean himself—even his fishing clothes looked good.

During my stay with Charlie, I had become fast friends with Horny Nick. I had known him, off and on, for several years, played cards with him a lot, and had made several trips to the city with him. I had also met his girlfriend, named Minnie, with whom he had lived for many years without benefit of clergy. He even named their dog after me.

Nick helped me out a lot with my fishing by explaining shortcuts and giving me good tips and advice like getting me up on my toes instead of walking around flatfooted. With his help, I gradually became a fairly skilled fisherman.

Charlie's personality was discouraging. Sometimes, he wouldn't talk for as long as ten hours. During one of these black moods, I asked him what the trouble was. He looked at me and said, "Don't talk to me unless I talk to you first." But there was always Nick at the dock to tell my troubles to. He had a very sympathetic ear. There were even occasions when he took Charlie's side. He would say that Charlie was a deep thinker and that running a boat, at times, was quite a problem, so that was probably the reason he was that way.

I had a close call with Charlie M. We were fishing down in the South Channel and had fished for twenty straight hours without any rest. We had a good trip of fish aboard and had just thrown the anchor. We had six hours time before the next set, which gave us four hours of sleep apiece, as each man had to stand two hours watch. I had the first watch, which meant that I would be twenty-two hours without any rest, and believe me, my can was dragging.

Charlie told me to cut two hundred pounds of bait and bait two tubs of gear. The cutting of two hundred pounds of bait and the baiting of one tub of gear would just about require two hours, that is, if you were real fresh, and I was pretty well spent. But on top of that, he said, "Here's my jackknife. When you get through with that, scrape some of the herring scales off the walls." I believe I told him he could shove the knife he knew where.

During my watch, the fog closed in, so that you couldn't see twenty or thirty feet ahead, although the night had been clear earlier. It seems that when it is clear, you never see any other boats or ships, but as soon as the fog comes in, you can hear them everywhere. After a while, you get used to the pattern, and, sure enough, I heard a big dragger off in the distance sounding its horn. They usually sound their horns at three-minute intervals, and, from the sound, I could hear that he was bearing down on us quite rapidly. I woke Charlie up. He came on deck and being a seasoned fisherman, knew what the situation was right off. He took the compass reading on the dragger's last blow and knew that it was going to be quite close. He started the motor. In a situation like this, you don't dare move one way or the other until you see the other boat, and then you hope that you have time for evasive action. I finally saw the boat looming high above us. Charlie put the boat in gear, and it missed us by only eight or ten feet. We got quite a sloshing from its wake. Charlie said, "Let's get the hell out of here."

While I was fishing with Charlie Mathews, my friend, Horny Nick was fishing with Babe Miller, who was the high-line fisherman of the fleet. In commercial fishing language, this means the boat that does the best. And Babe was very good, but in my opinion, he was a louse. Nick was particularly enthusiastic about the prospects of going swordfishing, and he was telling me all about the forthcoming trip that they were to make to George's Bank. I had never seen a swordfish before in my life, with the exception of a slice on my plate, and I had no idea how you fished for them. He gave me a brief rundown.

One man stood in the pulpit on the bow of the boat with a harpoon, one man steered the boat, and several men climbed up into the mast and stayed up there all day, watching for the elusive fish. When the fish were sighted, they signaled the wheelsman by a bell, and he proceeded in the direction of the fish, while the harpooner tried to stick the fish. He told me his particular job was called head-mastman, which meant he was on the highest point of the boat. And so, they started out with the tide that night.

Two mornings later, Red woke me up and told me that Nick had been killed. The mast had split in two, and the mast and all the men on it crashed into the sea. They picked the men up, but Nick died a short time later. Little did I know when they left for that trip that it would be the last time I'd ever see Nick again.

This was quite a shock to me, as we had become very close. I can remember getting dressed in a suit, and about the only time a Cape fisherman dresses in a suit is either for a funeral or a wedding. And there is not much difference between either one, I guess. He was buried in Harwichport, in a very beautiful little cemetery. I used to visit it quite often the first couple of years, but as time goes on, you just don't bother anymore. I drank quite heavily for a week. Then I looked around me at some of the other derelicts, stopped feeling sorry for myself, and got back to some real hard work.

"Is that story of the boat missing you by eight to ten feet in the fog another fish story, slightly exaggerated?"

"No. That big boat almost rammed us. If Charlie hadn't started the motor and turned, we would have been run down. It was a much bigger boat than ours, and the wake it was throwing tossed us around pretty good."

"It must have been really hard to lose your friend, Nick."

"He wanted me to go on that trip, but there was something that bothered me about it. I looked at the boat when Nick was explaining swordfishing to me and said the mast needed some more stays. You know what a stay is?"

"Yeah. It's the wire that goes from the mast to the hull to stabilize the mast."

"The mast didn't look secure to me. I told Nick that, but he told me not to worry, everything would be just fine. I didn't like Babe Miller, the captain, either. I had never fished with him, but there was something about him I just didn't like or trust."

"So you were right about the mast?"

"It looked that way. The mast snapped while Nick was high up on it. I really liked Nick. We didn't fish much together, but we did a lot of things on shore together. I really missed him, and he was the first friend I lost, so it was really hard. It never got easier losing my friends, but I guess I got more used to it."

Chapter Eighteen
The *Pat-Er-Glo*

The *Pat-Er-Glo* was a boat that was built by Captain Ernest Parsons of Boston, who at one time, had been a high-line skipper during the dory fishing era. The *Pat-Er-Glo* was named after his three children Patty, Ernest, and Gloria. She was a beauty, finest in the Harwich fleet, forty-two feet long, with a fourteen-foot beam and a beautifully comfortable fo'c's'le. At the time, I never realized how much time I would spend on her.

Captain Parsons bore the distinction of being one of the only skippers off the East Coast who never lost a man or a dory in his long and successful career. So this *Pat-Er-Glo* was just a sort of toy for him to play with in his retirement. I couldn't see how he could say he was retired. He fished harder and longer and caught more fish than most of the fishermen half his age. Red was one of his crew members, and they got along pretty well, as Red was a good fisherman and was making plenty of money.

It was obvious that Captain Parsons, who was maybe seventy-two or so, could never keep up the pace, and everyone was waiting for the inevitable. He had a complete collapse and had to go to the hospital for about a month. He left Red in charge of the boat; he did well and caught quite a few fish.

Captain Parsons soon sold the *Pat-Er-Glo* to my old friend, Dan Ballou, who a few years earlier had set me on the course for Harwichport. He didn't have a crew, so he asked me if I thought Al was capable of running the boat yet. And I said that I thought he was, and I also asked if I might go along. Dan said he would love to have both of us, but not to expect too much work from him, as he had a heart condition. He said he could cut bait, steer, cook, and do various other small tasks, but Al and I were young and vigorous. Dan Ballou was an exceptional man in that he owned the boat, but he never gave Al a hard time and left the running of it completely up to him.

This was Al's first time as a skipper, and he was learning by trial and error. On the first few halibut trips, we got very few fish in comparison to the other boats and set on the wrong type of bottom, but we soon learned from our mistakes and finally came up to par with the other fishermen.

Halibut fishing is about ten percent savvy and ninety percent luck, and luck is something I don't usually have. To give you an idea of your chances of setting into a school of halibut, take an offshore chart of the grounds we fished and divide it into a couple hundred squares, with there never being more than four or five of these squares having a school of halibut in them at one time. You can see how chancy it could be. Some boats would have one or two halibut, some none at all, and half the boats as many as fifty halibut. The halibut season came and went, and we were getting along very well. They were really happy days.

We started pollocking amongst the rips. This particular day, Dan had prepared a beautiful dinner for us—fried pork chops, mashed potatoes, and apple sauce—the whole works. As Al and I were eating the pork chops, we noticed they tasted gritty and there were a few hairs in them. I didn't want to hurt Dan's feelings, but I said, "What the hell happened to these pork chops?"

"Well, I'll tell you, Tiggie," he said, "I was frying the pork chops for a half an hour, and you remember that rough rip you just went through? Well, the whole plate fell onto the deck and into the coal pail, so I kind of picked them up and dusted them off a bit. I guess I didn't do too good a job."

About two hours later, Al was steering the boat, keeping ahead of the tide rip, the pollock were biting beautifully, and Dan was working two lines. I was working three lines, when I noticed Dan didn't look too good. The next thing I knew, he was down on his knees, and I could see that he was having a heart seizure of some sort. I helped him up to the engine box, and we laid him down, resting his head against the bulkhead. We managed to get his heart pills out, and he took a couple. Al insisted that we get started for home immediately.

But Dan said, "Nothing doing. If I'm going to die, I'll never make it to shore anyway, and I can't think of a better way of dying than watching Tiggie catch pollock."

Can you believe that? And with pollock at two cents a pound! Soon after this, Dan had to give up fishing, and he left the boat in Al's hands.

Chapter Nineteen
Unpleasant Tasks

One day, as we were coming back from the Mussels, it was very foggy and dead calm. Al was steering, and I was dressing fish. We had only had a mediocre catch of about twelve boxes, so I wasn't hustling too much. The next thing I knew, Al was hauling the boat hard to port (or to the left) almost knocking me overboard. I yelled at him, "What the hell?! Are you crazy or something?" Then I noticed that we had almost had a collision with a motor-sail boat. It was just lying there dead in the water. It was about thirty-eight feet long. Al made a circle around it, and we hollered several times, but nobody appeared from below.

Al pulled up alongside of it and said, "Tiggie, go aboard it."

I looked up at Al—any time I talked to Al, I always had to look up at him, as he was nearly a foot taller than I—and I said, "Why do I have to go aboard?"

Al's answer was, "I'll tell you, Tiggie! I'm the captain, and you are the crew, and that makes me the boss. Now you just take your Wop ass and take a look-see!"

I jumped on the deck of the boat and looked down into the fo'c's'le, where there were two empty bunks and a couple of lockers, which I reluctantly looked into expecting to find a body. There was food on the stove that had turned moldy in the pans. It became apparent that whoever had been on the boat had been alone and had fallen overboard without being able to catch up with the boat again. Al threw me a tow line, and we proceeded to tow it into Harwichport, where we tied it up to the dock and then called the Coast Guard and state police.

Al and I went aboard to look it over after tying the motor-sailor up at the dock. There were several checkbooks and a wallet on the table. The checkbooks had large amounts in them for balances, but there was only $9 in the wallet.

Al said, "We ought to take it 'cause we'll only get accused of stealing anyways."

But we didn't touch anything. The man's name was Humphrey. He owned a big drug concern in this country and was quite wealthy, as his sister informed us at a later date.

The investigation by the Coast Guard and the police entailed several days and tied us up for quite a while. We realized that we were entitled to some salvage money, but it took us over a year of paperwork and about five years of aggravation before we got $300 apiece from it. His body subsequently washed up on Nantucket.

We finally talked Red into coming along with us, as he was having a little trouble with the boat he was on. We knew he was quite foolish but thought we'd have a little fun anyway. Red was a very fast baiter. He had a peculiar habit of sticking the hook into the bait and not pulling the point, or barb, through. His method was completely different from Al's and mine. Al said that he didn't believe the fish could get hooked the way Red was baiting. Red told him that his tub of gear would catch as much fish as anybody's; besides which, it was easier to throw as the hooks didn't catch onto each other. From then on, for the next three days, Red would count the fish in Al's tub, mine, and his own, and they averaged about the same. Al was convinced that it was a better method, and consequently, most of the fishermen in Harwich and Chatham bait by that method.

During one particular trip for halibut, we were coming back in the middle of the night with about fifty-mile-an-hour breezes—a southeaster. Our course was northwest for home, so we were like a giant surfboard keeping just ahead of the waves most of the time.

Al said to us, "I'm just as glad that it's dark and we can't see the size of some of these seas."

Red and I were in the stern of the boat dressing the big halibut and codfish. I was closest to the stern. I happened to look up and saw a tremendous sea, which was going to hit us. Red was in front of me with the knife in his hand and several big halibut, so I couldn't go that way. I jumped on the stern and climbed up the mast. As it was, I still got two boots full of water. After the foam and spray and everything settled, the cockpit was full of water. Red hollered to Al that I had been washed overboard, but I was safe.

"I bet you saw rogue waves a lot out there," I said.

"Yeah, we did," Tiggie responded.

"Bruce and I were in Costa Rica once when we had one of those experiences. We were fishing in an open boat."

"Al thought I was washed overboard that time," Tiggie interrupted.

"Are you the only one who can tell a story here?"

Tiggie took a bite of his muffin, so I thought I could start my story again. I managed to get through it, but there was no comment from him.

"I was a lot more agile to get high up on that mast."

"I guess I should consider myself lucky that you kept quiet long enough for me to tell the story. I'm supposed to sit here and listen to you every day and not add anything, huh?" I said with my best hurt expression.

"I was listening. I didn't mean anything by it."

I remembered when I could give him a hard time, and he gave it right back to me or vice versa, but he was getting too sensitive to do that too often now.

Wychmere Harbor wooden boat fleet

Wychmere Harbor

Johnnie Barker on right

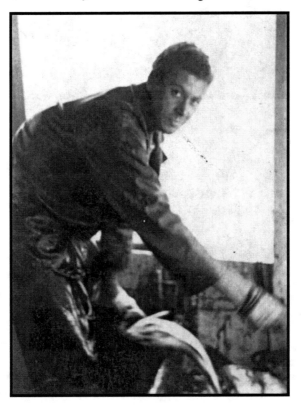

Al Hanson

Al Hanson, left, and Charlie Chase with hat

Al Hanson and Red Moran on *Pat-Er-Glo*

Al Hanson and Red Moran with tub trawl

Al Hanson, tall one, with Red Moran on *Pat-Er-Glo*

Al Hanson and halibut before steadying sail

Red Moran, with back to image,
Al Hanson and Tiggie on *Pat-Er-Glo*

Crazy Red Moran on *Pat-Er-Glo* stabbing shark

Being towed in on a dory

Two-man dory fishing in 1950s with Captain Parsons

Dory fishing

Pat-Er-Glo in Wychmere Harbor

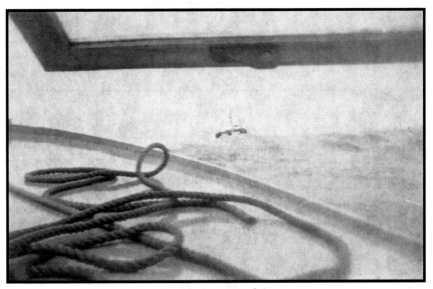

Heading out to fish

Fishing for swordfish in between halibut sets

Fishing off Chatham

Fishing shark hauled up

Fred Chillis, Tiggie's cousin, with halibut (250 pounds) at Wychmere

Jackie on *Pat-Er-Glo* with 50-pound codfish

Mr. Fish and Red Moran on *Pat-Er-Glo*

Mr. Fish on *Pat-Er-Glo* was going to medical school

Heading to the Mussels

Red Moran and Tiggie on *Pat-Er-Glo*

Pat-Er-Glo at Wychmere Harbor

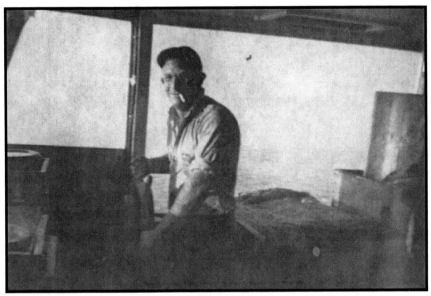

Red Moran on *Pat-Er-Glo*

Al Hanson on *Pat-Er-Glo*
(he died at sea when thirty-three)

Towing boat into Wychmere Harbor

Herbie Maggio and Tony Bonacorso (relatives of
Tiggie) fishing with Tiggie on *Pat-Er-Glo*

Herbie Maggio after shooting shearwater

Herbie Maggio, Tiggie's cousin, with halibut

Red Moran on *Pat-Er-Glo* (he later committed suicide)

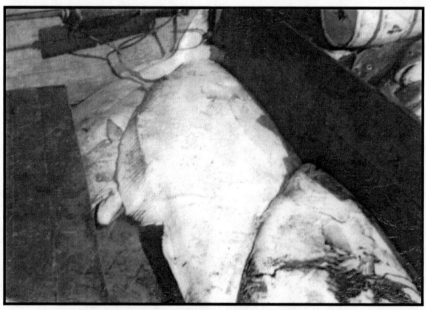

Halibut fishing on Babe Miller's boat off Nova Scotia

Swordfishing on *Terra Nova* with Babe

Grenadier, a deepwater fish, caught on Babe Miller's boat

Tiggie hauling back cod in shark's mouth

Tony Bonacorso (Tiggie's uncle) fishing with Tiggie

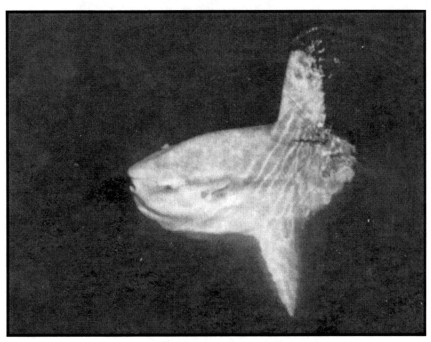

Oceanic sunfish found off Corsairs Canyon

Tiggie with blue shark

Old wooden boat railing

Tiggie on Walter Young's boat

Stone Horse Lightship off Monomoy

Chapter Twenty
Superstitious?

Some of the best times on the *Pat-Er-Glo* were spent by the side of the dock watching the girls, the tourists, and the dock-side activities. This particular summer, there was an artist who used to hang around the dock. Her name was Pat. She wasn't really pretty, but she had about a forty-inch chest and very rarely wore a bra. After a week or so, she had become very friendly with all the fishermen and used to come aboard the *Pat-Er-Glo* quite frequently.

One of the things that fishermen think of as a cardinal sin is if a girl walks through some of the gear that you are working on or sits on a bundle of it. This particular day, we had just rigged a new tub, and Pat stepped all through it. Al told her, in no uncertain terms, that this was considered bad luck and not to do it again. She then proceeded to tromp around in it a little bit more. Al picked her up bodily and threw her overboard. She swam up and down the channel a couple of times and asked a couple of fishermen to help her up on dock. It was quite a sight to see her soaking wet, her clothes clinging to her, and no bra. In fact, some of the older fishermen sitting along the dock managed to get both their eyes open.

That night, we went fishing and lost the tub of gear that she had stepped in. Al was furious. The next day that we didn't go fishing, we had to replace it. Along came Pat on the dock; she jumped into the boat right on the gear again. This time, Red threw her overboard. Same scene again, only this time, there were five or six more fishermen than there had been the previous time. By the end of the week, the benches were full of fishermen, making bets as to whether Pat would get another dunking. It kind of put a little excitement in the old fellows' lives.

Pat was a very friendly girl. In fact, she bestowed her favors upon many of the fishermen—that is, if she liked them. If she didn't like you, you couldn't touch her with a ten-foot pole. One of the fishermen was telling me that she was, undoubtedly, one of the fastest girls that he had ever gone out with. He said all you had to do was get her near a bed or a blanket, and she would trip you and beat you to the fall, always ending up beneath you. At the end of the summer, when Pat left, a little of the sparkle went out of the eyes of the older fishermen, and some of the younger ones would reminisce about her through the cold winter.

The three of us fished together for another year and a half and did fairly well, but like all associations, it inevitably came to an end. Red was getting to a point where he wanted to be a skipper again and run his own boat. And Al and I were not getting along fourteen carat. So it was just a matter of time before we went our separate ways.

"Do you know why there are such superstitions about women and boats?" I asked Tiggie.

"Not really." Tiggie had been talking about women in general and Pat in particular. "She wasn't all that pretty, but she was stacked. She used to wear these knitted tops with pretty large mesh. She was, what do you call it—a..."

"An exhibitionist?"

"Yeah. An exhibitionist. She loved those mesh tops or tight shirts. And it just added to things when she got thrown overboard with the wet shirt clinging to her. She had a room next to mine at Mrs. Nickerson's. My dog, Suzy, used to go out the window of my room and into her room, walking over the clean sheets with muddy paws.

"I made $100 because of Pat."

"How'd you manage that?" I asked.

"She was leaving the Cape and needed money, and I loaned her $100. All the boys on the pier said I was crazy, and each of them bet me $10 that I'd never see the money again. I had put a time limit on the payback and went to the post office every day, but nothing came. The next-to-last day, there was a letter from New York, and it was from her with a $100 money order. I went down to the dock and waved the letter and money order in their faces and told them to pay up. So I made a hundred bucks on the deal."

I never got an answer from him about women on boats and superstitions, though.

Chapter Twenty-One
Off to George's

I came down to the dock one morning, looked aboard Dick Chase's boat, and saw Johnnie Costa, Dick Chase, and Al Hanson with charts spread out over the engine box and knew right away they were cooking up some kind of a trip, and knowing Al as well as I did, I knew it would be in some distant spot or place. I figured maybe forty or fifty miles some place, never realizing that it would be about two hundred miles roundtrip, quite a feat for boats of this size and class.

Dick looked up at me and said, "We've got a good trip planned for you, Wop. We are going to George's Bank."

When I heard this, I was planning a hasty retreat. Al Hanson reached up and grasped me by the ankle and said, "At least listen to the idea before you go off."

They were being overly sweet to me. Since it was coming from them, I realized they were going to pour sugar on and sweet talk me into going. I said, "I'll listen, but I doubt I'll be going."

Al said, "Why?"

I replied, "Because I'm yellow, and I don't care who knows it."

There had been only one other boat from our fleet that had ever gone that far and fished this particular spot. It was Babe Miller. He had made three or four real successful trips as well as a couple of brokers—a broker being a trip that you don't make expenses. It was taking a calculated risk on the weather, and you would just have to hope the weather stayed good for at least three days. Al Hanson was running the *Pat-Er-Glo* at this time and had Bobby Our for crew. He told me that he had talked Bobby

Our into going, and Bobby was a very good friend of mine. Al had told Bobby that they might run into a little difficulty in getting me to go along, and Bobby told Al to "...tell the Wop he had better go, or I'll kill him." Not wanting to get killed, I agreed. I would be going with Dick Chase.

The next day was spent making final preparations, getting ice, nearly a ton of bait, food, and the rest. We had a different problem than Al's boat. We had a gasoline engine, and the capacity of our tanks was nowhere near as much as would be required for the trip, and so we had to get two fifty-five-gallon drums and tie them in on the stern. When we eventually had to pour it into the tank, it was quite a job with the boat tossing and rolling, and we lost a lot of gas. The *Pat-Er-Glo* was diesel driven, which meant it burned less fuel than a gasoline engine, so Al and Bobby didn't have the same problem as we did.

We steamed, or ran, for twelve hours. Al was ahead of us in the *Pat-Er-Glo*, and they stopped to take soundings with the sounding lead. We came alongside, and Dick asked Al what particular type of bottom we were going to set on.

Al said, "Black and brown pebbles with bits of coral growth on them."

The first sounding was pure sand, and like on the land, sand is found in a desert, and there is very little life in the desert. It is the same principle in the sea—a sandy bottom isn't very good. We steamed in various directions for over eighteen hours taking soundings every so often without any sign of pebbles or stones—nothing but sand, and it was quite discouraging. We had been gone from the dock for thirty hours, and we hadn't set a hook yet. Also, we knew that our gas was running low and if we didn't set soon, we would just have barely enough to get back to Harwichport. Johnnie called Al on the radio and told him to stop as he wanted to powwow for a few minutes. We ran alongside of Al, and Johnnie told him that we had to find something quickly, or we would have to start back; our gas situation was getting quite critical.

We had been drifting for probably fifteen minutes when Johnnie happened to throw the sounding lead over the side and haul it up. At last, there were the elusive pebbles with the coral growths on them. He shouted to Al to take a sounding.

Al looked at the lead and said, "This is the place, boys."

He put a marker buoy over the side—this you do when you are fishing in a small area. Our boat set to the east of the marker buoy, and Al took the western set. Both boats set six skates apiece.

After setting the gear, we let it set for three hours—we had to wait till the tide slacked a little, since George's Bank is famous for its swift tides. Johnnie, Dick, and I had a standard bet when halibut fishing. We used to pay a dollar a fish. We had six skates in the water and would get to haul two apiece, so chances were equal.

I hauled the first one and didn't see a fish and handed the end to Dick. He hauled five in rapid succession. Then it was Johnnie's turn, and he landed four or five, also. At this point, I was out about $10, but the way the fish were coming, I was anxious to get at the rail and haul again. I didn't get a fish again and handed the gear to Dick, swearing quite profusely.

Dick said, "Let a man show you how to catch them flat ones," he said, and he began to bring in ten more.

Johnnie came up with eight more, and I was elated because we had a nice trip on board and would make a few bucks even if I was out $28 in bets. The fish were all lying aft with their white bellies and were quite a sight.

The weather report we got wasn't too hot and coupled with our gasoline situation, we thought that we had better get underway for home. Dick and I cleaned the fish, and we steamed for ten hours before we made the Pollock Rip Lightship, and the sea and the wind were building all the time from a northwesterly direction. By the time we got to the dock, it was just about half a gale, and it blew for three straight days. We just got by, by the skin of our teeth. Al got to the dock first, and we were half a mile behind, just approaching the breakwater when we ran out of gas. Al had to turn around and tow us in. When we hit the dock, I told all hands concerned that that was last trip to that place that I would take.

111

Chapter Twenty-Two
The Bad Trip

Red and I went on a trip in pursuit of the mighty halibut down to a place called the Pumpkins with a man named Harry Randall, an old-time fisherman from Boston. Al Hanson (who had finally bought the *Pat-Er-Glo*) and Bobby Our were going to join us. I had many misgivings about this trip as the barometer had been quite low and unsteady. It had been overcast for several days, but there was no wind at all. I couldn't quite put my finger on it, but I had a bad feeling about this trip, and how right I was.

It had seemed in the last year or so that Al's judgment on weather was bordering on recklessness; it was one of the particular reasons I had quit fishing with him. Yet, in a way, he still seemed to hold the reins. This was a constant source of irritation. Red listened to Al, and we argued about Al setting policy for our boat.

The trouble with this set-up of the two boats fishing together was that the *Pat-Er-Glo* could steam into twenty-five-mile-an-hour breezes wide open, and the boat we had, the *Viking*, had to slow up in any breeze at all. So, when we got caught in a breeze or fog, we became separated, and, if it was a good breeze, the *Pat-Er-Glo*, would get back to Harwichport hours before us, and we would have to ride out the worst of it.

On the way down, it took seven hours to get there, and we just had time to make one set of six skates. You never set gear in the dark when halibut fishing as the halibut do not bite at night, although haddock prefer night sets. But if you set before dark and don't haul until night, you do fairly well sometimes. There is one little drawback in this method,

112

though. For some reason, when you haul fish at night, when the fish see the lights from the boat, they really get violent. And if they happen to pull the gear out of your hand and start to run with the line, there is a hook every eighteen feet, and you have to make sure you duck in the right direction.

We finally got the gear set about 5:00 p.m. that afternoon. As this was late spring, there would only be two hours of daylight to fish instead of the preferred three hours, but the tide wouldn't be slack for four hours, so we wouldn't be able to start hauling till 9:00 p.m. We had chow, did a few chores, played a little cribbage, and got a weather report, which said fifteen to twenty-mile southeastern winds, which wasn't too bad at all; it also called for a fair wind home. But often, successive weather reports seem to get progressively worse, and I didn't think this would be an exception. Up to this point, there was not a breeze, and the sea was oily calm, but the overcast sky had an ominous look to it.

We got the gear hauled and had eight or ten fish of between fifty and one hundred pounds and about a thousand pounds of codfish besides. Al Hanson on the *Pat-Er-Glo* had a similar catch. We had just enough fish not to call it a good trip but not exactly a broker either. What we really needed was another set like it to top it off and give us a little gravy. So Al and Red decided that we would set anchors out and see what daylight brought forth.

The next weather report that we got at midnight gave southeast winds increasing from twenty to twenty-five miles per hour, but there was still not a breeze where we were.

I was all set to head home without making another set, saying to Red, "We could make good time with the smooth seas."

Red then said, "Won't we feel foolish getting to Harwichport tomorrow, and it's still calm. Besides, what do you want to be called, 'chicken'?"

By the time dawn broke, that elusive breeze had finally struck at, I would say, about twenty-five miles an hour from the northeast, not the southeast like they had predicted. Northeast was the worst direction we could have, as it would be hitting us on the starboard side on the way home, and the sea seems to build up much more rapidly when the wind is from the northeast quarter. We had the radio telephone on, talking to Al on the *Pat-Er-Glo*, and he said he had been in contact with two or three of the other boats from Chatham and that they were going to turn around and go back as they didn't like the weather report.

But Red said, "We're here; we might as well stay and set three skates anyway. We'll get home; we always have."

Harry Randall and I asked him how come he didn't consult with us as we also had a say in it. There ensued a short violent quarrel in which I told him he could shove the boat he knew where.

I walked aft in a huff and made ready to set the gear. Red steamed a little distance from the *Pat-Er-Glo*, and we began to set. All the while we were setting, Harry Randall was growling and griping to me as if it was my fault.

I said, "You got anything to say, go say it to that red-headed bastard up there."

The gear was set, and we would have to wait three hours before we started to haul. Red turned the radio on to see if he could get another weather report, and this time, it was a beauty. It gave northeast storm warnings for winds up to fifty to sixty miles an hour.

Red looked over at me, kind of turned pasty white, and said, "Hit me if you want to, but for Christ's sake, don't say I told you so."

We started to haul the gear as soon as the tide started to slacken up a little. Because of the wind against the tide, the boat was very difficult to handle, and consequently, we had a very, very stiff haul. By this time, the wind had picked up considerably, blowing at least thirty-five and gusty. We finally finished hauling the gear. The *Pat-Er-Glo* had finished about ten minutes earlier and was lying alongside. Al and Red talked for a few minutes, deciding which course they would take. Al would lead, and we would follow. I knew how this was going to end up, as the *Pat-Er-Glo* was a much better boat than the *Viking*. We kept the *Pat-Er-Glo* in sight for about half an hour, and then it became rainy and foggy, and that was the last we saw of them that trip, making me feel completely alone, not that they could help, but, as they say, misery loves company.

Red had the wheel for the first two hours, and the wind increased to a point that I couldn't judge what speed it was. When we had first started home, we had had a head tide; that meant that the tide and the wind were flowing in one direction, and the seas wouldn't crest so badly, but when the tide went against the wind, they broke and you had a tide rip effect everywhere.

At this stage of the game, as the seas kept on increasing, you had to hold one hand on the throttle and man the wheel with the other, and each and every individual sea was a challenge. If you were between two big seas, you had to get out of the trough of the sea and halfway up the crest, so that they wouldn't break over you. If you got too far up on the sea, you fell through it and stood a chance of breaking a plank or pounding some of the caulking out of the seams. Therefore, whoever was at the wheel had his hands full.

Red and I swapped off and on. Harry took the wheel once, and we hit a sea wrong, fell through another one, hit with an awful crash, and held our breath for a few minutes expecting the water to rise above our knees at any moment. But the *Viking* was built rugged, even though the design was lousy. Red didn't let Harry steer anymore.

At this point, Harry lost all his nerve, and you could see he was coming apart at the seams. Harry told Red he was going to beat his goddamned head in, and I told him he wouldn't do any such thing out here. But if he waited till we got in, that is **IF** we got in, I would help him. In the meantime, we would all have to cooperate if we were going to make it.

We had left the fishing grounds at 10:00 a.m., had been steaming for ten hours, and hadn't seen a buoy, land, or either the Stone Horse or Pollock Rip Lightship. We had Al on the radio telephone, and he said he was just coming around Monomoy Point. He had just seven miles to go across Nantucket Sound.

Red told him he had no idea where we were, as he had to constantly change course for each huge wave. Al wished us luck and said he would stay aboard the boat all night when he got to Harwichport and keep the radio turned on. He said it might give us a little comfort if not much help, but he could at least do that.

About two hours later, a huge sea hit the bow and broke all the windows out of the trunk cabin on the port side. I rushed into the cabin, surveyed the damage, and knew that things had to be plugged up or we would be in serious trouble. I stuck my head out of the fo'c's'le and told Harry to break up one of the fish boxes. At this point, Harry was a gibbering idiot, and I had to do it myself. I stuffed blankets and other bedding into the three portholes and nailed boards across to hold them in place. It did the job.

After nineteen hours, we finally approached the Pollock Rip Lightship. We established radio contact with the lightship and inquired about the wind velocity. They said it was blowing between fifty and sixty, and the forecast was for it to continue for two more days.

The lightship was approximately one hundred feet long, and once in a while, the sea would get between us and the lightship, and all you could see was the top of the mast, but none of the hull of the ship. At this point, the skipper of the lightship informed us that he was going to dump some diesel fuel over the side, and this would smooth the seas and keep them from breaking over us. They did this for several hours, and he told us he would have to discontinue this as he was exhausting his fuel supply. He said he didn't think it was possible for us to avoid many more seas, and one was bound to hit us the wrong way and do us in.

He made a suggestion that they put a cargo net over the side and throw us a line, and we put our life jackets on and go into the water and up the side of the lightship. Of course, this meant losing the boat, but since it was insured, we could always get another boat, but one can't get another neck. Harry was shouting and hollering that he wasn't going into the water, so I told Red we were going to have to talk it over and decide one way or another. Red and I were young, strong, and agile, but when we looked at poor old Harry, we realized that he probably wouldn't make it.

Red said, "We are all going to make it or none of us will." Then he informed the skipper of the lightship that we were going to stay with the boat.

He asked the skipper what the wind velocity was at that particular moment. The skipper said forty knots, and he figured that that would be the least it would be for the next two days, and if we were ever going to have a chance of making it, we would have to try soon.

Red figured that the tide should turn in about half an hour, and with the tide and the wind together, the seas would be long, but they wouldn't be breaking, and we might just be lucky enough to make it. From the Pollock Rip Lightship to the Stone Horse Lightship, it ordinarily took us forty minutes. In the *Viking* that night, we were like a huge surfboard. We made it in about twenty-two minutes. It was quite a ride. We finally got around Monomoy Point and into the lee of the land, and it was duck soup from then on.

When we got to the dock, I informed Red that from now on he would have to use better judgment than this, or I would go elsewhere. Harry Randall grabbed his clothes, boots, and everything else, and I never did see him again.

"You have a couple of stories about storms. I guess if you've been on the water long enough, you're bound to get caught out there when you're not supposed to be there," I said one day.

"It happens more than you'd like," Tiggie responded.

"Is it because people take too many chances?" I asked.

"That's part of it, and one of the reasons I never wanted to own my own boat. If you own a boat, you're almost married to it. You have to make payments on it, and you have to pay your crew, and you have to make a living from it. That puts pressure on you to go out when you know better or stay out longer than you should."

"What about the times you don't stay out on purpose, but the weather becomes flukey?" I asked.

"When I was fishing, they didn't have the weather forecasting they do now. I don't think anybody really knew what the weather really was offshore. So weather could come up without any real warning. It happened all the time. Even if you got good at forecasting yourself, you could get fooled."

"You talked about the men on the lightship pouring diesel fuel to calm the seas. Did that really work?"

"Yeah, for a while, close to the ship, but when we got out of the slick they made for us, it was almost as bad as it had been," Tiggie responded.

"That's something I have a hard time with—purposely pouring oil into the water."

"I don't think anyone would think of it today, but back then, we didn't know about oil damage. And it might have been the thing that saved our asses out there."

"I didn't know the lightships were manned. I thought they were just anchored there."

"No, they had a full complement of men," Tiggie said.

"Can you imagine being stationed on a lightship in the middle of one of the honking northeasters we have around here? Do you think they airlifted them off in really bad storms?"

"I really don't know. I don't think I'd like to be there, though. When any of us got into trouble, they were there to help out the best they could."

Lightships were an important navigational aid before the days of LORAN, radar, sonar, and satellite navigation. They remained anchored on station, flashing their beacon and sending radio signals over the water. Nantucket Lightship was the first ship encountered for the transatlantic ships, and it also signaled the sharp right turn necessary for ships going around Nantucket Shoals and heading to New York or ports south or sharp left to Boston and ports north. It was in a precarious position.

"There was something comforting about seeing the lightships," Tiggie continued. "You knew there was someone there, and even though they may not be able to help, it made you feel better just knowing they were out there. When we were caught out there and saw the lightships, we knew we were close to home and might just make it."

"Can you imagine being in a storm that blew the lightship eighty miles off station in hurricane-force winds and fifty-foot seas?"

"Those guys earned everything they got," Tiggie said.

The lightships are no longer in service, but they are still in the memory of those who share a fascination with them through Websites. The Stone Horse Lightship was located about a half mile from the southern tip of Monomoy Island and indicated a course direction was necessary if a vessel were using Pollock Rip Sound according to the Lightship Sailors Association. From 1951 to 1963, the ship used was a 102-foot, steel "whaleback hull" vessel with a 25-foot beam and 11.3-foot draft. She was powered by a 315 horsepower diesel engine and had a maximum speed of 8.2 knots. She had an illuminating apparatus of two 375-millimeter electric lanterns of 13,000 candlepower each, a six-inch air siren for fog driven by two 40 horsepower kerosene engines and a 1000-pound hand-operated bell. She was retired from duty in 1964. Her engine and lighting apparatus had changed over the years, mainly switching the power component from kerosene to diesel and kerosene to electricity for the lanterns, but the hull was the same.

The Nantucket Lightship was even larger at 148 feet 10 inches with a 32-foot beam. She was the largest lightship ever built. She was in service until 1975 when she was decommissioned and sold to Nantucket Lightship Preservation, Inc. She was restored for use as a mobile floating museum. She had twin illuminating beacons on each masthead of 500-millimeter lens electric lanterns. In 1959, she was blown eighty miles off station in hurricane-force winds and fifty-foot seas and was out of communication for several days due to water-damaged electronics. Both lightships were replaced by lighted horn buoys.

Maritime history buffs have researched stories connected to the lightships. The Nantucket Lightship 117 sank in 1935 from a collision with the ocean liner *Olympic*, sister ship to the *Titanic*.

According to an article in the *Cape Cod Times* (September 2004), Captain Eric Takakjian of Fairhaven, Massachusetts found the ship in 1998, and his recovery crew raised the 1,200-pound signal bell a week earlier. When the lightship went down, the captain and two crew members survived, and five men were lost. One of the survivors, C.E. Mosher, said, "We saw the *Olympic* loom out of the fog [at night] a short distance away. The visibility was only five hundred feet. A crash was inevitable. I sounded the collision alarm. We all donned life preservers. Then we waited."

"When you were steaming back—excuse me, jogging back—you said you had to adjust the throttle for each wave. That must take incredible concentration," I said to Tiggie.

"It does. Whoever is at the wheel has to really pay attention. If you go down the face too fast, you can get buried in the trough, and you have to get back up on the next wave."

"What happens at night when you can't see the waves?"

"It's a matter of instinct and feel then," Tiggie answered.

I mentally imagined the experience it takes to gain that instinct.

"What happens when the seas are in all directions?" I asked.

"You just have to hang on and hope for the best. There's stuff flying all over the place. When the windows get blown out of the pilothouse, it's a real nightmare, because then, there's the rain and the seas, and it's just plain miserable."

"I've never been out in really nasty weather," I offered.

"Consider yourself lucky." I knew he meant it.

"Did you get seasick?" I asked.

"In those conditions, you don't have a chance to get seasick if you want to survive. It's miserable enough without that. But I was generally lucky there. I didn't get seasick. I've been with guys who did, though, and they had a real rough time."

"I'm still thinking about what it must have been like to be coming home in a storm jogging for almost a full day and night, trying to keep the boat from getting buried in a trough, throttling back and forth depending on whether you were climbing or descending a wave, and hanging on the whole time. It's hard for me to imagine."

"I'm glad those days are over," he said.

Chapter Twenty-Three
The Last of the *Pat-Er-Glo*

Halibut season was approaching, and after a winter of planning where to go, a place seventy miles off Provincetown called Cassius' Ledge was looking good to Red and Al, but that would be about one hundred miles from Harwichport. I told Red in no uncertain terms that I had no intention of going one hundred miles from home port in this little piss-pot he called a boat.

We fished closer to home, and at the start of the season, we had moderate success, no really big trips, but we were making wages. When the season starts, you pick up a few here, or a few there, but prolonged fishing means you have to keep going further and further offshore. Pretty soon, our expenses were exceeding our gross stock, and you could see the handwriting on the wall—give up the halibut or take the longer trips.

One night, Al invited Red and me over to his house for a few drinks. I knew something was up with him inviting both of us at the same time and seeing several bottles on the table and charts spread about. I guess they figured that if they got me loaded, I'd agree to go anyplace with them, but I wasn't buying any part of it. I would drink their goddamned liquor, look at their charts with them, and dream about the big schools of halibut that were out there someplace, but if it was further than forty miles, I wasn't going.

Babe Miller's boat, the *Terra Nova*, the biggest boat of the fleet, was well able to make the trip, but in my opinion, the *Pat-Er-Glo* was not in that class. The two boats finally left Harwichport, the *Pat-Er-Glo* and the

Terra Nova, without Red or me. That same night, Red and I made a short trip nearby, did quite well, and picked up five big fish. We were in radio contact with Al later on that day, and they said they had just arrived on the grounds. Bobby Our and young George Payne were with Al. Al said when he looked back at Bobby, all he could see were his big, dark eyes staring at him, and he heard Bobby telling him he'd better get him home safely or else. It was the last time I was ever to hear Al's voice.

Red and I got in that night, and he said, "It doesn't look like we'll get out tomorrow fishing. The weather report isn't so hot." He said, "The barometer is quite low, and I'm hoping that Al won't get in any trouble weather-wise."

The next day, the wind increased to thirty to forty miles per hour. We turned the radio on numerous times during the day hoping to hear Al and Babe Miller talking but could hear nothing.

That night came and went, and Red woke me up the next morning about 9:00 and told me he had heard the Coast Guard talking on the radio. He said that the *Pat-Er-Glo* had gone down and one man was lost, but they didn't say who. Red said that we should go down to the Coast Guard station for further information.

Finally, all the facts filtered in. During that last night, the wind had increased to over seventy miles per hour. Although it was early April, it snowed all night, reducing the visibility to zero, adding to the misery of the rough seas and pounding. The Coast Guard was in contact with the *Terra Nova*, and it wasn't till then that we knew who was lost. The wind had broken off the riding mast, and Al and Bobby had gone to lash it to the side. This act cost Al his life.

Babe told the Coast Guard that the *Pat-Er-Glo* had been leaking all night, making her low in the water, sluggish, and hard to handle. Finally, one sea hit her wrong and capsized her. Young George Payne was at the stern of the boat and was thrown clear. Bobby Our was pinned under the boat, and it was only a miracle that he eventually got out.

It was months before they found Al's body. He had become ensnarled in the mast, the canvas, and all the lines that were wrapped around it. A dragger's net pulled him up that way. He was identified not only by the mast but by the contents of his pockets, one item being his lucky silver dollar.

Red and I were quite shocked, and for myself, I still feel that a little of me died along with Al. We had good times and bad times together, got along well and got along poorly, but I always considered him a dear friend. Even Red had a few tears in his eyes, about the only time I ever saw him cry. He took it rather hard, along with about most everybody else. Things never did seem quite the same at Wychmere Harbor from then on.

I was the one asked to identify Al's body, and it was one of the hardest things I've ever done in my life, to see his partially decomposed body and find that lucky coin in his pocket. The memory haunted me for decades...It still does.

"That's a horrible and really sad story," I said to Tiggie. "I can't believe that you had to fish in his pocket to find his lucky coin. God, that must've been awful."

"It was. He was half decomposed, but his clothes were still okay, and that was really the only way to identify him. You couldn't tell by his face—it wasn't there anymore."

"Yechh. Where was the boat, or where was he? How could you find the boat offshore?"

"It wasn't offshore. It was near Billingsgate Shoal."

"Billingsgate Shoal?" I ask incredulously. "That's in Cape Cod Bay. How the hell did it end up there?" I asked.

"Apparently, they were in touch with the Coast Guard almost the whole time, but the storm was so bad that the Coast Guard couldn't get a good fix on their location. It was snowing and sleeting, and the wind was howling, and the seas were really high. They were off Stellwagen someplace (Stellwagen Bank, now a National Marine Sanctuary located more or less north of Provincetown), and they missed the buoy off Provincetown that would have gotten them east of the Cape. They literally got blown into Cape Cod Bay."

"And the Coast Guard didn't know where they were?"

"No."

"So how come it took so long before they found him, and you had to make the identification?"

"They found the boat and saved George Payne and Bobby Our but couldn't find Al. They didn't find him for quite a while after that. But it was months later. Going into his pocket and finding that coin was just about the worst thing I've ever done in my life."

"What did you do with the coin?"

"I threw it the hell overboard as far as I could," he said emphatically.

"It sounds like Bobby Our was pretty lucky," I continued.

"He was. He was in an air pocket when the boat capsized and survived. Somehow, he was able to get himself out from under the boat. And he stopped fishing not too long after that and went into the earth-moving business and still owns the company. His brother, Jackie, stayed with fishing and was one of the best. He's gone now, too. They're all gone now. I don't know why I'm still here. What's the point?" he asked morosely.

"You're too ornery to let go yet. Besides, you can't go until I'm finished with this thing."

"Well, you'd better hurry up. I want it done before I die."

"You've been saying that every day. You're just going to have to wait."

Chapter Twenty-Four
Dwindling Numbers

One morning at the dock, I was sitting there when I saw Red walking towards me arm in arm with a girl. The girl part wasn't unusual. The part that was unusual was that he had a suit on; fishermen seldom wore suits on Cape Cod unless it was for a funeral or a wedding. This morning, Red went whole hog. He even had shoes on, although I believe his rubber boots were not too far away, as he had said on numerous occasions he felt naked without them. He walked up to me and introduced me to, of all things, his new wife.

This came as quite a shock to me. After a few minutes, I was able to swallow again and congratulated him on his marriage. Problems soon emerged, though, when his wife became the shore skipper.

If we went fishing for haddock and didn't do too well and another boat did better halibuting, she would tell him he ought to go halibuting because they were doing better. We would put the halibut gear aboard and the bait, make a trip or two. In the meantime, a few boats would hit some haddock again, and she would say to him, "What the hell are you doing fooling around with them goddamned halibut again?" And this procedure went on and on causing considerable hard feelings between Red and me.

After the passing of Al, Red and I fished together for about a year. The work was quite hard when you fished just two men, and Red was considering taking on another man. Good men were hard to find, and there didn't seem to be any likely prospects around, but we kept our eyes open—Chris Myland came into the picture.

Chris had a boat of his own called the *Tuffy II*, named after his dog, which was a little unusual as most boats were named after the fisherman's wife or children. The *Tuffy II* was a fairly new boat but had gotten off to a bad start. The man who had originally owned it had been drowned, along with his crew members, while coming over the Chatham bars, and the boat had acquired a bad reputation. Chris didn't have a crew of his own and was inexperienced in fishing, so he asked Red if he could come along for experience. Red asked me if it would be all right if Chris came as it would mean a little extra work for me breaking Chris in. The idea appealed to me; Chris was a giant of a man, and I was more like a shrimp, and I could just see me bossing him around and giving him orders. But Chris was a smart boy, caught on rapidly, worked well, and fit right in.

The halibut season had just started, and we were fishing in a place called the Edge of the Ground, which was approximately fifty miles from Monomoy Point. The aggravating thing about this particular spot was the difficulty in locating it with sounding lead. During this period, we had no sounding machines, and it was a piece of ground on which you need not be very far off to catch absolutely nothing while another boat on one side or the other of you would get a load of fish.

We were going with another boat called the *Ronnie*, run by Dick Chase with Bobby Our and another guy named Murphy as crew. The plan was for Red to sound out the bottom and set the gear first, and then Dick would set on one side or the other, whichever he preferred. We proceeded to set, and Dick set one string on either side of us. Dick judged the tide a little wrong, and it carried him across one of our strings of gear. That meant he would have to haul his string first because we were under him, and it would have been impossible for us to haul the combined weights of the two strings. After the customary time of about three hours, giving the fish a chance to bite on, Dick hauled the string and took fifteen large halibut off it. One was a monster of about three hundred pounds dressed weight, which would make the fish about 350 pounds in the round.

We watched him haul two or three big fish aboard, and we assumed we would have similar fish. We were looking forward to all the nice halibut we were going to get. We hauled the whole two strings and got two little halibut of about twenty pounds apiece. We talked to Dick on the radio, and he said he had twenty-six large halibut and about a ton of codfish, the best set he had gotten this year so far. Our spirits aboard our boat were rather low since we just barely made expenses, whereas Dick and his crew made a couple hundred dollars apiece.

I told Red that I wasn't keen on going down with the *Ronnie* again—let them find their own goddamned fish. So Dick and his crew went to another spot, and Red said he would try a little spot he had always wanted to try but hadn't been able to find recently. After much looking and sounding, we managed to get located, put a marker buoy on it, and set the gear out.

Red started to haul, broke the anchor out of the bottom, hauled twenty or thirty feet of buoy line, looked at me with a foolish grin on his face, and said, "Tiggie, I got a big one on." He got the fish halfway to the boat five or six times and had to give it line again and again. It was one of the roughest battles Red had ever encountered with a halibut, and I could see Red was pretty near whipped himself.

Finally, the halibut was spent, and the three of us managed to get him in the boat. When he hit the deck, he was very wild, thrashing and banging his tail. Crazy Red picked up a hammer and repeatedly hit him in the head till one of the eyes was all shattered and hanging out of its socket. This big, beautiful fish that had probably roamed at will for fifty years or so and had fought so gallantly for its life didn't deserve this kind of treatment. I told Red that if he hit it again, I would hit him in the head with the hammer. We almost got into a very bad argument. Chris stepped in, and our tempers subsided.

This was one of our best sets. We got twenty-eight beautiful fish. Nine of them came on the one line of seventeen hooks, which was the most that I had ever caught on one line.

The next trip was very frustrating as we set in three different places and had only one codfish and one hake. We were about ready to throw in the sponge when Red asked us if we would be willing to try three more skates on the edge of the grounds. We would have to set it just before dark and haul it in the middle of the night. We had a complete broker, so we agreed we were willing to take the gamble, not really expecting very much. We set and lay by the gear till nearly midnight. It was my turn to haul. As soon as I got the anchor off the bottom, I could feel the trawl was alive with fish. The next hour was a mad hassle. We had seventeen large halibut and two thousand pounds of large codfish. Too bad we couldn't have set there the first day and gotten an excellent trip out of it.

But if you've been in fishing long enough, you know you just can't give up; you have to keep trying. In this instance, it paid off handsomely.

After that trip came a period of terrible weather—we put bait, ice, and food aboard, only to see it spoil and melt away three consecutive times, and we couldn't get out at all.

Red's marriage was going very, very badly. His wife was insistent that he get a job on the land, which Red would never consider—he had worked along the waterfront and the sea since he had been thrown out of school many years before. His wife constantly harassed and badgered him until his life was unbearable. He called me nearly every night on the phone. We would discuss the weather, the possibility of getting out the next day, and various other conditions.

Three nights went by without a call from Red, and I hadn't seen him at the dock at all. I began to get a little anxious, so I called his wife, and she said she hadn't seen him for four days. She figured he was off sulking someplace as they had had a big fight. But after a full week, I had the nagging feeling that Red might have done something foolish. I looked in all the places that I knew of where he might possibly be. I looked up his old girlfriend and inquired around Hyannis but still nothing.

The next morning, I got a call from his wife. The police had found his car in the woods at Brewster. He had run a hose from the exhaust pipe into the car and ended his life.

Now, with Al and Red gone, my morale was at a very low ebb. I started feeling sorry for myself, which gave me an excuse to drink excessively. I got involved with a married woman, and I could see I was heading for a lot of trouble. Chris tried to talk me into running the *Tuffy II* and getting back to fishing, but I would have no part of it. I could see this married-woman deal was going to get rather messy and was trying to look for a way out, when Bobby Our told me he was going to take a swordfishing and halibuting trip with Babe Miller off the coast of Nova Scotia. Babe still needed another man, so he asked if I wanted to go along. I still didn't like Babe, but I realized that I had to get away, and this would be a way out.

"My God. First Al and then Red," I exclaimed the day after reading the story. "That must have been really hard."

"It was not the best time in my life. Red was a crazy bastard, and I guess I sort of knew he'd come to a strange end, but I never thought he'd take his own life."

"What was the woman like who was his wife? She must have been really something to have married him, from what you've told me about him."

"She was a miserable bitch. I think she caused his death."

"So you said."

"She said she got him a job painting for \$60 a week," Tiggie explained. "Lots of times, he made that in one day. He wasn't about to leave a boat and work onshore anyway. Red wasn't happy with her, and I told him I had a solution to his problems, but he wouldn't do it."

"What was your solution?" I asked.

"Hit her over the head with a ball-peen hammer and take her to the canyons in a thousand feet of water. They'd never find her."

"He wouldn't go for that, huh?"

"No. Instead, he did himself in."

"What made them get together? He sounds like he wasn't exactly first prize either," I suggested.

"I don't know. I was having enough women problems of my own."

I was realizing that there were some threads of conversation that he was just not going to get into with any depth. Relationships with women fit into that category, but from what I could glean, they were intense—both high and low.

Chapter Twenty-Five
The Long Trip—Swordfishing

I finally agreed to go on a long trip aboard the *Terra Nova*, a larger boat than the rest of the boats in the fleet. At fifty-five feet, she looked much bigger with the long swordfish pulpit and the thirty-foot mast. I knew I would like the boat, but I wasn't sure I would get along very well with Babe, the skipper whom I had known for many years but had never fished with directly—I heard he could be a real bastard.

The rest of the crew included my close friend, Bobby Our; Charlie White, who I had heard was a good fisherman and did his work with a smile but who had a tendency toward drinking a lot; and Jackie Crosman, a Chatham fisherman whom I had seen several times but didn't know well. I had heard he was a likeable fellow, maybe a bit irresponsible, who also drank a lot. It sort of looked like it would be an interesting trip.

Getting the boat ready for the sea was no small task. Charlie, the cook, and I were designated to procure the food supplies, something right up my alley because of wartime experience as a mess sergeant. The trip was to be split into two segments. The first half would be about seven-days duration going after swordfish. Then we would put in at Yarmouth, Nova Scotia. There, we would refuel, take on food again, buy our halibut gear (it was much cheaper than Stateside), fish for a week or so for halibut, and then head back to the Cape. So we needed food for ten days. Jackie and Bobby loaded the fuel and the ice—approximately ten tons—while Babe checked out all his electronic equipment.

We left the dock at 3:00 in the afternoon. I had a few misgivings about the departure. It was the last of June, and the tourist influx had begun, which meant plenty of pretty girls and much nightlife, and I was about to miss all this for about three weeks. But as the boat left the land, the land being a magnet and the offshore grounds being another magnet, the further offshore we got, the more the attraction of the offshore magnet began to bear on me, and I looked forward to the trip more.

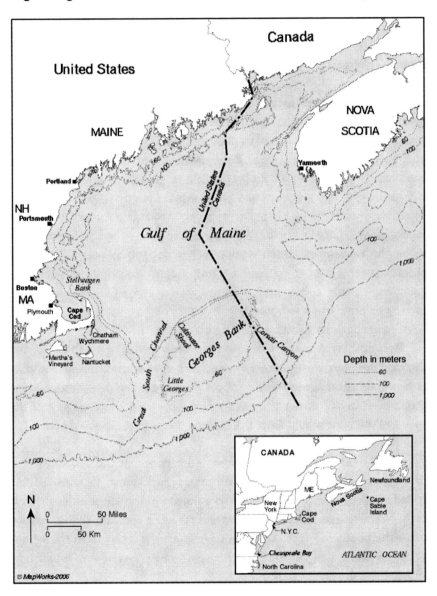

Gulf of Maine and George's Bank

This was a beautiful afternoon—one of those rare days when the sea was smooth as glass. About twenty miles at sea, we came onto a vast school of giant bluefin tuna blended in with schools of porpoises. You could look in any direction and see these huge fish breaching. Most of the tuna were single fish, but the porpoises were in groups of ten or twenty, all jumping in unison. We watched the beautiful scene until the sun finally set and then were treated to one of Charlie's wonderful suppers. The watches were set at two hours per man. We would have to steam all night to get to our destination—the southeast part of George's Bank—well over 120 miles from Harwichport.

While we were eating supper, Babe explained the duties and fundamentals of swordfishing, the bulk of the explanation directed at Jackie and me since neither of us had ever been swordfishing. Babe would be the striker or the harpooner. Bobby would be on top of the mast as the head mast man, and he would be the one to guide the wheelman to the swordfish—he had a button and could signal the guy who was steering. The signals were three beeps for straight-ahead, one for port, and two for starboard. Charlie took the port side and Jackie the starboard. I was to be the wheelman, which wasn't such a hot job as you were in the pilothouse of the boat by yourself and couldn't see or hear what was going on. I could also visualize myself getting the signals all mixed up, turning to port when I should have been turning to starboard, making a wrong approach to a fish and getting blamed for it.

Swordfishing was not like any other type of fishing I had done, and the fundamentals were quite different. When you are cruising, the boat always goes at one speed—wide open. The wheelman never touches the throttle—slowing down or speeding up—because the changing of the speed of the boat would alert the basking fish, and they would sound [go deep] and you'd miss your shot.

The striker or harpooner throws the harpoon at the swordfish; the dart comes off of the harpoon and has one hundred fathoms of line coiled up along the deck attached to a fifteen-gallon wooden keg that is in the wheelhouse. As the fish is hit and runs the line out, the wheelman turns the boat away from the line, so it doesn't get caught in the wheel. When the line is all run out, he throws the keg overboard, supposedly letting the fish play himself out.

The boat carries a dory, which is laid on the deck. The next step is to put the dory over the side, and a man rows up to the keg and picks it up. He has a little roller arrangement on the bow of the dory, and he has to haul the fish up till he gets it to the side of the dory. He also has a long-bladed knife called a lance, and he tries to make several passes through the gills of the fish, causing it to lose much blood, and it soon dies. Once in a while, you get a swordfish that doesn't die so easily, and it will charge the dory, trying to get at its antagonist. When the sword comes through the bottom of the dory, it usually misses the man in the dory, but swordfish puncturing dories happens quite often actually, every season.

After the fish is dead, there is still the problem of getting it into the dory, and this is no small feat for one man considering that swordfish run from one hundred fifty pounds to eight-hundred-pound monsters, dressed weights. The dory man also has to fight off sharks as one or two bites in the swordfish ruins its market value.

The fisherman rows back to the boat coming up alongside. The boat has a boom with block and tackle, and a line is put around the swordfish's tail. It is hoisted up on the deck, the head is cut off, it is gutted, the tails and fins are removed, and it is thoroughly washed and put in the hold and buried in ice. The swords are usually saved for souvenirs.

Charlie White was an expert on dories, so the job of fighting, killing, and actually landing the swordfish fell to him. Jackie Crosman was adamant about wanting to go in the dory, but Babe told him to keep his shirt on—he'd get the chance—but not for three days or more. No one else wanted the dory job—I sure didn't want any part of getting into those cranky things.

At night, the motor is shut off (unless it's foggy, and watches are necessary), and the boat drifts all night while the weary crew, who have spent fourteen hours at the wheel, on the pulpit, or hanging on the mast, get some sleep.

The next day broke, bright, calm, and clear. We finished breakfast rapidly, and the hunt was on again. Bobby sighted a fish and told Babe it was a huge one. He gave me the signal, the approach was perfect, and, just as we were upon it, Babe hesitated in throwing the harpoon. He looked up at Bobby and said, "Don't you know a shark when you see one?" Then he looked down at the fish a second time and saw that it was a swordfish of about five hundred pounds with its sword broken off. The lost fish was probably worth $300. Bobby and Babe exchanged several violent words, ending with Bobby calling Babe a stupid bastard, and Babe pointing the harpoon at him and saying, "Come down and say that." All I could think of was the $50 that would have been my share.

We did not land another fish till the fourth day. It became apparent that Babe couldn't hit the side of a barn door with a harpoon. One day, he missed eight large fish, probably worth over $1,000. Tempers were pretty well frayed. Bobby asked him why he didn't get his fat ass out of the pulpit and let somebody else take a shot at it.

Babe replied, "Not while I'm alive and still captain of the *Terra Nova*."

About the second day out, I noticed a marked increase in the number of boats—maybe fifty to seventy in all—around us in every direction. Most of the boats came from Canada with the exception of one or two from Nantucket and possibly a half dozen from the New Bedford area. Now, with this many boats all on the outlook for swordfish, there were many incidents of two or more boats sighting the same swordfish at the same time, and then the race would be on to harpoon it. With each fish worth $100 or more, it was a dog-eat-dog situation, sort of like one of those chicken games, with both boats heading for the same spot, neither one giving way. When it seemed like there would be an inevitable crash, one would veer off to one side and give up the chase. Later on that night, when the fishing would be over, the winning skipper would usually rub it in while they were talking on the radio.

The weather had been beautiful and ideal for days, calm and sunny. Sunny weather was absolutely essential as the fish came to the surface and basked in the sun. The smooth surface made it very easy to see the swordfish's dorsal fin as it cut along the surface. There were also numerous sharks, and after a while, you became an expert in distinguishing between the two. An oceanic sunfish could fool you, though, because their dorsal fin was very similar, but that was the only similarity. The sunfish was completely round, just about all head, no tail whatsoever; they swam by flopping from side to side. They had very small mouths, and I was told that they fed exclusively on jellyfish, although I couldn't imagine how it could get any nourishment out of them as they were over ninety percent water.

All activities of the fleet ceased as the sun went down, and the boats would huddle in a group just drifting for the whole night. There would be much talk on the radios, comparing notes on how many fish were landed, and we could see that we were doing terribly. Most of the barbs and animosity were directed at Babe, and he was becoming very unpopular with everyone.

The Canadian fishermen really loved fishing, the sea, or anything pertaining to it. Numerous times, they would get in their dories and row to one boat or another for a visit, often bringing musical instruments, playing for a while and singing a few songs and then rowing back to their boats. Charlie White and Babe were originally from Canada, and they knew many of the other fishermen.

Jackie Crosman finally got to have his chance to land a swordfish. We managed to get three fish, and our spirits were lifted somewhat. Jackie prevailed on Babe to let him land one, and Babe said the next one was his—and it was a huge fish of five hundred pounds or so. But a very peculiar thing happened. Babe struck the fish with the harpoon, and it floated right to the top as if it was dead. Apparently, the dart had pierced its backbone, and it just lay on the surface stunned. Babe told Jackie to jump into the dory immediately, but Charlie White told Jackie to be very careful as the fish might come to at any moment. Babe also knew this, but he had a mean streak in him, maybe actually hoping that Jackie would get in a little trouble since Jackie had been so anxious to land a fish.

Jackie jumped into the dory. It was a graceful leap, giving the appearance that he had done this all his life even though he was a novice at it. He rowed like hell up to the fish. The fish was about as long as the dory and was just lying there, dead in the water. He rolled the fish into the dory and was standing there admiring him, when the swordfish came to. The fish thrashed, jumped, broke one of the floor mats in the dory, and knocked one of the oars overboard. Jackie was standing near the head of the fish and was doing some rather fancy legwork to keep from getting banged up. He managed to get the lance and plunged it into the head of the fish several times. In the meantime, Babe was laughing—it was a great big joke to him. Charlie White was shaking his head saying, "I knew that was going to happen." The rest of us thought it was a rather dirty trick to play on Jackie.

Chapter Twenty-Six
Ashore in Nova Scotia

We managed to land ten fish in seven days, and Babe said that he thought we would head into Yarmouth, Nova Scotia. I was beginning to feel a little crummy with no shower for days and little water to even brush our teeth. The fo'c's'le was beginning to smell pretty rank with five men in it, none of whom had bathed in over a week, so I looked forward to getting on land and cleaning up again.

We ran all night in a thick fog to Yarmouth, a nerve-wracking trip. There were so many boats in the area that it was just about a miracle that we didn't collide with one of them. We did not have radar—they were still pretty expensive for fishing boats—but we had LORAN, a new navigational instrument. The next morning, we broke out of the fog right at the entrance of Yarmouth Harbor, and though he was terrible with a harpoon and had a surly personality, I hated to admit that Babe was an excellent navigator and fisherman.

After sounding his siren several times in the harbor, we tied up the boat at the dock where quite a few fishermen greeted us. Babe and Charlie knew many of them and introduced us, and out came the bottles. Charlie and Jackie would never pass up a drink, and I could see that this was shaping up to be quite a drinking bout. Bobby and I decided to leave the boat.

The main street along the waterfront in Yarmouth was unpaved and had a railroad track running down the middle of it. The cinder-type dusty road was full of ruts and holes. We saw a huge fish-packing plant and several boats unloading their fish.

Bobby said, "Let's go look them over."

They were in the process of taking out a nice catch of halibut. The skipper recognized Bobby—he had met him on another trip—and he invited us aboard. It was a beautiful boat, along similar lines to Babe's, and the crew was a happy-go-lucky bunch, eager to make friends. I remember one guy named Black Zack, whose wife came down to the dock and asked him if he was coming home before he went out again. He said, "No." I thought this was quite peculiar as he had been at sea for twelve days. Being a little curious, I asked him about it, and he said, "If I go home, I'll get no rest at all, and I might get the wife pregnant again, and I think fifteen kids are enough."

The skipper invited us up into the plant to show us how they culled or graded the various sized halibut. The fishermen got different prices for different size halibut. Fish over one hundred pounds were classified as large halibut; those from one hundred down to forty pounds were classed as medium fish; from forty down to ten pounds were chicken. The small fish brought the best price usually. I didn't think about it at the time, but it seems a shame that the small fish got the best price when they had not had a chance to mate. But the young fish were the most tender and in highest demand.

The buyers had a little gimmick to drop the price. If a fish had more gray on its belly than white, they called it a gray halibut. The gray didn't impair its eating quality, just the looks. The buyers frequently pointed out various fish lying on the deck of the plant, saying that one was a gray or another one was a gray. Usually, you got about half the price for grays that you normally got for the whites. Once in a while, a halibut would have just a little patch of gray near the tail, and an unscrupulous buyer would push it aside, calling it a gray, and when the skipper left, the buyer would put it in with the white fish, thereby making a huge profit on it. Fishermen needed buyers, and buyers needed fishermen, but animosity often developed between the two, fishermen believing they were always getting the short end of the stick.

Bill was watching the culling of his fish, and it was obvious that he didn't like the call on some of the cull. In fact, he was smoldering mad. He looked up at the buyer and told him that if he picked another gray out of what Bill considered white fish, he was going to take that goddamned hook away from him (the hook used to drag the halibut around) and jam it in his ass. From then on, the cull went a little better in Bill's favor.

Later in the afternoon, plans were made for a party at Bill's house that night, and our whole crew was invited. Babe had never taken a drink of hard liquor in his life until he was forty, but he made up for it from then on and was a hard-drinking man. There were about twenty of us at Bill's. We drank all the hard liquor and all the beer they had and were starting on a couple of gallons of red wine. Mixing all those together, you usually ended up pretty sick. I stopped at the liquor.

About 2:00 a.m., Bobby and I decided to leave. One of the fishermen offered us a ride, which we declined as he was obviously drunk. But he insisted, and we didn't want to seem unfriendly so we accepted, and what a wild ride it was. He had a brand-new station wagon, and he was driving quite fast. He sped down a steep hill leading to the dock, drove onto the dock, and stopped just inches from the end of it. We almost went over into the drink, car and all. Believe me, Bobby and I were glad to get out of that car.

We walked over to where the boat had been left, and all we could see was the top of the mast of the *Terra Nova*. When we had landed, the tide was fairly high, but now, it was low tide. They had a rise and fall of over twenty feet, which was about four times as much as we had in Harwichport. Bobby and I looked over the edge of the dock and could see we weren't going to go aboard the *Terra Nova* this night. So we stretched out on the dock and slept there for the night.

The next day, we were to run a complete string of new halibut gear that cost half of what it did in the States. We had lots of help rigging the gear, maybe twenty of us working on it, and the work went rapidly.

Babe said that we would take off the next afternoon. He told Charlie and me to go get supplies, telling me to keep my eye on Charlie—making sure that he didn't get loaded or take off and shack up with an old girlfriend or something. I assured him that I would get him back in good shape and told him not to worry about it.

We hired a cab, and he took us to the ship's store, a perfect delight and nothing like our supermarkets. The proprietor and his family lived in the back of the store, and we could see he was very anxious to please, knowing that we would place a large order with him. The meats were excellent and about half the price they were at home. We loaded up on steaks and pork chops and some very excellent veal. As I was busy picking out the meat, periodically, Charlie would disappear. Each time he would reappear, he'd have a stupid grin on his face. Finally, the shopping done, I looked for Charlie and asked the proprietor where he had gone. He said he was in the kitchen in the back of the store talking to his wife. I walked into the kitchen to see Charlie finishing up the quart. Looking at me with a big grin, he said, "Well, are you finally done?" Babe was not happy when we got back.

The next morning was spent putting five more tons of ice aboard and four or five hundred pounds of frozen herring for bait. I asked Babe how come we had so little bait, and he told me after the first set we made, we would keep six or eight of the big codfish or cusk—a member of the codfish family that are fairly good eating but are of almost no value, seldom exceeding two cents a pound. We would take the codfish and cusk, fillet them out, and cut them into strips and use that for bait after the first set.

Bobby, Charlie, and I had finished with the ice, and Babe noticed that Jackie wasn't around. In fact, Jackie hadn't even slept aboard that night, and none of us had any idea of where he could be. Babe was just about in a rage when Jackie came staggering down the dock carrying a pretty good load and made the statement that he had been having such a good time that we could sail without him—he was going to stay. Babe told him to get his ass aboard the boat. Bobby and I jumped up on the dock, carried him aboard, and locked him in the fo'c's'le, keeping him there until we cleared the port.

Chapter Twenty-Seven
Halibut off Brown's Bank

We steamed all that late afternoon and through the night, and at daylight, we arrived at the halibut grounds on Brown's Bank. The depth of the water would vary from one hundred fifty fathoms to four hundred fathoms—well over two thousand feet deep at six feet to a fathom. This was to be a new experience for me as I had never fished over one hundred fathoms. Babe, Bobby, and the rest of the crew talked about the different species of fish we would catch, and, believe me, some of them were real weird looking.

On the grounds, there were about twenty Canadian boats. Babe talked to some of them over the radio phone, asking them how they were doing. They replied that they were doing fine. From the looks of the number of boats and their flag buoys scattered about, it looked as if we might have some trouble finding a place to set, but we finally found a little clear spot, got set in, and waited for the gear to soak or give the fish a chance to bite on. We steamed around for several hours looking for swordfish, which also were in the vicinity of this halibut ground, but we didn't even sight one.

We hauled the gear. It was loaded with codfish, and nearly all of them were over forty pounds up to sixty pounds, huge, beautiful fish, which we had no use for whatsoever, as we couldn't keep them on ice longer than two or three days. We kept only a half a dozen for our next baiting; the rest were thrown overboard, doomed to die, because when they came up from that depth, they got the bends. Their stomachs hung out of their mouths, and they would just swim along the top of the water eventually being eaten by the sharks.

About the only fish I know of that can swim up from that depth and back down again without any visible effects is the halibut. I have seen them come off the hook right at the side of the boat after being hauled off the bottom, two thousand feet down, and swim away without any apparent ill effects. We also got seven halibut that set which was pretty poor.

The equipment required to fish at such a depth needs some explanation. The most important thing you have to have is a hauling machine. The line goes through two sets of wheels, which have grooves. When you have a lot of tension on the gear, it sinks into the grooves. The hauling machine is run off the main engine by a series of belts. The buoy lines are five hundred fathoms long or three thousand feet. It constitutes such a huge pile of rope that the one who coils it stands in the stern of the boat and walks the rope around and around him until the coil is knee-high. If you were to take the three thousand feet of line or rope and stretch it out on level ground, and you were on one end of it, you would be unable to pull it by hand, so a hauling machine is necessary. But the bottom where we were fishing was very steep and covered with rocks and huge coral formations the Canadians called "wire trees," so, even with the machine, half the time, you couldn't even get the gear back, usually resulting in the fishermen parting the line and losing the gear and the fish.

The next set was the best one we got the whole trip. We set two hundred hooks, and when we started to haul, we realized we had a load of fish on. The hauler was groaning and squeaking, and we could barely move it. It took over three hours to get the buoy line up before we saw one hook. Charlie White was coiling, and Bobby and I were at the rail to gaff the fish. We got the anchor in the boat, and all we could see were halibut, hook after hook, as far as we could see down into the water. We only got ninety hooks back, but took over seventy-one halibut off the ninety hooks, which was some sort of a record, and most of the fish were over one hundred pounds. We were up to our waists in fish—huge, thrashing fish. Jackie was piling some of them out on the outer deck, trying to give us a little more room to work in, as we figured we were going to fill the boat with this one set.

However, like all good things, it was too good to last. We hauled up a huge wire tree of coral, and it had cut our gear off. It wasn't so much the loss of the gear, but, more than likely, we lost close to one hundred big halibut, which would eventually die on the trawl, probably worth about $2,000. I said to Bobby, "I'll remember this trip for the rest of my life with all the halibut we saw. We're lucky to see maybe thirty or forty on a two-day trip off Cape Cod."

We also caught, along with the halibut, codfish and an occasional tremendous-sized cusk, much larger than the cusk off Cape Cod. When they came to the surface, their skin was full of air bubbles or blisters, and they popped and hissed because of the difference in pressure. I was talking to one of the Canadian skippers over the radio telephone, and he asked me what I thought of the huge cusk we were catching. Did we ever see any that size off Cape Cod? And I told him that I caught a cusk off Cape Cod one time that was so big that I took a picture of it, and the picture weighed eight pounds. There was complete silence for two or three minutes on the radio, then he finally called back to me that he wasn't about to admit that Cape Cod cusk were bigger than the Canadian cusk, but he would go along with Cape Cod fishermen, who were undoubtedly the biggest liars.

Up to this point, the weather had been excellent. We had a little fog, but had no wind other than the ten or twelve-mile-an-hour breezes, but we got weather reports that the wind was going to pick up from the nor'west and become gusty. We were too far from land or port and spent a very sloppy day riding it out. We had a chance to rest a little, work a little on our own equipment, play some cribbage, and really sit down and enjoy some of Charlie's nice cooking at a leisurely pace, which was unusual on a fishing boat as everything was done on the run.

Chapter Twenty-Eight
Once a Louse, Always a Louse

The next day dawned brisk and clear, and the wind had died to a whisper. Bobby and I cut the codfish up for bait and made the set. We saw a couple of swordfish, chased them, and got one of them, then went back to the gear and began to haul. We had eight or ten huge halibut; three fish over two hundred pounds and six or seven feet long were bitten completely in half. You could see that it was just a single bite on each one. The mouth of the shark that did this had to have been at least two or three feet wide. I had seen and killed many sharks, but I couldn't visualize anything as big as they must have been.

Some of the Canadian fishermen claimed that these kind of sharks were what they called ground sharks, which meant that they lived exclusively on the bottom and, therefore, were never seen. They said that there were times when they would eat pretty nearly all the halibut. Luckily, this was not one of those times as they only ruined five of the fish. We saved the halves, and when we got back to Harwichport, we cut them into halibut steaks and split them up amongst ourselves.

Some of the other fish we caught were real oddities. One was a wolffish; it was very similar to a saltwater catfish, which bears absolutely no resemblance to the freshwater catfish. The wolffish flesh was like molded jello—if you laid it on something and shook it, it quivered for quite a while. We also caught black dogfish, which had scales on them unlike the usual dogfish we caught, which had none. Some of the Canadian fishermen said that if you got stuck by one of the spines on these dogfish, it was very painful and usually ended in a serious infection. One spine was located just ahead of the dorsal fin, and the other was near the tail. We handled these devils rather gingerly.

We caught numerous large crabs unlike anything we had ever encountered off of Cape Cod. I imagined that they were edible, but no one had the guts to try one. We even got a few skates that I couldn't identify.

But the weirdest thing of all was a fish that I later identified by a picture; it was called a grenadier. The fish was approximately ten pounds and had a round body in the middle that tapered away to a long rat-like tail. The head was fairly small, having a small, almost toothless mouth. The eyes were huge, with no pupils, giving the appearance of being opaque. It was covered with diamond-shaped scales, which were as sharp as razors.

I knew several of the fish biologists at Woods Hole, and I set aside several of these specimens, packed them away in ice, hoping to bring them to the biologists when we got into port. But for no other reason than being mean, Babe threw them overboard. Boy, was I pissed and let him know it, long and loud.

Babe came up on deck one time, while Bobby and I were watching a school of porpoises play around the boat. Among them were several small baby ones about three feet long, cute as all get out to watch. Babe came up and looked the situation over and took off. He had gone forward to the swordfish stand, picked up a harpoon, and came back. He plunged it through the head of one of the baby porpoises. It cried and made all sorts of noises, and the other porpoises went wild, and so did Bobby and I. Bobby nearly hit Babe in the face, and I called him a lousy bastard. Of all the fish stories I have heard, from various fishermen, I have never heard of anyone killing or hurting a porpoise for no reason at all. I made up my mind that I would never sail with him again.

The next two or three days we had fair fishing, and the hold of the boat was beginning to fill up. We agreed that we shouldn't leave such good fishing and that we should stay on till the fishing petered out. But the next night, we received a radio call from Bishop, the fish buyer at Harwichport, who said the prospect of a good price looked good for the next couple of days, so we should get in and make the market. Bobby and I argued that we were on good fishing grounds and that while we were there, we should stay and finish out a couple more days. Babe had to have his own way in everything, and so we were on our way home.

A day later, we took out the fish. We had sixteen thousand pounds of halibut and two thousand pounds of swordfish. All the halibut were over one hundred pounds. The heads were cut off. One of the greatest fish delicacies is halibut cheeks. The texture and flavor is very similar to bay scallops. Al Paine, who used to run Thompson Brothers Fishmarket on the docks, offered twenty-five cents a head, which would amount to about $25 to split among the four of us. The usual custom was that the captain let the crew have the money derived from the heads, but Babe said he wanted a boat's share for the heads or we couldn't sell them. I looked at Bobby. He looked at me. We both got a fishfork and pitched the whole $25 worth overboard into the harbor.

This great big, handsome price we were supposed to get for the halibut came to nineteen cents a pound, which was about half of what we usually got. I think that somewhere along the line, a different price was agreed to between Bishop and Babe, thereby cutting the crew out of their fair share. We found out later that the Canadian fellows, fishing along with us on Brown's Bank, got twenty-five to thirty cents a pound for their fish in Boston, and they had to be trucked a long distance. It looked like a fishy deal to me. Bobby and I picked up our share, which was $500 less $150 for taxes. We walked away with the whopping sum of $350 for twenty-one days of excruciating labor plus much aggravation.

Babe moved away to Point Pleasant, New Jersey, got one of those easily acquired loans from the government for boat improvement, and eventually lost his boat. It was sold at a public auction. He went fishing on another boat, not as a skipper, though. One winter night, the boat went down with all hands. Babe's body was never found.

When I reminded Tiggie of the story, he laughed and said, "They sure liked to drink when we were there."

"Because they were fishermen?" I asked.

"Maybe."

"I thought it was interesting that you caught codfish that were useless to you except for bait. But your comment about the cod being wasted was sort of telling, too. It must have been hard to throw them overboard."

"It was," Tiggie said solemnly.

"Brown's Bank sure is a long way from Cape Cod," I suggested.

"Yeah, it is."

"There was one part of your explanation of the gear used for halibut fishing I'm not sure about."

"What do you want to know about?"

"You talked about the buoy line and how it was coiled."

"Yeah. The person who brings in the buoy line walks it around him in the stern of the boat."

"Whoa," I said, making a "T" with my hands, giving him the "time-out" sign. "What do you mean, he walks it around him?"

"The line has a buoy on one end and an anchor on the other just like cod trawl line. But there's four hundred fathoms of line. That's 2,400 feet. And it's thick line because it has to be so strong to go down so far. You can't coil something like that like you do thinner rope—it's too heavy. So the only way you can coil it is to lay it down so you start in the stern and walk in an ellipse around and around and around until the rope is about knee high."

"The guy doing this is standing in the middle of a coil of rope that is knee high?"

"Yeah," Tiggie said matter-of-factly.

"And this is done off Brown's Bank, a piece of water nearly as notorious as George's for lousy sea conditions."

"Yeah," Tiggie said again. "What's the problem you're having?"

"One false move, and the guy is over the side," I said.

"One false move in any part of fishing, and you're over the side. You try to be careful, and you don't think about that or you wouldn't go," he answered.

I just shook my head at the thought of it.

"I was talking to Bill Amaru the other day," I said. Bill is a commercial dragger fisherman out of Chatham—he drags a net behind his boat rather than setting long lines of hooks. He is a former member of the New England Fisheries Management Council, the body that sets fishing regulations. "He said that it was true that there was price fixing going on. You guys weren't just dreaming that and being paranoid."

"We knew it was going on, but there was nothing we could do about it."

"Bill said that one of the biggest buyers, O'Hara, actually went to jail for it. He said that the buyers would get together in a restaurant in

Gloucester and decide what the price would be. It had nothing to do with the market forces."

"We were always getting screwed."

"Have you been back to Nova Scotia?" I asked.

"No."

"We went there years ago and watched a boat being launched in Yarmouth. It was quite a sight—this brand-new Novi boat..." I said, trying to insert a story of my own.

"The people are so friendly up there, or at least they were," Tiggie interrupted.

"They were very friendly when we were there, too. We tried to order a Novi skiff from a really good boat builder who had orders for three years ahead but..." That was the second time I tried to interject a story of my own that day.

"Those Novi-style boats were pretty good in a sea. But the bow was so high it was hard seeing over the bow sometimes. Have you noticed the flat bows on the boats in Chatham now?" Tiggie asked, off on another subject entirely.

"No. Why do they have a flat bow?"

"Chatham has a size restriction on the boat, and it's based on overall length, so if they chop off the point in the bow, they're not really losing anything performance-wise to the boat and the boat can be bigger. That's the problem with people who write the regulations and don't have a goddamn idea of what they're talking about. People are going to find a way around something anyway," Tiggie said knowingly.

I smiled remembering I had written lots of regulations, some of which kept Tiggie busy trying to find ways around them.

"I can't believe that story about Babe Miller and the porpoises."

"Neither could I. I was so goddamn mad I wanted to ram a harpoon up his ass. Those poor baby porpoises were crying, and the mothers were panicking, and all the time, he's there laughing. Who would kill a porpoise for no reason? What kind of a person would that be? They're so smart and so cute, and they never hurt anything."

"I bet you weren't too sad when you heard he died," I said.

"You never want to wish someone dead, but getting lost at sea seemed somehow appropriate for him."

Chapter Twenty-Nine
My First Time as Skipper

After my trip to Nova Scotia, I was without a boat or a job. Chris approached me one day and asked me if I wanted to run the *Tuffy II*. I wasn't too keen about it—I didn't particularly like the boat, and I really wasn't sure if I was capable of running a boat. Red had taught me a lot about running one, probably more than all the other skippers I had been with, but I hadn't had the experience yet. Unlike most fishermen, I hadn't considered or wanted to be a skipper because I did not want the responsibility. I had concentrated on being a good crew. But for most fishermen, the ultimate goal was owning your own boat. I told Chris that I would give it a try.

Chris said that he would come along with me. Those first two or three weeks were rather tough on me, and I made a lot of mistakes, which was to be expected, and did not get too many fish. When you first get to run a boat, it is as if you are on display, putting you under quite a bit of pressure for the first few weeks. You know that everyone is watching you and criticizing which just makes you nervous. I had many things to learn; the courses to the various fishing grounds, the various depths, the various species' habitats, the time of the year they were there, and most important, the tides and the various times during the tide cycle when fish fed. But I gradually gained confidence in myself, and things started to go smoothly.

The third crew member quit, and I was in need of another man. There was an old fellow named Edgar who lived on a boat that had a permanent berth at the dock. A huge fellow, who always had a grin on his face and a chaw of tobacco in his mouth, he occasionally filled in for a fisherman who was sick or couldn't fish for one reason or another. He had had many offers from other skippers since he was a top fisherman who knew all the facets of the business but had declined them all, stating that he didn't want to fish steadily. So I was quite surprised one day, when he came aboard and said, "Tiggie, I like your style. I would like to come aboard and fish with you and Chris." I told him to pack his bag and move right in that day. Edgar and I were together for about three years.

Edgar was not the biggest fisherman I knew, but he was by far the strongest. He could pick up a codfish of fifty pounds or better by the end of the tail, which is pretty difficult and almost impossible to grip considering how slippery the tail is. Or he would pick one up by the dorsal fin and chuck it the length of the boat without any apparent effort. He actually lifted up one end of the main engine and held it while Chris inserted some shims under it.

We got along famously that summer and caught our fair share of fish but didn't make much money as the top price we got for haddock all summer was only eight cents a pound; most of the time, it was only six cents a pound. That fall, we had a bad northeaster for two or three days forcing all the big Boston draggers to go back to port. If we could get out, we had a chance of getting a good price for our haddock, so we hoped for a break in the weather.

Bishop, the fish buyer, told us we could probably get twenty cents a pound for our haddock, an unheard-of price. We were the first boat out that night. We set our gear about half an hour before any other boat. The first out of six tubs of gear had about a thousand pounds, which was very good, but there was nothing but dogfish on the other 2500 hooks. As the other boats set later, they didn't see even one dogfish. Boats on both sides of me had good catches. Some boats stocked as much as $800 for that one day. We barely stocked $200.

As the week progressed, our catches increased, but the price also dropped. We got five cents a pound for haddock on the last day of the week. Naturally, that was our biggest catch on the cheapest prices. It inevitably worked out this way. I heard it called "supply and demand," but just once, I wished I had the big supply when the demand was high. We ended up catching more fish for the week than any other boat, but sharing up less.

One night, we had set our gear before daylight, and Chris noticed a big dragger bearing down on us; it looked like the dragger was dragging its nets. If it was, it would tear our gear all to hell. We approached the dragger and pulled up alongside of it, telling the skipper we had gear in this locale. The skipper told us to go to hell; he'd drag anyplace he wanted to. We lost just about all our gear and equipment, not to mention the fish on it and the time and work to replace it. We tried to sue the boat for loss of gear, but our lawyer told us it would be a hopeless cause, and we just had to absorb the loss.

As time went on, I started to notice that Edgar was very anxious concerning the weather, and he was always mumbling that we were going to get lost or I was taking too many chances. I knew a bit about his background. Years before, he had been run down by a steamer and had been the only survivor out of seventeen men, and he had been washed overboard a few times but always managed to survive, even though he couldn't swim a stroke. It was getting to the point where I would have to fire him or get another boat. Since he lived aboard the boat and had nowhere to go, I chose to get another boat.

"Did you like being the skipper?"

"After the first couple of trips, yes. I could put the boat on fish, and then it was okay. I took chances, but I didn't own the boat, so I probably was a bit more cautious than the captains who owned their own boats. If you got into trouble, though, you were the one in charge."

Chapter Thirty
Shipwrecked on Monomoy

There was one boat in the harbor that was fairly new and was owned by a man known as Peg Leg. Actually, Bishop had all the money in the boat, and Peg Leg was the owner on paper, but Peg Leg agreed for me to run the boat for him.

Peg Leg had lost his leg when he was seven years old. He was all shoulders, had a slim waist, a rather underdeveloped good leg, and an old beat-up peg leg and a cane about two and a half feet long. He was constantly slipping and falling on the boat, but he would bounce right back up again and continue with his work as if nothing had happened. I used to feel a little sorry for him and assigned him the lighter tasks, such as steering or baiting the gear.

The third member of the crew was Ken Devine. He was a very good fisherman, but he drank excessively. Whenever he took a couple of days off to go to Boston, promising to come back on time, he would be two or three days late. I would get very mad at him but would hold my temper, realizing there were no other men available.

I was beginning to know that there were a lot more problems entailed in running a boat than I had thought, such as knowing about the tides and the navigational end of it, but the worst part of all, and very difficult at times, was the pampering of the crew.

Nantucket Sound was full of mackerel nets and fish traps in the spring. The fish traps used to give us the biggest problems. We would leave the harbor, and half the nights, it would be thick fog and there were two fish traps right on our course. So, without radar, navigating would be done by knowing the running time to the fishing grounds, but we also had to know the running time to obstacles like the fish traps. We would run our time to the first trap, slow down, put our search lights on, find some of the poles, get by it, and so on to the second one. But every once in a while, I'd run into one, and maybe break a pole or get tangled in the net. It was quite a relief when the poles and traps were pulled up in the middle of July.

That fall and winter, the fishing was good, and to that point, it was my biggest year fishing. In fact, I almost made enough money to get by on. Towards the end of winter, there was a lot of work to be done on the *I'm Alone*—Peg Leg's boat.

Repairs made and gear rigged, we made several halibut trips to the grounds that were rather close and did very poorly. We knew that we would have to take two-day trips further offshore. Now that I was married, I would really have to fish in earnest, which meant taking many more chances. We decided the next trip would be to the edge of the ground.

The trip itself was strictly routine, a mediocre catch of ten halibut and a couple of thousand pounds of codfish. On the way home, there was a patchy fog, so I stayed at the wheel—it was my job to find the lightship and get around Monomoy Point. I made a perfect hit, made the Stone Horse Lightship, and was quite proud of myself, as, without navigational instruments, it was not at all unusual to miss the lightship by a mile or two on a seventy-mile cruise.

I had cleared Monomoy Point after standing at the wheel for seven hours, so I told Peg Leg to steer due north for Harwichport, as I was going to lie down for a few minutes. I had been lying down for about five minutes when there was an awful crash, and I flew out of the bunk onto the deck, landing on my shoulder. I couldn't imagine what the hell had happened.

I crawled out of the cabin and said, "Where in hell are we?"

He said, "I think I ran into Monomoy Point."

"How the hell could you do that?" I asked.

He said, "I guess I wasn't paying attention to the compass."

He kept trying to back it off the point, but I saw that we had sprung some planks, and she was rapidly filling with water. The water was quite deep off the end of the Point, and I realized that if we got off, we would probably sink and not be able to get to the shore since it was still early April and the water was still very cold. I told him to kill the motor immediately. I got off a mayday call to the Coast Guard on the radio telephone, giving the situation and our position and they told us it would be a couple of hours before they could get a DUK to us [a DUK was an amphibious vehicle used by the Coast Guard as a rescue boat, now used in several waterfront cities such as Boston, for tours by land and water].

There was a pretty good breeze going, and the boat was taking quite a pounding in the surf. We had just about all we could do to hold on and not get thrown overboard. We had to get off the boat soon before it started breaking up. I reached into the fo'c's'le and grabbed two or three blankets, threw them into the air, and the wind blew them way up onto the beach, high and dry.

I took a small trawl anchor, tied a buoy line on it, threw it up onto the bank, and made it fast to the boat so that we could have a sort of lifeline. Then I told Ken he should go first.

He said, "Like hell!"

I said, "Ken, we can't stay aboard the boat."

And he said, "You go first; let me see if you make it."

I grabbed the line and went over the side right up to my neck in what felt like ice-cold water and hauled myself up on the beach, safe and sound. I guess this gave Ken a little courage, because without any hesitation, he was over the side and soon joined me. Now came the problem of Peg Leg. He was nowhere near as tall as Ken and me (and I'm not much more than five feet). I knew with that wooden leg, he was going to have a little trouble getting up on the beach. Finally, after a little coaxing, he made his try and got halfway up on the line, then he let go of the line and came up the beach, like a crab on all fours, having a little difficulty with the wooden leg sticking in the sand.

The boat broke up faster than I expected—it was quite a shock really. The sides of the house went first, then various pieces of wreckage started to come ashore. The three of us just stood there lost in our own thoughts.

The boat was insured, so Peg Leg would come out all right, but I was thinking of all the work we had done on her in the last three months and the loss of our personal gear and the fish. But we did get away with our necks, which was something.

I told Ken and Peg Leg to give me a hand with some of the wreckage. It was quite windy and cold, and we were all soaking wet. We needed to erect some form of shelter—the Coast Guard would not be there for two hours yet. The boat went aground at midnight, and therefore, the earliest we could expect help would be 2:00 a.m., but it would probably be later. Ken and Peg Leg refused to help, so I made a shelter myself, using the wreckage and blankets I had tossed onto the beach. The two fools walked up and down the beach for about an hour, then, teeth chattering, they finally asked me how it was under the blanket.

"Not first class," I said, "but bearable." I said, "You bastards can freeze to death" when they asked if they could join me under the blanket, but I gave in, and we all huddled under the blankets for several hours. We finally saw the lights of the DUK approaching. They had a thermos of hot coffee and nice warm blankets, but it still seemed like a long, cold ride back to the Coast Guard station.

They had a police cruiser at our disposal, which took us to our various homes. The police cruiser left me off at my house.

I had made many mistakes in my life, but my biggest one was falling in love with a very beautiful, dark-eyed girl. I ruined a beautiful friendship by marrying her. The next eight years, we fought so much and so often that it made my years in the Army seem like a Sunday picnic. While I was single, I had thought I was leading a miserable life, but being married, I really knew what misery was.

I pounded at the door, and my wife let me in and asked what I had done wrong to be escorted by the police. So I told her I had gotten arrested for swimming on a private beach at night. She nagged me for several minutes, and I asked if I could please get out of my wet clothes, and then I would tell her about it. Even when I told her about losing the boat and the harrowing shipwreck on the beach, all she talked about was the fact that no money was coming in. It was just another episode in how our married life was.

"You talk about your relationship with your wife as being really awful. Red's was bad, too. Did any of your friends have good marriages?" I asked Tiggie one morning.

"Do you know anybody that has a good marriage?" he retorted.

"Yeah," I answered.

"Well, I sure don't. My second wife was even worse than my first. I don't think we spoke a civil word to each other for all the time we were together."

I've tried to put his relationships with women in some type of context, wondering what it was about him and his buddies and their women that they were constantly at each other's throats. I'm not sure, but I think it has something to do with initial attraction and security. Fishing was always an insecure occupation. Not only was there little money coming in for long stretches of time interspersed with relative abundance, where a portion was often spent in the local bars, but it was a very dangerous occupation, too, and the husband could get seriously hurt or die as a result. A safer bet was an onshore job that probably paid less overall but was steady and the man could be home. What's odd is the age-old thought that a woman could change a man once they were married, but for a fisherman who has the love of the sea in his bones, that's not going to change easily, if at all. Perhaps the chiseled physique of hard-working fishermen and inherent danger and a "living-on-the-edge" life are what attracted the women in the first place. I don't know. But, in listening to Tiggie and others, a happy home seemed to be just a delusion.

Chapter Thirty-One
The Move to Chatham

The Harwichport fleet dwindled down to three boats. Most of my friends had moved to Chatham, and Frank Thompson, who owned the dock, decided to close the dock to enlarge his restaurant business. I needed to move to Chatham, too.

I was completely unfamiliar with the Chatham bars, so I eventually got a site with Jackie Our, Bobby's brother. He had just gotten a new boat, new to him that is, having lost his first one on the Chatham bars. I figured that if he lost one, it was very unlikely he'd lose another.

Fishing out of Harwichport was one thing. We left a protected pond through a good channel to Nantucket Sound, and even though the Sound could get pretty snotty, it was nothing compared to the Chatham bars.

Every fisherman in the Chatham fleet had a story of a boat lost or a near miss over that bar. The boats had to go through a cut in the beach where the sand moved constantly, shoaling the channel so that it was never in the same exact place month after month. The surf crashed on the outside, and you had to fight your way out and then time your way in perfectly so you didn't have a wall of water breaking on your stern on the way in. It was bad enough when you could see what you were in for, but most of the time, the boats left at night or in the fog or both. The goddamn fog was the worst—even shining a light to find the channel buoys didn't help much. It was real easy to make a mistake going in or out of that inlet.

When I went with Jackie, the other crew member was Bobby Nickerson, a big, rugged kid, who was also a good fisherman. But no one worked any harder than Jackie, the skipper. He drove us very hard but would never designate a job he couldn't or wouldn't do himself.

I thought there were some characters at the Snow Inn dock, but the ones at Chatham dock had them all beat. Jackie was called the White Savage, not to his face, of course. There was Hungry Springs—they called him that because he bounced all the time; Pants—who always had his hands in his pockets jiggling something; Cupcake—an ex-Cushman baker; and the Band Aid brothers—their last name was Johnson.

The Chatham dock was a beautiful place. In the course of a summer, it had thousands of visitors. There were also a large packing plant, numerous fishing shanties, and, right opposite, a spit of land called Tern Island, which was one of the largest tern nesting areas on Cape Cod. These birds all came about the same time in the spring. Every night that you came down to go fishing in the summer, they chattered away through the night and were very noisy but not unpleasant, and you took very little notice of them. Then, some time in late September, you came down to go fishing, and there would not be a sound at all. They left soon after the tourists left, and we knew we would miss them all winter long.

Between the two fish companies on the dock, we had a place that we could hang out in, with an old potbellied stove and all. We passed the long winter hours working on gear around the stove and telling stories about fishing or about girls. There were a lot of real old-timers, and many were the times I pictured myself in years to come telling younger fishermen of our exploits. We all treated those old-timers with great respect, and a good fellowship was enjoyed by all.

One morning, the talk was about halibut. Very rarely did a day go by when the conversation didn't get around to halibut—everyone's favorite fish. Everyone tried to top the other fellow in his tales about them. Joe Stapleton had been a dory fisherman many, many years before. He stepped forward and said that he had heard some crap before in his life and many tall tales, but he had everything beat. He said there weren't any of us who had seen a halibut of any significance. He said one time, on the Grand Banks, they used to catch numerous large halibut but rarely kept them as they had a poor market value and were extremely difficult to handle in a dory.

He said he was hauling the gear one day when he realized that he had an exceptional fish on. After struggling with it for nearly an hour, he got it to the top; the fish had fought so hard that it just lay there dead in the water. He called seven of the other dories over, signaling them by holding an oar in the air. They came over and proceeded to cut eight dory loads of the choicest steaks off the halibut, cutting the rest of the fish loose. He looked around at everyone in the room and said, "That was a halibut, boys." And he walked out, slamming the door. That was the end of the halibut talk for a few days.

Halibut trip on *Jocelyn C*

Jocelyn C fishing in 2000 feet of water at Corsair Canyon

On Sten's boat with cusk off

Rick Gardner on *Jocelyn C* halibut fishing 1970s

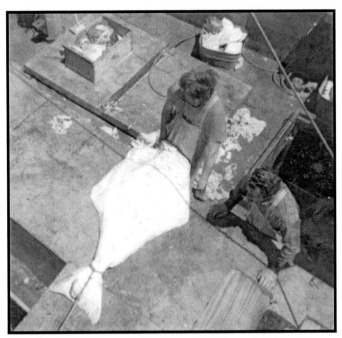

Rick Gardner and unknown mate on *Jocelyn C*

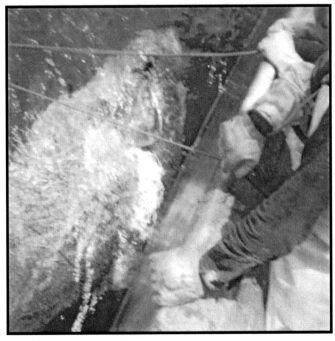

Sten Carlson with Greenland Shark

Sten Carlson on *Jocelyn C*

Sten on *Jocelyn C* with Greenland Shark at Corsair's Canyon

Tiggie on *Jocelyn C* 1970s

Chatham near fish pier

Tiggie

Squall at sea, *photo courtesy of Fred Bennet*

Working the gear, *photo courtesy of Fred Bennet*

Landing a flounder, *photo courtesy of Fred Bennet*

A day offshore, *photo courtesy of Fred Bennet*

Chatham fish pier, *photo courtesy of Fred Bennet*

Boats moored off the fish pier, *photo courtesy of Fred Bennet*

Fred's boat, *photo courtesy of Fred Bennet*

Iced up in the harbor, *photo courtesy of Fred Bennet*

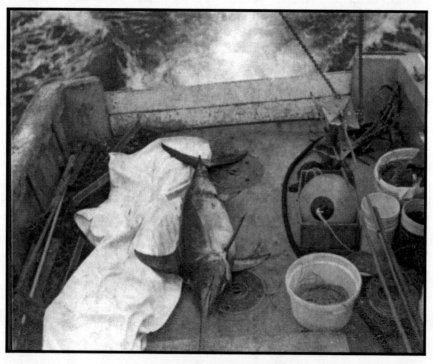

Swordfishing, *photo courtesy of Fred Bennet*

Fishing offshore, *photo courtesy of Fred Bennet*

Waiting for a meal, *photo courtesy of Fred Bennet*

Modern pilothouse electronics, *photo courtesy of Fred Bennet*

Jim Hammond, *photo courtesy of Fred Bennet*

Sea scalloping in the seventies, *photo courtesy of Fred Bennet*

Chapter Thirty-Two
Iced Up

One winter, the harbor was completely frozen over. All the boats were locked in about six or eight inches of ice, and the price of fish was sky-high. Some of the boys thought it would be a good idea if we cut some of the ice with ice saws and made a small channel for the fleet. Then we would run the engines of some of the boats creating a wake from the wheel. The tide might clear the harbor out, and we might be able to get out. It seemed like a hopeless task, but a few started in on it, and soon, it was a community affair. It did pay off handsomely, though, as a couple of days later, we were able to go out for three days in a row, and it enriched the economy of the town by about $15,000.

I had been fishing with Jackie Our for over a year and had been having difficulties at home. My wife was chronically ill, I had two small children, and I was having a tough time making ends meet. My relationship with Jackie had been worsening, as he had a violent temper, and it didn't take much to set him off.

One trip coming home from the Mussels, we had set six tubs of gear, but rather than setting with the tide, we set almost as the tide had turned, so we had about five tubs of snarl, which would require at least a day's work on land to straighten out. On the way in, Jackie and I were dressing the fish, and the other mate, Bobby Nickerson, was at the wheel. There was a pretty good breeze. We had just about finished with the fish and were washing the boat down when Bobby Nickerson hollered, "Look out!" A huge wave about twenty feet high was bearing down on the starboard side. It was one of those freakish, unexplainable seas that occur every so often. I guess they call them "rogue waves" now. We just barely had time to grab hold of the gunnel when it broke over us.

Jackie and I were nearly washed overboard, soaking wet, boots full of water, and about five or six hundred pounds of fish washed overboard, including the only halibut we had. Jackie gave a quick look around to see if anything else had been washed over. He noticed one wooden tub floating upside down. We knew there had been gear in it and knew the weight of the gear had turned it upside down, the gear sinking to the bottom. Jackie said, "I'll bet, out of the six tubs, that one was the only one that wasn't snarled." And he was right.

Shortly after that, I was unable to work long hours because I had to take care of my two little girls. Jackie told me I could have a site anytime I wanted one, but I had to quit and go quahogging, while a baby-sitter looked after the kids when I was working. Jackie eventually lost that boat, too, on the bar, very luckily getting away with his life and his crews' lives, also.

He fished a few months with a couple of other boats, but since he had been a skipper, he was bound and determined to get another boat. There were none available then, and it took nearly a year to have one built in Nova Scotia. He took a trip to Nova Scotia to try to buy a second-hand one. Naturally, there was much speculation among the fishermen as to what he would show up with. Finally, the word came that he had gotten a boat and would arrive in port the next day. All the boys were lined up on the deck as he steamed into the harbor. The usual remarks were going around—it sits too low in the water; the bow's too high, blocks the view, etc. As he pulled into the dock, we saw that he had a big sign nailed up on the side of the house, which read, "Here it is, boys, tear it apart."

Jackie had a lot of luck with this boat. He named it after his little son, calling it the *Wee John*. The price of radar became reasonable, and he acquired a set along with LORAN, a navigational aid, and the latest fish-finding and depth-recording equipment. He became one of the highliners of the fleet. Electronics were making a difference. Very soon, thereafter, sounding lines and dead reckoning became lost skills. Fishermen relied on the electronics to find their way to the fish.

One winter morning, I said, "You've talked about cutting ice around the boat. How did you do that?"

"What do you mean how did we do that?" he asked. "We took ice saws and cut."

"That's not what I mean. You're talking about saltwater ice in a harbor where the channel runs at a pretty good clip, so the ice is unstable."

"It's not unstable, and it was thick," he corrected.

"Okay, maybe unstable is the wrong word, but saltwater ice is usually thought to be dangerous, because it has to be so much colder for it to form in the first place. And you're talking about the harbor with a fast tidal current, not some sheltered salt pond."

"It was a real hard winter, and the ice was six to eight inches thick around the boat."

"So you cut around the boat?"

"No. We cut a rectangle in front of the boat leading to thinner ice."

"You did what?" I asked, taken aback.

"We cut a rectangle out on an ebbing tide and let the tide work the rest of it out to clear water."

"And you didn't break through and fall in when you got closer to the far side of the rectangle where the ice may have been thinner?" I asked. "You must have been pretty hungry to do that."

"We hadn't been able to get out in a couple of weeks, and money was getting pretty low. We were getting desperate and thought if we could get a couple of days with the price sky-high because no one could get out, we'd make it through okay."

"And did it work?"

"Yeah. We were the only boat out for three days and made real decent trips. Then a few more boats cut their way out, and the price dropped, but those first few days were good."

"The Coast Guard didn't cut the ice in the harbor back then?" I questioned.

"No, they didn't have the equipment they do today. If we wanted to get out, it was up to us."

"If they didn't have the equipment to break ice in the harbor, if anything happened to you when you were out there, they couldn't get to you either, could they?"

"No, we were taking a chance on that."

"You sure were," I said. I continued, "If the harbor was frozen, didn't the gear and rigging in the boat freeze, too? I can't imagine being out in that kind of weather."

"Yeah, it was cold, but not that windy, so it wasn't bad. We were dressed for it."

"I don't think you can put enough layers on and keep warm in those conditions. It's certainly not my cup of tea."

"You get used to it if you want to eat," he said matter-of-factly.

Chapter Thirty-Three
Walter Young

I needed to get back to fishing and was looking for a site when I was approached by Walter Young. I had known Walter only casually and was surprised when he asked me if I would like to fish with him. He said that I knew the offshore grounds well and he was very familiar with the inshore ones, so we could be co-captains. It worked out very well for three years.

Walter had worked with Dave Ryder, one of the most successful commercial fishermen from Chatham, who later became a selectman. Walter had fished with him for many years and said many times that he wished he knew only half as much as Dave did, but Dave had taught Walter very well. Walter was an excellent fisherman. He never got discouraged, and we went every day possible—and even a few impossible days.

Walter's boat was the *Hazel Y,* named after his wife who waited for us on the dock every night. They just had one child, a boy named Bubbie, who loved the ocean. He would go fishing with us every chance he had—on weekends, school vacations, and in the summer. His father told him, on numerous occasions, that he would have to finish school before he would let him fish permanently. The poor kid got seasick nearly every trip and used to take pills for it, but he did all the work allotted to him. Some weeks in the summer, he would earn as much as $150, which wasn't bad for a fourteen-year-old kid. One day, he dressed fifty-eight boxes of haddock, which is about 6,500 pounds or over three tons of fish, quite a feat for a boy of that age, and he was quite proud of it.

One winter, there were very few haddock around, and the weather was very bad. We couldn't get to the fish offshore, so we had to fish off the coast up Nauset way, catching mostly codfish. At that time of the year, the only bait the fish would bite was sea clams or mussels. We couldn't obtain any sea clams, so we had to use mussels, getting them ourselves, opening them, and baiting the gear. Some weeks, we would work a hundred hours, just barely making a $1 an hour. Most of the boats had a three-member crew—Walter and I did the work of three men. Numerous times, we would set more gear than the three-man boats.

Sometimes, we didn't get out for a week at a time. Then you'd have to be like a detective. You knew where you got fish the last time you were out, and you tried to anticipate where they would be this trip. Usually, out of twenty-five boats, someone would find them. The next day, the whole fleet would go to that spot, and there'd be a mad rush to find a place to set your gear. The fishing business is, as they say, "dog-eat-dog." This trip, Walter and I set on them and had about thirty boxes. The closest anybody else had was fifteen, so we knew the next day would be a mad scramble.

Customarily, we used to leave the dock at 3:00 in the morning, but Walter and I were going to outfox the other fellows, so we planned on leaving at 2:00 a.m. The only trouble with that plan was there were five or six other foxes among the fishermen. Once at the dock, it was chaotic to get the boat from the mooring, bring her to the dock, put the baited gear aboard, fill the water jugs, and take off before the other guys. We had a five-minute start on the other boats, and the *Hazel Y* was quite fast, but this morning, Walter ran it a little faster than usual.

We got there about fifteen minutes before the first group of boats, and we got our six tubs in the water before the first boats arrived. We cut the motor and let her drift, giving the fish a chance to bite on the gear and felt pretty damn smug about beating everyone to the best spot, patting each other on the back. It was my turn to haul the gear, and as soon as the anchor was off the bottom, I could feel that it was loaded with fish. But much to my horror, when I got the anchor in the boat, all I could see were dogfish sharks, one on every single damn hook, and each and every one of them had to be pounded off. The only fish we caught off the three thousand hooks were three haddock. The other boats that set later than we did got no dogfish at all and ended up with good trips. There must be some moral to this story, but I never could quite figure what it was.

Chapter Thirty-Four
For the Birds

Walter and I did numerous projects with the fish biologists at Woods Hole. In fact, they took a moving picture which was shown around the world to different fishing interests showing the whole process of trawling. We were also put in the commercial fishermen's review, which is put out by the U.S. Government. It sort of made us feel like celebrities even though we never got a dime.

One of the more interesting projects the biologists were working on was determining the blood types of the haddock. They were working on the theory that fish were like humans and had various types of blood, and they were trying to establish if haddock off Cape Cod had a different type than the ones found off of Nova Scotia. They knew that cod and haddock had different types of blood from each other, so they were trying to find several types of blood from the haddock. The first few attempts failed as the blood soured before they could get it back to the laboratory. Then they tried refrigerating the blood, but they didn't bring enough ice and had the same results. The third time, they were successful. Walter and I talked one of the men into taking some blood from a skate, which I imagine caused some confusion at the laboratory. Unfortunately, as with all scientific work of this nature, I imagined it would be years before we knew the results of it.

One time, Walter introduced me to a Wallace Bailey, who was the director of the Wellfleet Audubon Bird Sanctuary. He was a big, tall, husky sort of a guy, and I liked him right off. He questioned me about birds I had seen and was particularly interested in one bird, the white shearwater, or fulmar. He seemed elated when I told him I had seen quite a few in the last few days. He said they were not native to North America. He said that the last sighting was thirty years ago.

The next night, when we went fishing, Mr. Bailey joined us and brought another colleague as a witness because they were so rare in this country. They had several cameras with them, their lunches, and various other paraphernalia, decked out like they were going on a safari. Walt told them that they ought to turn in and get some sleep as it was a three-hour ride to the fishing grounds, but they were too excited to do any sleeping and were just about a wreck by the time we got there.

The fulmar is nearly as large as the seagull. Its body is a little shorter and stubbier, and the color is white. If there were a thousand gulls following behind your boat—which they do when you are dressing fish—you could pick out half a dozen fulmars among them by their bill, which is curved a little bit, and by their flight, which is much more rapid than a gull's flight, and they glide along the water with their wingtips just barely touching the water.

Soon after daylight, Bailey spotted three of them, and he and his friend just about went foolish. I guess they were about as excited as I would get if I got a ten-pound trout, so, bearing this in mind, I could understand their excitement. Walt just shook his head. The pictures didn't come out well, and they were very disappointed. I guess some of their friends didn't believe them, so another trip was planned.

This time, when they came aboard, they had a shotgun, and Bailey told me that he had gotten a permit from the government to shoot one and have it mounted and put in the museum as there wasn't one in the whole country. He also told Walter and me that there would be a quart of liquor apiece for us if we got the bird. Naturally, this made it much more interesting for us. Dawn came, and for two hours, we didn't see even one fulmar. We finally sighted two, but they wouldn't come near the boat. We finally enticed them closer by throwing fish livers overboard. Bailey picked up the gun and said, "I really hate to kill one of these birds but here goes." He fired at the two of them, missed them by a mile, and said, "I was afraid of that. I am a lousy shot." Why he didn't say that before he took aim, I don't know, because Walter and I were expert shots. That was the end of the bottle and the whole business, as we never saw another fulmar the whole day. I don't think Bailey ever did get the fulmar.

"You know," Tiggie said one morning when we got on the subject of birds, "after he missed those shots, we never saw one of those birds again. But at least he gave us a case of liquor. I guess that's worth something. We saw some other odd stuff offshore, too," he continued. "Have you ever seen a Ross's Gull?"

"I don't think so."

"You'd probably remember because they're so rare. Actually, they come from Siberia."

"Oh, you're trying to see what I know again," I said, recognizing the game.

"I was just checking."

"Yeah, right," I responded.

"Seriously, we saw one of those gulls, and when we told some people, everyone went crazy. Bird watchers came from all over the place to see if they could see it. I only remember seeing it once and never again. I wonder how it got here—that's a long way from Siberia. Storms blow birds a long way from their normal route, but this was really far. I wonder what happened to it."

"Maybe it found its way back to Siberia."

"I'd like to think so, but more than likely, something got it first," Tiggie suggested.

"Yeah, you're probably right."

"Did you ever see a dipkee?" he asked.

"What the hell is that?" I asked.

"It's a small black bird that often lands on land in a storm, but then it can't fly. Its legs are way back on its body, and it needs water to take off. So if you see one, you have to put it in a bucket of water and bring it to a pond so it can take off again."

"I have to look that one up. You don't mean a dovekie, do you?" I ventured.

"Yeah, that's it. What is it again?"

"Dovekie."

"Dovekie. Good. I was sitting on my deck, and two blue jays came. One of them was eating all the June bugs caught on the screens from the night before," he said, on a roll about birds this day.

"Blue jays eating June bugs?"

"Yeah, but then a hawk swooped down and got the blue jay. I couldn't tell what kind of hawk it was. Do you know hawks well?"

"I can identify a few of them but not all."

"There's about fifty kinds," Tiggie said.

"That's a slight exaggeration for our area, I think, Tig," I said, catching him.

"Well, there's a lot of them. With their white breasts and dark bands, it's hard to tell them apart."

"I know what you mean."

"Did I tell you I saw a family of quail this year? There were twelve of them. Haven't seen quail in a long time," the observant naturalist said.

"I saw some this year, too," I responded. "And heard them. Sounded nice for a change. I wonder what happened to them for so long. It's been years."

"My cats used to get them. Maybe now, since I don't have any outdoor cats, they'll stick around."

"I used to have a cat. His name was Gray—big, long-haired, all-gray cat..."

"Lou won't let me get another cat or dog. I really miss them."

"But then she'd be left with the animals," I said instead of continuing with Gray.

"I still want the company, though," Tiggie finished.

Tiggie and his dogs were constant companions for years. When I first knew him, he had Huskies, but during our conversations, he talked about the Weimaraners that he had earlier. His last dog died several years ago, and it was obvious that he missed having his dogs around him.

Chapter Thirty-Five
Crossing the Bar

Chatham Harbor is home to a fairly large fleet of fishing boats. Currently, eighty-two commercial boats moor in the harbor. A migrating barrier beach protects the harbor from the mighty Atlantic, but those who fish out of Chatham Harbor have to face the surf and constantly changing conditions of Chatham Inlet, one of the three most dangerous inlets on the East Coast, according to most sources. Nauset Inlet, ten miles or so north of Chatham, and Oregon Inlet in North Carolina are the other two nasty inlets, but when discussing the type of danger that each inlet poses, there's really not much difference among them—at least there's little difference between Chatham and Nauset.

The barrier beach in Chatham actually follows a cyclical pattern in its migrations. An inlet through the barrier beach will be formed usually in a storm event. The beach south of the inlet will be starved of sand for a while and breaks up into numerous sand bars. Eventually, the northern portion of the beach will begin to move south, shifting the inlet south, too, until there is one very long, continuous beach; the inlet will be the space between the beach and a barrier island called Monomoy Island.

In my book *Rowing Forward, Looking Back*, I described what happens to this particular barrier beach according Dr. Graham Geise, a leading Cape Cod coastal geologist. Dr. Geise wrote a report for the town of Chatham with illustrations of the beach dynamics. He showed that in the 1830s, the beach looked like it did in the 1970s; it was a long, thin beach. In 1846, a breach occurred that became a new inlet several miles north. All the sand in between the two openings broke up in the harbor and eventually migrated toward the land, and then finally, the beach migrated south again until the 1980s. In January of 1987, a northeast storm created a new inlet about a mile south of the 1846 breach. Now the same type of sand movement has been taking place since that storm in 1987. It is apparently a 150-year cycle, and 1987 was year one of the cycle.

One of the results of the sand movement is that a sand bridge formed between the land side and the old barrier beach south of the inlet, cutting off any water flow between the barrier beach and the mainland. Before the new inlet, boats could off-load fish at the town fish pier in Chatham Harbor, go around the "elbow" of Chatham, and moor in Stage Harbor, an indentation of Nantucket Sound on the south side of Cape Cod. Boats moored in Stage Harbor had a choice of going through the dangerous inlet or going around Monomoy Island. Now, those same boats have no choice—they cannot get to the new inlet—they have to go around. About fifteen commercial boats moor in Stage Harbor now.

A popular viewing area of the Chatham inlet is a parking lot across the street from the Chatham Coast Guard Station. Situated on a hill overlooking the new inlet, a person can actually watch geology in motion over time. Just going there a few times a year can show visible changes. Normal daily tidal currents change the sand patterns, and those who view the place in the summer may be lucky to see a few days of foamy surf, but summer is notoriously calm compared to the other seasons. At other times of the year, foamy surf is the norm.

Foolhardy souls in craft that should stay in protected water often tempt fate and go out the "cut," as some call it. Most of them return safely and confidently "knowing" the inlet. These people may even think they have a handle on the size and configuration of the bars in the inlet—they don't change that much in the summer.

But add a storm and watch out! A storm wreaks havoc. The channel could be filled in, relocated to a new place; sandbars could be higher than they had been before the storm, meaning more chance to go aground; offshore bars could close in closer to shore meaning a long parallel course broadside to breakers in the surf near the beach; and any other configurations of sand and water that Mother Nature throws at this particular inlet. Or, there could be a new inlet formed as happened in April 2007 after a three-day northeast storm pummeled the beach at the time of new moon high tides leaving a gash in the barrier beach one hundred feet wide and five feet deep by the time the storm abated. Whether this new hole in the beach will become the actual inlet is anybody's guess and only time will tell. What we do know is that as the prevailing winds shift in the fall more to the north and northeast, changes are more dramatic. Imagine a fishing boat having to negotiate this gauntlet twice a day, every day.

"Hey, Tiggie. I've been meaning to ask you," I begin one morning, "you talk about meeting your crew at the fish pier at midnight so you could get to the fishing grounds by dawn in order to set the gear."

"Yeah, when I fished out of Chatham, we left then or maybe a bit later."

"It was the middle of the night and pitch black when you left, right?" I asked.

"If we were lucky, it was pitch black. If not, there was fog."

"How did you know what the bar was like?"

"What do you mean, how did we know?" he replied, confused.

"Just what I said," I responded. "You're going out in the middle of the night when you can't see the surf. How did you know what you were heading into? It's bad enough when you can see. How did you know whether it was okay to go through the inlet?"

"The waves come in sets," he answered. "The biggest is usually the last."

"Yeah, I know that. But that doesn't tell me how big those three waves are in a set."

I knew that if you were going through the inlet and misjudged what you were doing and a wave broke on top of the boat, you were in deep trouble. The trick was to try to run the inlet without having a wave crash with all its power directly on top of you.

Tiggie sat there a minute, took a sip of coffee, and finally said, "You can feel the seas coming up through the boat through your feet."

"Like a sixth sense?" I asked.

"I guess so," he answered.

I was taken by his simple answer that conveyed so much to me. I thought of all the boats he said he fished on and knew that each boat was different. What he was saying to me, if I interpreted it correctly, was that a lifetime of experiences taught him what a boat felt like under him, and even though each boat was different, the feel of the water under the boat had similarities—enough similarities that he could tell whether they were in for a hard crossing or not. He couldn't see what was happening, so he developed an extension of the sense of touch.

It was automatic to him, and my question caught him by surprise. It was the best answer he could come up with. Whether other people who spend their lives in boats would answer the same way, I don't know, but the thought process that I could see taking place led me to believe that he had not thought much about it before, but it was the best answer he could give me. He was not telling me a fish tale. I was getting to know when he was telling me a yarn and when he was being truthful—this was one of the latter moments.

CROSSING THE BAR

One of the most aggravating and nerve-wracking features about fishing out of Chatham was the Chatham bars, which had to be faced twice a day, once on the way out in the dark and then again, coming in. If the seas had been rough all night and you had a rough passage over the bar and through the seas, it would just about spoil your whole day as you would be dreading the return trip through the surf, over the bar, and into the harbor. Boats had been fishing out of Chatham long before electronic navigation aids, but even the radar and sounding gear didn't help much. You had to rely on your senses to get you through safely. Many a boat has been lost on Chatham bar. In the dark, you had to listen carefully to the sound of the waves pounding the bar. I got to learn that the waves usually came in sets of threes followed by a sort of lull.

One night, the surf was just too rough to attempt a passage, so we waited till daylight, and it didn't look very good. You customarily waited for a lull in the breakers and then you let her go full throttle. Once committed, you had to follow through.

Walter watched the breakers very closely trying to figure out the pattern, and he asked my opinion of it. I said, "I have complete faith in your judgment. Anytime you are ready, let her go."

And so we started across. About halfway across, three monstrous seas loomed up, and it seemed as if there was no possible way out of this mess. Walter shouted to hang on. He didn't see how they could possibly miss us and not do considerable damage. But luck was with us, and each sea broke just before the bow, instead of on us, and all we got was a little foam and spray on us. We considered ourselves very lucky indeed.

We went fishing and had a pretty good trip of fish, but in the back of our minds was the dreaded thought of facing the bars again later in the afternoon, and to put a little icing on the cake, before we started home, a thick fog set in. We made the first buoy on the outer bar, and from the look of the swells—what little we could see because of the fog—it looked like it would be a touchy situation.

There were four or five buoys, and you only had a few hundred yards of error, so coupled with the fog and the rough water, it kind of gave you a parched throat. We both lit up a cigar, and Walt said, "Here goes nothing, Tiggie."

Walt made the first two buoys right on the button, then he veered hard to the starboard side, and a big sea caught us and gave us a good pounding. Walt looked at me and said, "Some goddamned thing went wrong with the steering gear."

It is things like that that make a fisherman wish he were a farmer at times. All day long, the gear worked perfectly, and it had to pick this crucial five minutes to break down. He gave it a quick look-see and saw that no temporary repairs would be made then, and we were being forced closer and closer into the breakers. We got an anchor overboard as quickly as possible, hoping that it would hold us away from devastation, but each succeeding swell would force us in closer. We decided we had to put another anchor out.

I got on the radio and put out a mayday call to the Coast Guard. When you did this, there was quite a formality that you had to go through which ran something like this.

"What is the nature of your trouble? Do you need immediate assistance? What is the length of your boat? Where is your home port? The captain and name of your boat?"

Then, if the radio man considered your situation precarious enough, he informed someone of higher authority, and you went through the same rigmarole again. Naturally, during all of this, we were getting closer and closer to the breakers, and it became a little upsetting. But you gritted your teeth, trying to keep calm and keep your diction understandable over the radio.

It usually took about twenty minutes for the Coast Guard boat to get from the dock to the bars, if the crew of the lifeboat was assembled at the station and they started immediately. I must admit I was a little upset, and, not meaning to be insulting to the Coast Guard, I told the chief they had better start for us post haste and not stop for any coffee or else we wouldn't make it.

It was nearly an hour before we could hear their boat in the fog, but it seemed like an eternity to us, and another twenty minutes before they could locate us and get a tow-line to us. They were just in time, because as it was, every second or third sea would break over us.

We finally got to the dock, and there was quite a crowd there—some of the fishermen had heard our distress call on their boat radios and had spread the word around. Walter's wife was among the spectators and was obviously relieved to see that Walter and I were okay.

The Coast Guard chief came aboard, angry about my remark about them stopping for a cup of coffee. I told him that I hadn't meant anything insulting or derogatory but was just expressing our precarious situation. But he still chewed me out for a few more minutes whereupon I told him he could go to hell.

Walter hadn't said a word yet, but then he spoke up and said, "That goes for me, too."

"There are so many cases of people who have trouble crossing the bar," I said to Tiggie. "Almost everyone I know who goes out of Nauset Harbor has a story of a near-miss. Sometimes, it's because of something like not paying close attention, losing focus momentarily, but I've also heard of a weird wave that comes out of nowhere. Most often, it's mechanical, though—something breaks down at the worst time, like what happened to you and Walter in Chatham Inlet. No wonder they're considered two of the most dangerous inlets on the East Coast."

"You get used to it, but it's not fun a lot of the time," Tiggie said, resigned.

"I'll bet," I answered.

"You know what I've been thinking about?"

"No, I haven't a clue. What now?"

"Anchors," he said.

"What about anchors?" I asked.

"You know all the anchors on lawns around here?" he asked.

"Yeah, what about them?" I responded.

"Each one came from a ship that was lost on the bars around the Cape," he continued. "There are hundreds of shipwrecks. A lot of the anchors came up in drags."

"What do you mean?" I questioned. "Wouldn't an anchor tear a net all to pieces? How would they get them on board?"

"The way the anchor lies on the bottom," he explained, "it wouldn't tear it apart. The top crossbar is perpendicular to the bottom that digs in so the rollers would roll over the top part and hook into the net part." He demonstrated the action of the net going over an anchor with his hands. "You'd know you've got something, but the nets are really strong—they hold thousands of pounds of fish, so it wouldn't tear it apart. I think we should find out where all these anchors came from. Find out the history of them. What boat did they come from and where did it go down? It would be a good story."

"How could you begin to find that out?" I wondered.

"When they come up, they usually have some sort of marine growth on them because they've been down so long. Knowing the growth on them, we could determine what type of bottom they were on." It was a rational methodology.

"Back to telling something about the bottom again?"

"Yeah. The trouble is most of them have been painted, so it would be hard to tell what was growing on them," he said, the reality of the enormity of the task sinking in.

"It's a fascinating idea," I offered. "I just don't know how to approach it. Besides, I have to finish this first," I reminded him of the task at hand with his book.

For the next couple of weeks, no matter where I went around the Cape, I began to notice anchors on lawns. I've always known they were a prized possession of those who had them, but I never focused on the sheer number of them within a twenty-mile radius of my house. I knew he was onto something and wished I could figure a way to find out the history of the boats that once had the anchors.

Chapter Thirty-Six
Summer's Thanksgiving

The dogfish became so numerous and savage that we had to resort to hand lines—trawl lines weren't working—and we were only doing fair. A new type of fishing—new to the boats in Chatham anyway—was introduced, called jigging. It was an artificial lure of about two-plus-pounds weight, made of lead with a huge treble hook on one end of it and the jig fastened on to a two-hundred-pound-test monofilament line and two rubber worms, one about three feet above the jig and another three feet above the first worm. This paraphernalia was perfected by the Norwegians and at times, was very, very effective.

This type of fishing, being new to us, was a little tricky at first. But being good fishermen, we caught right on to it and did as well as most of the boats. We let the jig sink and touch bottom and started to haul it back, and a big codfish would hit it, getting hooked in the damnedest places—mouth, head, or various parts of the body. You usually got a big fish on the jig, and while he was thrashing around, you got another one on one of the worms above the jig, and once in a while, you'd get a third on, sometimes hauling as much as one hundred pounds of fish at a time. There were times it was possible to get as much as five thousand pounds of fish, providing they were biting good.

The monofilament line had the advantage of deceiving the fish, going through the water rapidly, getting the jig to the bottom faster than the conventional cotton line, and having much more strength than the cotton line did. But it had its disadvantages, too. It used to have some of the worst snarls that you could ever imagine, sometimes requiring ten or fifteen minutes to clear each one, usually when the fish were biting—meaning the loss of six or eight fish—a costly delay.

Along with the cod, the fleet was catching one or two large halibut—some as large as two hundred pounds—because the jig simulated a herring, a natural food for halibut, instead of the sea clams we had been using as bait. I had never caught a halibut on a hand line, and for some reason, we weren't doing as well as other boats. Then, one day, it happened. I could see Walter had something on that was giving him a bad time.

He said, "I think I have a big halibut on."

He hauled it off the bottom three or four times, and each time, it took all the line out again. He told me I should get the harpoon ready, a piece of gear all boats carried in case a big fish were caught. I stood beside him, and about ten minutes later, we got our first glimpse of him, a fish about seven feet long. When he was two feet below the surface, I could see that he wasn't hooked very well and just as I threw the harpoon, the jig pulled out, but we managed to get him in the boat. He weighed over two hundred pounds and was worth $100.

Nearly everyone in the fleet had caught two or three halibut, but I was still to get my first one. They were all riding me quite hard, saying I must be doing something wrong. I had some near misses. One fish, about one hundred pounds, came within a few inches of the surface. I picked up my gaff and stuck it under its chin, and all hell broke loose. He almost hauled me overboard. I had one hand on the gunnel of the boat and the other on the gaff, but the gaff slipped out of my hand. Away he swam, gaff and all. Another fish struck the jig when I was working the line one-handed and caught me unawares. I got this terrific strike, and he immediately ran out the fifty feet of spare line that I had on the deck. The wooden spool holding the line hit me on the back of the head, taking some of the skin off my ear and pulling the line through my hand so fast that I cut one of my fingers which caused me to release it, losing the whole works.

Finally, I threw my jig overboard and got a hit almost immediately, but I also had a bad snarl. I took a couple of turns with the line around a cleat and casually cleared the snarl, which took about ten minutes. Wondering if I still had a codfish on, I started to haul it in. I could feel that I still had something on, but towing it around that long had taken most of the fight out of it, and it came along quite easily. Just before I got it to the surface, I was just about stunned to see a seventy-five-pound halibut, which I gaffed and hauled aboard. As it hit the deck, the jig fell away. As the fish was lying there, I could see it had quite a bulge in its stomach, and as fishermen are quite curious about the eating habits of fish, I cut him open to see what he had been feeding on. He had a small haddock, a small codfish, and a turkey leg in him. I found out later that the Band Aid brothers (their last name was Johnson) had thrown a turkey leg overboard two days earlier! You see some strange things offshore.

"That turkey leg is a pretty funny story. You and your halibut, is it true?" I asked.

"Of course it's true. Do you think I could make something like that up?" he responded.

"Knowing you?" I said laughing. "How long did you keep to jigging?"

"I told you, I don't remember amounts of time."

"Well, did you like jigging? I've always heard it said that jigging is a jerk on one end waiting for a jerk on the other."

"That's pretty much it. It was different, so it was good for a change. But I can't say I was crazy about it."

Chapter Thirty-Seven
Tragedy Strikes

The summer went, and fall came. Walter and his son were looking forward to the duck hunting. I had no enthusiasm for it as the best duck shooting was done in the real foul weather, and I could think of better places to be on a cold, windy day than in a duck blind. I went off-Cape one day. When I got back, I heard that Walter's son had drowned while duck hunting with his father, and his body had not been recovered. All the fishermen joined in a search the next morning.

It was a shock to me. It just did not seem possible. I was down at the dock with the fishermen at the crack of dawn the next morning. There were about twenty skiffs, two men in a skiff. I was hoping that one of us would find his body, but being as close to his son as I was, I was hoping that it wouldn't be me. There were helicopters and Coast Guard boats. After the third day, most all of the boats gave it up, leaving just Walter and the Coast Guard searching. Walter searched for a week and finally found him, lifting him out of the water himself. I really don't know how he could do it.

I didn't talk to Walter for about eight or nine days as there was nothing that could be said. I believe it was one of the largest funerals in Chatham, and I don't think there was a dry eye there. Fishing aboard the *Hazel Y* from then on was never quite the same, and that spring, I went back to quahogging for a spell.

Chapter Thirty-Eight
Sten Carlson

Tiggie spent several days over the winter talking about fishing with Sten Carlson, a different type of fisherman than Tiggie was used to.

He started one morning. "My wife, Louise, had another sister who was married to a guy named Sten Carlson. He was a real intelligent guy who had never been fishing offshore, so I took him on a trip to show him how it was done. We still didn't have electronic fish finders then, so when we got to the grounds, I took out the sounding lead to read the bottom. I told him that if we saw gray sand, it was barren; pebbles were better, but stones were good."

"When was this?"

"I told you, I don't remember dates." He fished with Sten after he dictated his stories about the first twenty years of fishing, so I figured it must have been in the late sixties or early seventies.

"But you were still fishing offshore. You hadn't started the quahogs and bass fishing yet?" I asked, trying to get some sense of what period of time he was talking about.

"No, I was still fishing out of Chatham."

"Okay. Continue."

"One day, we went to one of my favorite spots, threw the sounding lead overboard to check our location, and did pretty well. I told him that we'd probably come back on our next trip, and he asked how I'd find the same spot. I told him I just knew where it was. He said, 'Sure,' but I knew he didn't believe me that we'd be at the exact location. A while later, I looked over at him. He was swearing that he'd lost his knife overboard. I'd lost countless knives over the side but rode him a bit on his clumsiness anyway. He was green at this. The next day, we went back to the same spot."

"You knew it was the exact same spot?" I interrupted. "No fish finders, no sounding machines, and you knew? Did you have LORAN by then?"

"It was before we even had LORAN A, I think," he responded.

"So he doesn't believe you, right?" I asked.

"I tell him," Tiggie continued, "to throw over the sounding lead. I knew we were right where we should be, but he didn't believe me. I knew we were right on target, but Sten didn't buy it. When we hauled back the gear, I made a believer out of him, because his goddamn knife came up in the trawl. He said I was just lucky, so I proved it to him a second time.

"We often used old coat hangers to attach a flag to the buoy line. After the flag was attached, Sten asked me what I wanted to do with the extra coat hangers he had, and I told him to fire them over the side. A few days later, we brought up coat hangers in the gear.

"It's hard to explain how to find a particular piece of bottom in all the area we covered when there are no range markers or any way to know exactly where you are. We took soundings all the time and could actually 'read' the bottom. The charts would give us depths. They would show ridges and troughs. We would time how long it took to get to a particular location. Knowing the direction we were heading, how long it took to get to a favorite place, and what the tides and winds were doing, and then adding the bottom type that showed up on the lead line, we could put the boat where we wanted to be."

"How the hell could you do that?" I asked skeptically. "The tides and currents and wind are different all the time, and you must have to adjust the speed for the conditions."

"I don't know how to explain it," he said rather frustrated. "I got to know that stuff really well. It comes from experience and skill—some fishermen were just better at it than others. A lot of guys couldn't figure out the tides. It's one of the hardest parts to understand. But I was good at it."

"It follows the same as the inshore, doesn't it?" I queried, interested in this topic but not understanding it very well.

"No, the tide runs generally north and south."

"What do you mean north and south? Is that the longshore current along the back side of the Cape?" I wanted to know if we were using the same terms for different forces or different terms for the same forces.

"Yeah, maybe. We always called it the tide."

"Does it follow the phases of the moon? Are there tide charts for offshore?"

"Not really."

"You're kidding," I said. "Then how do you know whether it's running north or south or when it's going to change?"

"It's hard to explain."

"So you leave Chatham, steam all night to get to where you're going by dawn, set your gear, and haul back at slack tide so you don't have so much tidal pressure against you, and you have no tide charts telling you when all this is going to happen? You just have to learn it?" I asked.

"That's about right," Tiggie stated. "That's how all of us did it."

"That's quite a skill, you know, since everyone now has to have all the electronic toys to do that for you," I stated.

"I know. And I was good at it," he replied unabashedly.

"I don't doubt that for a second."

The conversation drifted back to Sten.

"Sten saw what I was doing and decided fishing wasn't such a bad living, and next thing I knew, he came back to the Cape with a big, sixty-five-foot boat named *Jocelyn C.* It was so big, he had to keep it in Harwich until Chatham officials finally relented and let him berth there. I went with him a few times to show him the ropes, and he caught on pretty fast.

"Sten wasn't like most fishermen back then," he continued. "He had gone to Yale, and he liked to try different things.

"Back then, fish weren't handled very kindly, but the Norwegians had found ways to preserve fish quality. They made it efficient, too. So Sten saw this and had the Norwegian-type gear loaded aboard his boat.

"A lot of people thought he was a pain in the ass because he had all this fancy equipment aboard his boat. But then, he got top dollar, and pretty soon, most of the fishermen changed how they were handling fish, and Chatham gained the reputation for the highest quality of any port.

"Sten was different from most fishermen. He wasn't afraid to talk to anyone. He could talk to fishermen and talk their language but just as easily, he could talk to the scientists at Woods Hole."

"I talked to Quig [Gerry Quigley, a mutual friend who was very close to Sten] about Sten, too," I said. "He said Sten was also curious and wasn't bound to doing things just because that's the way they'd always been done, so he experimented a lot with gear and with places to try. Jerry said that you guys had always put the gear over the side using a stick to get the hooks to flow out straight without getting tangled, but Sten devised a chute that made it a lot easier. He said at first, all the men laughed and made fun of him, but when he came in highliner a few times, the other guys took a closer look, and before long, all the fishermen had new chutes aboard their boats."

"He's right," Tiggie replied. "They all use them now. They don't bait the gear as they go offshore either. Now the boys hire someone to bait the gear on shore, and they take it all done. They don't use the same tubs either, and they don't use the stiff line that we did. It's all different."

"Yeah," I said. "Bill Amaru said the same thing. He said they use a limp line like parachute cord now, and it gets dumped into a fish box, and they don't have to bother coiling it at all. Bill said that Sten was an innovator but that he wasn't always very well liked."

"That's true. He wasn't," Tiggie said.

Tiggie continued with stories about Sten. "Did I tell you about the time he got a fish hook in his leg?"

"Yeah, but I may have missed something," I said.

"Sten was a rugged fisherman," he began. "One time, we were halibut fishing. When the hooks come, even though they are eighteen feet apart, they come fast. Sten took one in the thigh. When that happens, you have to cut off the shank and pull it through. Sten took a swig or three of bourbon and told me to cut the hook shaft and 'worry the hook' out. Somehow, it always fell to me to do the nasty work like that."

"That's a term I never heard of before—'worry the hook.' And it hurts just thinking about it," I offered.

"I cut off the shank and pulled the huge hook through his thigh—he didn't move or even twinge, but he did go lie down. The next morning, I asked him how his leg was, and he acted like nothing had happened."

"Real macho, huh? The hook goes in one place and cuts through and comes out another place." I shivered involuntarily at the thought.

"He was just that kind of guy."

"You said he was curious about things you saw offshore, too. Did you see anything really strange?" I asked.

"Yeah. We brought a shark on board that we hadn't seen before. In fact, it wasn't like anything anyone had ever seen before. Sten described it to the scientists at Woods Hole, and it was a really rare thing—some kind of black shark. We took a photo of it and brought it to Woods Hole and got a letter back from them saying it was a false cat shark, something that had rarely been seen. We found it in two thousand feet of water. It didn't have any teeth, and the dorsal fin wasn't like other sharks. [Tiggie used his hands to demonstrate.] It goes up a bit but then tapers down the length of the thing. The scientists asked us to save one and bring it back if we ever caught another, but we never did."

"Did you have any close calls fishing with Sten?"

"We were fishing in the shipping lanes a lot, so yeah, we had quite a few close calls. One time was really weird, though. We were way down south near the canyons off George's [Bank]. We almost ran into an aircraft carrier in the fog. At nearly the last minute, high above us, we could see the lights, and we were able to back down and avoid the collision."

"An aircraft carrier?" I asked in amazement. "That must've been some scary. By that time, you had radar, didn't you?" I asked, knowing he was talking about fishing in the seventies.

"Yeah, we had radar, and this blip is on the radar. As we got closer, it got bigger. I called down to Sten, but he didn't come up on deck and told me to take care of whatever it was. I'm looking at the radar, and this thing is taking up most of the screen. Finally, I called Sten a few names and told him he'd better get his ass on deck. When he finally came up, he took one look and yelled at me for not telling him what the problem was. You couldn't see anything for the fog, and there was no noise either until the thing was almost on top of us. It was too close for comfort, I'll tell you."

"Did you ever find out why it was there?"

"We were near the canyons off George's, and the Navy was having maneuvers. There was a submarine there, too. It was way out of the normal shipping channels. They never would have seen us, that's for sure."

"How long did you fish with Sten?" I asked.

"Off and on for probably eight to ten years." He surprised me with some actual time estimates.

"We had one trip that was really super. We went way the Christ down to Corsair Canyon south of George's. We got into a school of big halibut, and when we got back, we were the highliner of the fleet. We brought back 125 halibut. It was the biggest halibut trip anyone had ever had. It's still the record for Chatham. We went back, but Sten had mentioned it to one person in Nova Scotia, and when we got back there, it had been cleaned out. I figured we could have made nearly a year's living on those fish in a few months. Now, it's Canadian."

"It's over the Hague Line?" I asked. The Hague Line is a boundary established by the World Court in The Hague, Netherlands in 1984 to set the jurisdiction between the United States and Canada. It was a controversial boundary when it was set and remains so, both sides claiming they had been cheated of highly productive areas traditionally fished by their country. Canada gained the Northeast Peak, a productive sea scallop area while the United States gained the Southwest area, known to be productive for cod and haddock.

"Yeah. We couldn't fish there again now. Those bastards have the whole place," he remarked, referring to the Canadians.

"Well, they have that particular canyon, anyway. Did you fish for anything else with him?"

"Sure. We fished for cod and haddock, and he was often the highliner, but he was really good at getting halibut and was the highliner for halibut most of the time. We went to George's, and all the canyons searching for halibut. It was the fish we both liked to catch the most."

"You said that you caught the most halibut of anyone else in Chatham. How about the other fish?"

"I hold the record for the most haddock caught on four tubs of trawl—20,000 pounds."

"That's impressive."

"Yeah, and I also hold the record for the biggest catch of cod, too, again on four tubs of gear—22,000 pounds, and they were all big, big cod."

"Anyone come close to you lately?" I asked.

"How could they with the restrictions now?" Tiggie shot back.

He had a point. Fishermen are allowed one halibut and are severely restricted in the amount of fish they can catch and the number of days they can fish. All of those restrictions were unheard of when he fished.

Change came quickly to the offshore fishing fleet. Otto Zavatone, who demonstrated coiling the gear, said he got his first boat, the *Annie Z*, in 1970 and was using a lead line. Three years later, he got a second boat with all the latest electronic gear—depth recorder, radar, and LORAN were the major components. LORAN C was the biggest leap forward. The depth recorders took the place of lead lines as the machines could differentiate between hard and soft bottoms. But it was the LORAN that made such a huge difference. LORAN meant once someone had the bearings for a certain fishing location, they could find it consistently and in any weather. They didn't need to know about running times, engine speed, tide, or wind—all considerations in earlier times. All that mattered was getting to the coordinates. And once there, other boats followed so that "secret" spots were no longer secret. Coordinates were even sold, or so it was rumored, so that the whole complexion of the fleet and of the practitioners changed dramatically. Anyone could go fishing, and that included weekend warriors—people who worked at other jobs during the week and went fishing on the weekends—people who may not even live on the Cape. All they needed was a boat with electronics. Otto told of finding one of his sweet spots in the fog and working it for a few days while others tried to find him. Finally, someone did find him and told his buddies by radio where he was and that he had found Otto. The next day, there were twelve boats there and five draggers, the big boys, as Otto called them. He asked the blabbermouth why he thought others didn't listen to the radio, too, and asked him if he was happy because now he had ruined it for everybody.

The flood gate opened in a hurry, and more and more people entered the fishery. But the methods changed, too. The Brownell line was no longer available, and what was available was difficult to coil. Sten had introduced the chute rather than the heaving pole, and Mustad, the primary hook manufacturer, introduced modified "J" hooks and then circle hooks. Circle hooks don't lie flat on the gear and are difficult to line up properly. They are tough to bait, though they hold bait well. They also hold fish well, but they are more difficult to use in handling the gear.

The line is more like parachute cord—strong, but not conducive to neat coils. The gear gets messed up, but that is the way it is. The change in gear necessitated shore-based baiting where people are now hired just to bait the gear in inland warehouses.

After passage of the Magnuson-Stevens Act in 1977, foreign fleets with mammoth factory trawlers were no longer plying the waters off George's Bank, and many thought that establishment of a two-hundred-mile limit around our shores in 1983 would protect our resources. But it hasn't worked that way. In the intervening time, groundfish stocks have plummeted from our own fishing fleets forcing ever more stringent regulations on the fishing industry. No longer is it possible to bring back as much fish as the boat can hold without sinking. No longer is it possible to land a two-hundred-pound halibut, or if you did find one that size, you'd be hailed a conquering hero. Sharks, once a major headache for Tiggie and his friends, are now fished heavily to compensate for the lack of cod. Haddock, once so plentiful, took a nosedive in abundance but are making some recovery. The management councils, established by the Magnuson-Stevens Act, set the regulations after often acrimonious debate on each and every point of a recovery plan. Paperwork for fishermen, including detailed record keeping, the task many people got into the business to avoid, has increased dramatically. The new required skill is the ability to wade through all the regulatory prose just to figure out what can and can't be done without having the catch, or worse, the boat, confiscated.

Between the gear, navigational aids, and regulatory climate, the fishing industry does not resemble the industry of Tiggie's day. The skills Tiggie mastered so well are no longer necessary, but if a fisherman were out in the fog and something happened to the electronics, the captain may wish that he had learned those skills, just in case.

Tiggie shook his head sadly when he talked about the current status of the fishery.

"I wouldn't want to be doing it now," he said.

PART IV – INSHORE FISHING

Chapter Thirty-Nine
Weir Fishing

Each spring, fishermen look forward to the new season. Money is usually tight after the winter, and they anticipate an infusion to their personal finances. Fishing is still slow often, but one fishery has been taking place on the Cape since the Native Americans lived on its shores: weir (or trap) fishing. The method and trap configuration has changed little since the early days.

Obtaining the necessary permits for fish weirs, even though it is a traditional fishing method, is challenging. New licenses are nearly nonexistent; current weir fishermen have either kept the business in the family or bought it from a license-holder.

Tending traps can be profitable for the short season they are in the water, but it is a back-breaking way to make a living. I was lucky to be an invited guest one day—I was grateful for the opportunity and thankful I didn't have to do it every day. The men who do are rugged individuals.

Trap Fishing

During many springs, about the only possible way to make any money in Harwichport for a fisherman was to cut brush, house paint, or tear up poison ivy patches—fishermen had to eat like other people. But there was another alternative—trap fishing or fish weirs, and the pay was real good, about $10 a day, which was $2 more than you got cutting brush, and it meant working on the water.

A fish trap is netting hung from poles made from thirty to thirty-five-foot-long hickory trees, weighing approximately three hundred pounds apiece. The reason they use hickory poles is because they grow straightest, and the base on the trunk part isn't too thick. It if were too thick, they would be too heavy and unmanageable, after lugging them around all day—not that these are exactly easy to lug around. From the shore, they are packed on the boat, set in the water, and pumped into the bottom by jet pumps. The pump is tied to the pole at the base, and the force of water washes out a hole, and the pole settles into it to a depth of four or five feet, until the next storm comes along and knocks them all down. A fish trap has approximately 150 of these poles.

If you were in the air looking straight down at it, you'd see a long string of poles called a leader, leading to a sequence of two heart-shaped enclosures. The leader is in relatively shallow water. The fish swim up to the suspended net, and while many of them could swim right through because of a fairly large mesh, they shy away from it. They don't want to swim in even more shallow water, so they follow the leader to the double hearts. The fish swim within the first heart and come to a break in the netting at the point of the heart which leads them to the second heart. Once inside, they can't find a way out again. The second heart has a net on the bottom as well as the sides.

Every day, you get into the trap with a boat approximately twenty-eight feet long and haul the last heart-shaped net by hand, until you purse the fish up in one corner. Then you reach in with dip nets and save the edible species, and discard the trash, which used to be most of the catch, but these days, there isn't much thrown back. When I fished the traps, the edible fish caught in this type of fishing were basically herring, which arrived the earliest, then the mackerel, followed by squid and butterfish. These were the staples, but now, you can add scup and black bass to that list.

One species found in traps is the sea robins that make an audible sound, and when you get thousands of them together, it creates a roar. They are almost valueless, though. Then there is always our friend the dogfish shark, numerous types of skates, once in a while a sting ray, occasionally a giant sea turtle, and sometimes a whale.

My first trap fishing was with a couple of fellows by the names of Fred Powell and Boney Eldredge. Their first year of trapping, they made the grand sum of $600 between them. They got all old equipment, old nets, cracked poles, and other junk that the other trap fishermen had discarded. But this particular year, things were looking up for them. Two weeks after setting the trap out, they were getting fifteen to twenty barrels a day. A barrel is comprised of 175 pounds. So they were landing 2500 to 3500 pounds a day. They realized that they needed a little more help, and I went with them. They had a very successful year and always said that I was the one who brought them luck.

Loons have been known to get trapped sometimes, and it does seem peculiar to catch them in a fish trap. They swim into the trap and as they require a long distance to take off into the air, they can't escape. One foggy morning, I was the lookout in the bow, and as we approached the trap, I told Fred that I could see a half dozen loons in the trap.

He said, "Jesus Christ. Not those goddamned things. Now we have to go all the way back to Harwichport and get a shotgun."

I said, "What the hell are you afraid of, a few little birds?"

Fred said, "More so than a fifteen-foot shark."

I kind of thought he was pulling my leg as I was kind of green in this business of trap fishing. But he turned the boat around and headed back to port.

On the way in, he explained to me that loons are quite dangerous because as you are hauling the trap, and they get cornered, they will run up on the netting and try to stick their bills into you, which are quite long and hard. Some fishermen have been stuck in the legs at various times by them. He told me on various occasions, they had stuck their bills into the side of the boat three quarters of an inch. He said if there was only one in the trap, we would be able to handle him between the three of us. But six would be just about impossible, so that was the reason for the gun. When we got back to the trap, they had finally managed to get out of the trap and had disappeared. That just made our day two hours longer.

Most years, the biggest volume of fish caught in the trap is squid. I remember reading at one time that more tons of squid are eaten around the world than any other fish, or it is at least one of the leading fish consumed. Anybody familiar with squid knows they expel an inky substance when aroused or disturbed. I knew this myself but never realized the range of the squirt, as much as four or five feet, so you can understand when you pick up a net full of them, and all of them are squirting and spitting in different directions at once, you get hit in the face quite often. Sometimes it is just plain water, as the squid probably has run out of ink, and sometimes, you get hit with the real gooey, gooey black ink in the face.

When you get hit in the face, you look at the guy nearest to you and ask him if it is white or black, and if it's real, real black, he will look at you with a sly grin on his face and say, "Tiggie, it's just water, plain water." Then you reach up with the back of your hand and wipe it off, you think, until your whole face is black. This is repeated probably a dozen times during the day, and the sun bakes it on good and hard. By the time you get to the dock, you look more like a coal miner than a fisherman.

It got to be quite interesting each day to see what oddity would turn up that day. One day, Fred had bought a new fish fork, which was used to pin the twine under the gunnels of the boat, and he said, "We are coming up in the world—this is the only piece of new equipment we have in the whole operation." As we were pursing up the traps, we got a glance of something huge and flat. Boney identified it as a huge stingray; it was my first look at one. It had a long whip-like tail about seven feet long, and probably weighed about 125 pounds. The problem was how to get it out of the trap. Boney said that he would put the fishfork into its head and guide it over the rim which was a foot above the water. He got it up to the rim all right, using the new fishfork, but the weight of the stingray caused him to lose his grip on the fork, and away it swam with the fork protruding from its head, sort of like a periscope.

Fred said, "The only new fork we have, and we lost it the first day."

Another time, I noticed the huge swirl and turbulence in the water ahead of us. I thought maybe it might be a large shark. But usually, the sharks showed near the surface, and whatever was creating the swirl was quite deep, and we didn't get to see it until we had the trap halfway hauled. It was a huge sturgeon, which dressed out 475 pounds, which would have been five hundred pounds live weight. Fred and Boney said that it would be a difficult problem getting it into the boat, as the tail and back of the sturgeon was very bony and sharp, and they could inflict a severe wound. Also, a flick of the tail could break an arm or a leg and, for sure, set you on your can. We got him in the corner of the trap, tied lines around his tail, which was quite a chancy procedure, around his middle and head, and all three of us tried to pull him into the boat. After much huffing and puffing and groaning, we got him aboard, and he thrashed and pounded for half an hour before he finally expired. The armored plate enclosing his body was very tough, and you usually learned to dress a sturgeon with an ax or a hatchet, cutting the tail and fins off and splitting it down the middle of the belly. Once in a while, you got a sturgeon with ripe caviar in it, which brought a fancy price. But as luck would have it, this was a male fish. After much work cleaning this monster, hauling it up on the dock, loading it aboard a truck, and shipping it all the way to New York, we got $8 for it, about twenty cents a pound, hardly worth the effort.

One of the prettiest things you could see in the trap was a huge school of butterfish. These were real money-makers. Sometimes, you got as much as forty cents a pound for them. To look into a trap and see four or five thousand pounds at a time, all silvery and jumping in unison, and also knowing that you were going to get a good price for them, made them very attractive indeed. There is only one little source of irritation pertaining to butterfish, and that was when you got them in your dip net, they thrashed around so vigorously that their scales, which were very, very small, flew in all directions, and any time they landed on you, they dried and stuck. At the end of the day, you looked like you had been sprayed with aluminum paint, and as the sun beat down upon you, you almost felt as if you had a mask adhering to your face. It was almost comical to be covered in both black squid ink and butterfish scales. Luckily, there were no mirrors on the dock.

As the season progressed, the nets seemed to get heavier and heavier because of the various growths, seaweed, slime, etc. that clung to the net. It was getting to such a stage that something had to be done, and as green as I was at trap fishing, I mentioned that fact to Red. He replied that we would do something about it the next day. In the morning, as he got out of his truck at the dock, he told me to get the three rug beaters that were in the back and bring them along. I couldn't figure what the hell the rug beaters were for, but, before the day was over, I knew; believe me, I knew!

It was probably one of the hardest day's work I had ever done. We took all the netting, a small section at a time up to the gunnel of the boat and beat the hell out of it, knocking the slime and crap off it. Some of it required vigorous wallops. We did this for hours, till I lost circulation in both arms from swinging. As you knocked this crap off, it flew in all directions, into your face, in your hair, and dried like a mud pack on you, but finally, the chore was done.

Occasionally, a giant tuna got into the trap, and they were very difficult to handle, especially ones over five hundred pounds. Most of them had to be shot in the head with a shotgun, which was quite effective at close range. They were huge, beautiful fish. I felt deep remorse for them, wondering how this big beautiful fish happened to end up in this trap and meet such a fate as this. Tuna fish ranged thousands of miles, and it just made you wonder when you looked at a map how he ever got up in this corner of Nantucket Sound.

Another species that was caught by the trap fishing nets was the giant sea turtle. Some of them were up to 1500 pounds. Once in a while, the fishermen would bring one in to show the summer tourists, but because of their huge mass, when they were out of the water, they soon died if you didn't turn them over on their backs. I'd seen quite a few treated this way and felt quite sorry for them. I guess you could say that I am kind of soft, but I could see no reason for doing this, so that a bunch of gaping tourists could look one over, and the poor thing being carted off to be thrown in some dump someplace. Most fishermen can understand taking fish or any other product from the sea, so long as it is used for food or another useful purpose, but this was useless and senseless. I never brought in any myself, and I wanted no part of it when others wanted to bring one back to the dock.

I fished several springs trap fishing, but it was mostly a fill-in capacity. And about a month or two at a time was about all I could take at this very low pay.

Chapter Forty
A Little about Quahogs

The wreckage of the *I Am Alone* remained on Monomoy Point for several years, a reminder to other boats to give her a wide berth. It was completely covered over with sand eventually, leaving nothing but a memory.

I realized that I would have to do other kinds of work to supplement my income. I was married, and fishing was sometimes poor and sometimes good, but the money was very unsteady.

Over the years, I had tried to land jobs such as house painting and cutting brush but wasn't very satisfied with the work. I really hated working onshore. About the only line of fishing that I had not done was quahogging. Some fishermen did very well at it, working at it only part-time, so I decided to take a stab at it.

I inquired about what equipment I would need and was quite surprised when my friend, True Davis, told me it would require about $300 worth of gear. I didn't have $300, but my friend said I could use his equipment to start with and then buy a piece at a time when I made some money. He had a plan of how I could get some money—he needed somebody with him for a couple of days getting oysters and would pay $20 a day.

The next morning, I was to meet him at 5:00 a.m. at Round Cove in East Harwich. When I arrived, he was already in the skiff waiting for me. He said time was of the essence—we had to hustle. I figured it was probably because of the tide, or something of that nature. He rowed the skiff across the harbor to a flat covered with oysters.

He said, "Now, pick up just the live ones, throw them in the skiff, and work like hell because we have to get out of here by 7:00."

The work wasn't too hard, and I knew the oysters weren't going any place. I asked him what the hell the hurry was.

"Why the seven o'clock deadline?"

He told me we were stealing the oysters, and we had to get the hell out of there before the warden got up. This set me back a little. As a kid, I didn't even steal green apples without botching the job. But he told me it wasn't exactly stealing, more like poaching, and that if I was going to survive on Cape Cod, I would have to do a little of it. He said most fishermen poach a little in hard times.

Quahogs came in various sizes. The ones from two to three inches were called littlenecks and brought the best price, usually better than fourteen cents a pound; the medium-sized ones, three to four inches, were called cherrystones; the large ones, larger than four inches, were called chowders and seldom brought more than five cents a pound. Anything under two inches was classed as seed and was illegal to take. You had a two-inch ring made of either brass or steel and put the quahog through the ring lengthwise. If both ends touched you could keep it. All others, which fit through the ring, had to be thrown back as seed. [Now, the size limit goes by thickness—it has to be at least one inch rather than the two-inch length. The new size means that they can take smaller quahogs now that used to be called seed.]

True told me that I had to get a commercial shellfishing permit from the town and a bed certificate from the state, which gave me the right to sell my quahogs. The bed certificate specified what areas I was allowed to fish in, as certain areas were polluted and restricted. I was beginning to think that, between the expense and red tape, I'd be lucky if I broke even.

The gear consisted of a sixteen-foot skiff, an outboard motor, and the rake, called a basket-type rake, having about eighteen teeth that were two inches long. It had a basket affair above the teeth to hold quahogs attached to a twenty-six-foot wooden handle. You would anchor your boat bow and stern and throw the rake about fifteen feet in front of you, working it slowly in the bottom with the pole resting on your shoulder—your shoulder was always sore.

I fished in Pleasant Bay. The first two or three rakes yielded a lot of quahogs but very few of the legal size; they were all seed, but I could see that there would be plenty of quahogs here in a couple of years. I struggled through the whole day and came up with $7 worth. I was unable to work the next day because my shoulder hurt so badly. I was quite discouraged, but old-timers told me that after the first week or two, your shoulder toughened up and it was not so bad.

One day, while raking, I found a spot that was better than anything I had come across so far. I was raking away like mad when True Davis came along in another skiff and said to me, "I've got a drawer full of money at home. Do you want me to bring you some of it?" I didn't know what the hell he was getting at. He told me I was fishing on his private grant. He had gotten a shellfish grant from the town years before that gave him the right to grow shellfish in an area that no one else could fish in. He leased the area for his exclusive right. I had known he had a grant somewhere in the bay, and I also knew that it had to be marked with two signs, but I didn't see any signs.

He said, "You see that iron stake in front of you sticking out of the water?"

I said, "Yes, I see it. I thought somebody put it there because there were good quahogs near it."

He told me some kids had broken the signs off. I said that I wouldn't fish there again.

I stuck with quahogging for about a year, seldom making over $50 or $60 a week, but along with trawling, I managed to get by. That winter, my boat was frozen in at Round Cove, and I couldn't go quahogging.

When I started that spring, I noticed that the seed quahogs had grown just a fraction of an inch, and where I had been making $12 or $14 a day, my take went up to $30 a day. I had the whole bay to myself, but I knew it was too good to last. The first one to join me was a fellow by the name of Young Jim Chase, a legend in Chatham as one of the best quahoggers.

The first day Young Jim Chase came down to the bay, I didn't know who he was, and on the way in, I stopped and introduced myself. He grunted several times, finally saying his name. It was many, many months before Jim became anywhere near sociable. He would keep to his part of the bay, and I would be on mine. Once in a while, we'd exchange a nod in passing.

Quahogging was very good. I had my own skiff and several rakes but didn't have a very good outboard motor. One morning, I came down to go fishing, and someone had stolen my skiff. I was mad as hell, did a lot of vigorous swearing, and had to borrow a skiff until I could find another boat and motor to buy.

As quahogging improved, there would be another fisherman every week or so until there were as many as eighteen of us there. Consequently, the quahogs were being harvested faster than they were growing, and you were constantly looking for new spots and places, but I was getting to be a very good quahogger and had a knack for always turning up a new spot.

Chapter Forty-One
Accidental Bounty

The best spot that I found was more of an accident than anything else. I started out of Round Cove, got halfway across, and my motor conked out. I just couldn't get it to run, so I started to row the rest of the way, a considerable distance. I kept getting madder and madder at the motor, and I said to myself, *I'm not going to row you around the whole goddamned bay.* I picked up the hammer, hit the motor several times, and threw it overboard. A couple of guys on the shore saw me throw it overboard and eventually fished it up, and it ran for years afterwards.

While rowing, I was still smoldering, and I broke one of the oars, so I had to take the rake off of my pole and pole out of the harbor like a gondolier. Outside the harbor, I could feel what felt like stones or rocks with my pole. Was it possible that they were quahogs? I anchored my skiff and threw my rake over. After you quahog for quite a while, you can tell the difference between stones and quahogs by the sound they make when your rake goes over them. I knew these were quahogs, but were they seed or legal ones? I hauled the rake back, and it was nearly full of beautiful littlenecks, almost all legal.

What had started off as a terrible day was a blessing in disguise. I got rid of that aggravating motor, and I probably never would have found the spot, although we had gone over it every single day. I made $80 that day, fished there for three weeks, bought a brand-new motor, and managed to save a couple of dollars towards the slack times.

By the end of the summer, the quahogs had gotten pretty slim, down to $18 to $20 a day, and the fishermen started to drop out one at a time. By the time the fall came, it was down to eight of us.

While working, I made a little discovery. When you rake, you disturb certain marine worms, and the flounder gather around your boat to feed. Flounders were a very good price that fall, and some days, the flounders brought in more money than my quahogs.

I could usually get sixty or seventy pounds around my boat while quahogging, attracting the ones in a certain radius. But I had another little gimmick. I would knock off about an hour early and go visit each quahog boat, on the pretense of doing a little talking. While I was talking, I would have my little hand line going catching fifteen to twenty big flounders quickly then moving on to the next boat and repeating the same thing. I got away with this for about two weeks. Then they caught on and said, "Tiggie, talk, but don't put a line over."

Chapter Forty-Two
Pulling the Wool Over

As fall ended and winter drew on, the trawling was terrible and the quahogging was worse. I had used up what reserve money I had and was flat broke.

One night, one of my friends from Chatham was telling me how badly off he was, and I told him my situation was the same. He told me that he was going to poach some quahogs in one of the planted areas and asked if I wanted to go along with him. I didn't like the idea of it, but we had to have something to eat—we had no money at all. I was rather jittery that night as we approached the flats. This type of digging was done when the tide was out and was called dry scratching. As my eyes became accustomed to the dark, I noticed several shapes. It looked like other people doing the same thing. I told my friend that there were other people there besides us.

He said, "You don't go near them, and they won't come near you. You probably know them all anyway, but you gotta eat, so you do what you have to do."

The outcome of all this poaching was that when they finally posted the place or area to be opened for shellfishing, about the only one who showed up opening day was the warden—everyone else knew the quahogs were all gone.

One bitterly cold night, a friend and I were going poaching in Little Round Cove. We rowed across to the opposite shore, hauled the boat up, high and dry, and made a few steps, and I thought I saw something standing in the grass. My first reaction was that it was a person, but eventually, we recognized it as a blue heron. I picked up a stone and threw it at the bird. It circled overhead for about five minutes, making the most awful racket that you can imagine. My nerves were getting quite jangled. The police used to come down around the cove and check it two or three times a night, putting their spotlights on all the boats and looking everything over. We had poached about $15 apiece worth of quahogs. It was so cold that the cove was starting to get a coat of skim ice, making the rowing extremely difficult. Halfway across, a police cruiser approached. We both lay down in the bottom of the boat. It was right then and there I decided I would never do any more poaching again. I believe that was the hardest-earned $15 I ever made in my life.

That spring and summer, more quahoggers came into the bay than ever before. Some of the new quahoggers, who were real green at it, were soon getting more quahogs than the professionals. We knew that they had to be taking a good percentage of seed quahogs that would just fit through the ring. Most of them were too clever to be caught by the warden. They had various methods of ducking the warden, such as putting quahogs in a bag, dumping it overboard, and coming back and hauling it up at night. There was always a ready market for them, which encouraged the stealing.

Most of the honest boys were in favor of forming a shellfisherman's association. That way, we could bring pressure on the buyers not to buy the seed, and even bring a little strong-arm pressure on the SOBs who were taking the seed. We had a meeting of about twenty of us. They unanimously elected me president, stating that I couldn't be a crook if I was the president of the association. I don't actually believe that we really accomplished very much, but we did tell a couple of the boys to straighten up or else, which they eventually did.

One day, we heard that Jim Chase had had a heart attack, and for a quahogger to have a heart attack, he just might as well be dead. Jim Chase had done nothing else but quahog all his life. The fishermen were speculating whether he would ever get back to it again. Finally, after three months, he came down one morning to go quahogging—it was rather pathetic to see. One of the boys offered to carry his outboard motor and put it in his boat.

Jim looked at him and told him, "If I can't do all this myself, I've had it. I have to find out by trying."

Most of us steamed out of the harbor at the same time right behind Jim. We could see that just about everything he did was an effort. He finally got his boat anchored, threw his rake, hauled it halfway in, sat down, and called over to one of the boats. They took him home, and the rest of the boys took his boat in. He never came back to the bay.

True Davis, who was running a sea clam packing plant, had always been a nervous type, sometimes requiring sleeping pills to sleep at night. One night, he took an overdose and died. The ranks of the fishermen were being decimated.

Finally, I had gotten to the part in his stories when he was talking about quahogs—the type of fishing he was doing when I first met him. I thought of all the times he told me he never did anything wrong—never stealing or poaching. I thought of the times he read me the riot act because I was checking his catch for the day, blasting me with, "Why don't you check those other crooks?" And here, in his own words, he talks openly about poaching. Poaching had become a way of life—the fishermen knew it was illegal but rationalized that it was okay because money was tight. I just chuckled when I read it because as an enforcement agent, we knew what was going on, too—we just had to catch the fishermen in the act, and they were cagey devils.

"You knew exactly what you were doing," I said to Tiggie when the conversation got around to poaching. "It was just a game to you guys—see what you could get away with. Besides, you felt you weren't hurting anybody, right?"

"Well, we weren't."

"Did you think it all belonged to you?" I asked.

"No, but if we didn't get them, somebody else would."

"I can't tell you how many times I heard that line," I said.

Tiggie had talked one day about the thousands of pounds of fish he was bringing in all the time. He was saying how all the fishermen tried to outdo the others in the fleet and bring back more fish than the next guy. It reminded me of an essay I read years ago that became a classic reference for anyone studying or working with resource management.

"Did you ever hear about a guy named Garrett Hardin?" I asked.

"No. Who's he?"

"He wrote an essay in *Science* magazine in the 1960s that described what happens to a common resource."

"What do you mean?"

"Fish, or shellfish, for that matter, belong to everybody, right?"

"Yeah," Tiggie acknowledged.

"That means they're a common resource. He wrote something called 'Tragedy of the Commons.' It's fascinating because he shows the human nature of people who use or harvest common resources. He talked about a pasture, used by several ranchers, that could support a certain number of sheep. If each rancher had the same number of sheep, they all could use the pasture just fine. But if someone added sheep, there would be less for the other guys. But rather than decrease the number, the others would increase their flock, too, so that the first guy wouldn't get it all. Eventually, they'd all lose because the pasture would be overrun with sheep and couldn't support them all. It's the same thing with fishermen," I explained.

"We're just trying to make a living."

"Yeah, I know," I said. "But when you went out, there was competition among you, right?"

"Yeah. Everyone wanted to be the best."

"And when you first started fishing, there were a lot more fish around than when you stopped, right?"

"Yeah. There were more people in it. Those goddamn factory trawlers came in and wiped everything out."

"But look what happened after the factory trawlers left. The boats got more efficient, right?"

"Yeah, I guess so," he said.

"Well, nobody goes out with just a compass, a watch, and a sounding lead anymore, do they?" I asked. "Everybody has the machines—the radar, LORAN, sounding machines, fish finders, GPS, VHF radios, cell phones. Fishermen today couldn't do what you did. Most of them would be lost without the gadgets. They don't know how to do without them."

"Them goddamn guys couldn't find anything without all the machines," Tiggie said.

"Exactly. It started with LORAN, right?"

"Yeah, then radar."

"Both of them came in after World War II, right?" I continued.

"Yeah, but nobody had them for a long time, because they were too goddamn expensive."

"Did you read the article in the *Cape Cod Voice* [August 2004] about the woman who enlisted in the Navy during World War II and served at the Coast Guard station?"

"No, I didn't read about that."

"Her name was Helen Abrahamson, and she had the duty of operating the top-secret LORAN navigation equipment. The article said she and a few others went to MIT for training. Do you know what LORAN stands for?"

"Something to do with navigation," he suggested.

"Long Range Aid to Navigation. The article said it came into use in 1942."

"We didn't know anything about LORAN for a long time," Tiggie acknowledged.

"So, when did you start using radar?" I asked. "When you were fishing with Sten?"

"I guess so. His first boat didn't have radar, but the *Jocelyn C* did."

"I bet," I suggested, "since Sten wasn't one to follow the pack, that he added sounding machines and fish finders pretty quick, too."

"He was the highliner."

"That's exactly what I'm talking about. Then, when he came in with the most fish, others bought the equipment he had, too, right?"

"Yeah, so what's that got to do with it?"

"The better the equipment, the more fish you catch. The more fish you catch, the more money you make. If fish production can keep up with harvest, there's no problem, but if harvest exceeds production, there's a big problem. Why do you think the fishing industry is in such a mess now?"

"Too goddamn many regulations. You can't make a living now," he said.

"Regulations, yes. But the efficiency of the boats and the gear is like adding more sheep to the pasture—everyone wants to get a bigger slice of the pie and the pie is only so big," I said.

"You never used gill nets, did you?" I asked, changing the subject a bit.

"Those goddamn things? No, they kill more fish that you don't want. I always hated them. Such waste. For nothing. They kill everything that swims by and gets caught in the net."

Gill nets are walls of mesh stretched out over large areas to catch fish as they swim by. The fish get caught in the mesh and die. If the nets are not tended regularly, the fish can be dead for several days and be of poor quality by the time they reach the market. The method causes heated debates among fishermen who use one of three basic fishing methods: longline, like Tiggie used; gill nets; or draggers. All methods are efficient to some extent, and each fisherman has his own reasons for using one method over the other. All fishermen want the method used to be the most efficient, so he can catch the most fish with the least effort, increasing the bottom line of the business, although all fishing is grueling work.

The regulations put in place over the last two decades have eliminated an individual's ability to catch the most fish of everyone in the fleet—become a highliner. Now, they can only fish a certain number of days or harvest a certain amount of a particular species. As stated earlier, the industry is completely different from Tiggie's days fishing offshore and is hardly recognizable. About the only thing that is the same is the need for boats and a fisherman's desire to spend his time on the water.

"I bet the gillnetters weren't fond of you either," I opined. "Isn't it just competition, though?"

"I don't think so," he said.

"What about the draggers? What do you think about them?" I asked.

"They're not as bad."

"Why? I always hear about them tearing up the bottom."

"That's what everybody says, but I don't think it's true," he said adamantly.

"Why?"

"We could still get fish after the draggers went through. And there were a lot of places the draggers couldn't go where we could fish."

"If it was too rough for a dragger, wouldn't your line get tangled up in the rocks?" I asked.

"Sometimes we had to cut the gear free but not that often."

"So draggers are okay with you?"

"Yeah."

If I really tried, I could probably bring the conversation back to the tragedy of the commons. I don't know if Tiggie understood what I had been trying to say—the conversation wove around a bunch of other subjects as it usually did. I decided it was enough for the day. Another time, I might bring it up again. Or maybe, like other times we'd talked, he'd think about it, and I'd hear about it from him, often when I least expected it.

Chapter Forty-Three
Cassabooboo

Orleans had good prospects for quahogging, and I had been looking for a place to rent in Orleans for about two years but found it nearly impossible to rent there. The quahog situation in Harwich had rapidly deteriorated in the last few years, due to overfishing and too many seed takers, and the regulations were becoming unreasonable. The restrictions and regulations in Orleans were just about nonexistent—that is, until I moved there.

Most towns had a regulation that stipulated you had to be a legal resident of the town for six months before you could obtain a commercial shellfish permit, which was a good idea to a point. It kept some of the summer transients from encroaching on the resident fishermen's living. But I considered myself a little bit different, as I had been fishing, off and on, the last eighteen years right in the next town. To the selectmen, the town boundaries were sacred, and it made no difference to them that I had lived in the next town.

I waited for about four months and went into the town office to talk to the selectmen about it. Believe me, I didn't have a very good welcome. In fact, the chairman of the selectmen gave me a very difficult time, hardly letting me get a word in at all. They eventually made me wait to within two days of the six months time. I guess they thought they were giving me quite a break.

With my permit in my pocket, I moved my skiff and quahogging equipment from Round Cove across Pleasant Bay to a little harbor in Orleans called Quanset Pond. While coming across Pleasant Bay, I had to pass through the fifteen-boat Orleans quahogging fleet. They had known that I was going to fish there. As I went by, I waved and said "hi" to them. But my greeting was met with complete silence. Only one waved back and smiled, with a big foolish grin on his face. He had on a wool cap and his earflaps pulled down over his ears, and it was the middle of June.

The next day was my biggest day in value of quahogs that I ever got in Orleans, $72 worth. I said to myself, "This is the place for me." I didn't realize that I might never approach that figure again. Naturally, the word had gotten around that I had had a good day, and it was whispered in the shellfish warden's ear that I was probably taking seed. So I was checked three days in a row, and the rumors subsided.

Gradually, the fishermen began to accept me and would say hello in the morning. Like all Cape Codders, they are a little wary of strangers at first. Some of them I liked; others I didn't trust at all. The conversation always got around to the taking of seed, and they thought the biggest thief of all was Cassabooboo, the guy who had said hello to me the first day. It was later proven that the ones who accused Cassabooboo of taking seed were really the ones that needed to be watched.

Cassabooboo and I became friends. We liked each other right off the bat. I finally asked him what the idea was of wearing the wool cap in the middle of the summer with the earflaps pulled down, and he said that he had an inner ear trouble, which had plagued him for years.

I got through the summer and fall with only moderate success, and in the late fall, we were just about making grub money. Some of the other fishermen had long since given it up, but we hangers-on had to figure how we were going to get through the winter. We had fished all summer and fall in Pleasant Bay. The town had closed many of the good areas to save for a winter fishery, but we already desperately needed money, let alone what we needed for the winter to get by. The fishermen began clamoring for them to open up these other areas.

Orleans had a funny idea pertaining to regulations on the shellfishing industry. They had a shellfishing advisory board of about four members, and none of them knew anything about shellfishing or had anything to do with it. Yet, they dictated policy to us, constantly imposing ridiculous regulations and rules. We had consistently tried to get a fisherman placed on the board but had no success. Whenever there was a meeting pertaining to shellfishing or appropriation of money, fifty or sixty people showed up and maybe six or eight fishermen. Usually, rules and regulations were jammed down our throats that just about made it impossible for us to function.

One proposal was to open a place called the "Narrows" that they said had $37,000 worth of quahogs which would give us many days of fishing at two bushels per day. Other areas were closed, and the plan was that when that area was depleted, another area would be opened, and we could fish the new area. It looked good on paper with them sitting behind their desk telling us how plain and simple it would be. They almost made you feel as if they were doing you a favor.

Cassabooboo said to me, "You have heard of pipe dreams, haven't you, Tiggie? Well, watch how this one develops."

Opening morning on the Narrows was a sight to behold. About ten fishermen showed up—the other four or five didn't even bother to go as they had been poaching all summer in this area and knew that there wasn't anything there in the first place, let alone $37,000 worth of quahogs. You could hear the swearing and cursing for half a mile around in any direction. They cursed the shellfish advisory board, the selectmen, and the warden and said that from then on, they'd fish any goddamned place they wanted to, regardless of the regulations, and everyone spread out trying to find a spot of quahogs. I was a little reluctant to join them, but Cassabooboo said, "They can't do anything if we all stick together."

I went up to the head of Little Pleasant Bay to a place called the River, stumbling onto a spot right off, getting my limit of two eighty-pound bushels of littlenecks in an hour. The second day, two other fishermen spotted me. The third day, Cass came along, and I knew that this spot wouldn't hold out much longer—I was getting crowded out, and I would have to go exploring again.

Chapter Forty-Four
Caught in the Mud

There was a large body of water above this place called Meetinghouse Pond, and I asked Cass if he had fished there before and how he had done. He said that it was only mediocre, and the bottom was all muddy and covered with marine grasses and a plant called sea lettuce. It was nearly unfishable with our type of basket rake. But I had been a fisherman long enough to know not to take anybody's word for anything, so I made my mind up to check it out myself.

The limit had been changed to two bushels of littlenecks, and no limit on the medium and large size, as this class was only incidental. If you got your limit of littlenecks, it would give you about $26, and you might come up with $3 or $4 worth of mixed stuff. In my first try in Meetinghouse, I got my two bushels of littlenecks, but I was coming up with $10 or $12 more a day extra of mixed quahogs.

I also noticed something quite peculiar: Every time I went off the hard bottom with my basket rake, I would come up with a few beautiful quahogs in the mud and weeds. I had remembered some fishermen in Chatham talking about a type of rake that was used exclusively in mud and weeds. I made some inquires around the Chatham dock, and one of the fishermen said that he thought that Dick Chase had a small one, so I asked if I could try it out. He hedged a little while but reluctantly let me use it, making me promise upon a stack of Bibles that I wouldn't forget where I got it, as they were hard to come by and very expensive. I picked it up at his house that night, and like a kid with a new toy, I looked forward to trying it out in the morning. The next day, I got my limit in about two hours, also getting three bushels of mixed quahogs, which gave me about $45 for two hours of work.

I had Meetinghouse to myself for a whole week. Periodically, a fisherman would come up and try, but because of the mud and grass, he would soon give it up. Being a bit cagey, I would never lift my rake out of the water so that they could see the type of rake I was using. Finally, one day, Cass came chugging around the corner with his inevitable grin, pulled up alongside my skiff, looked in the boat, saw all the quahogs I had and said, "Tiggie, you are on a regular bonanza." He said he had been trying every place he knew the last three days, and he hadn't even come up with an eating limit. He asked if it was all right for him to anchor beside me and try his luck.

I said, "Sure, go ahead."

He hadn't seen my new type of rake, which I had purposely left submerged in the water.

He threw his rake in and hauled it back, and it was full of muck and grass with just one stinking quahog. He repeated this performance about five times, finally slamming the rake down on the boat and saying, "How the Christ can you possibly get any quahogs in this damned place?" I bet him a dollar that I would haul up at least forty on my next rake.

He said, "Impossible."

I hauled my rake in, and it was filled to overflowing with quahogs.

He said then, "What the hell kind of contraption is that?" He looked it over and said, "I'll see you tomorrow." He hauled his gear and went home.

The next morning, I started bright and early, and about a half an hour later, Cass came along. In the bottom of his boat, he had a huge mud rake weighing nearly fifty pounds. He told me he had remembered seeing this type of rake in Falmouth, and he had rushed off to go there the day before to buy one. He put it on his pole and asked me if I would show him how to use it. I had a few tips, but I was still learning myself. One thing I learned I shared with him—I said that this bigger type of rake worked much better drifting with the wind. We made several tries; the rake was very heavy, and we were quite awkward with it at first, but we finally got the knack and did excellently.

I bought a big rake just like his, and we did very well for the next two months, keeping the rake a secret from the rest of the fishermen. Finally, the secret got out, and some of the old-timers, who couldn't handle a rake this big, tried to get the selectmen to outlaw it. They didn't get that through, but the limit of mixed quahogs was dropped to one bushel, quahogs that they would never have been able to get with the type of rake they were using. The advisory board claimed that the quahogs left behind would be there for spawning stock, and it was good that they were there. We didn't buy it.

One fisherman gave us a particularly hard time, complaining to the warden all the time that Cass and I were taking seed. We were constantly checked but never had any in our possession. This guy even went so far as to threaten us with a gun one time. The chief of police said he couldn't do anything unless he actually shot at us.

Cass said, "If you find us shot, then you'll know who to look for, but that won't do us much good." It never came to anything, luckily.

When cold weather came, one of the rules of the town was, "No quahogging when the temperature is below thirty degrees." But most winters, the temperature usually got above thirty about 10:00 a.m. in the morning. So Cass and I would usually have our coffee together and start to fish around 10:00 a.m. The weather could change abruptly, though.

One particular day, we were trying a different spot about three miles from the landing where our cars were kept, when a northwest gale came up. There were winds of fifty to sixty miles an hour pounding us all the way home, and the temperature dropped to ten or twelve degrees. We nearly swamped the boat and looked like a couple of glazed donuts; the spray froze on contact with our oil cloths. It was a very, very close call and reminded me that you don't have to be offshore to get in trouble on the water.

From then on, it really got cold. Meetinghouse Pond froze over completely, and there were very few places of open water. We would go from one spot of open water to another, dragging our skiffs across the ice to get to the next open spot. We broke a lot of ice with our boats, and before the freeze was over, we had just about ruined two good skiffs, puncturing one big hole in mine. We seldom made over $8 or $10 apiece a day—hardly enough to pay for the wear and tear on our equipment.

The following spring, the warden came out one day and arrested us, saying it was against the law to have our mud rake in the water while the outboard motor was running. Even though others had been doing the same thing for a couple of weeks, the second day we did it, our licenses were lifted. The warden took our licenses away on a Thursday, and our hearing with the selectmen was not till Monday, causing us to lose four days work each, plus we had to hire a lawyer to represent us, which cost us $75. We had quite an argument in the selectmen's office, and Cassabooboo was told to leave the room, and in fact, ordered to get the hell out of the building. But we had an excellent lawyer who got our licenses back.

Chapter Forty-Five
Spooky Days

I had fished in Harwich, Chatham, and Orleans, and boy, was each town different. They were different in the areas they had to fish in and in their outlook toward fishing and fishermen. Harwich had the least area to fish, a small part of Pleasant Bay, a couple of ponds on the south side of town, and Nantucket Sound. Chatham had probably the most area and best shellfishing areas, and they had an attitude that supported the fishing industry, probably because of the fish pier and the great shellfishing. But I never wanted to live there. There was something about it I just didn't care for. Orleans was a compromise. It had Pleasant Bay, Town Cove, and Cape Cod Bay, and I could still fish offshore from Chatham if I wanted to because it wasn't far. Besides, Orleans and Eastham, the next town, had an arrangement where I could live in Eastham, which was cheaper, and fish in Orleans, a good deal all around.

Quahogging was good in Pleasant Bay when I first went there. Most of us had stayed in what was known as Big Bay most of the time and were doing okay, but more and more fellows got into it, and the amount of quahogs got fewer and fewer. There was no seed. So we all had to find new areas. Some fishermen couldn't cut it and got out and started banging nails, but some of us stuck with it. The mud rakes helped in the ponds, and I stayed a while in Pau Wah Pond.

Pau Wah was a small pond. On the north side, there was a creek that led to a big, overgrown cranberry bog, so there was fresh water flowing into the pond most of the time. The edge was a bit hard bottom, but not very far offshore, it changed to deep muck.

Pau Wah was eerie to fish in. Because it was a small pond, it often froze over in the winter, but because there was fresh water running into it, sometimes it didn't freeze very solid, and animals fell through the ice. I raked up hundreds of bones from deer, foxes, and other critters, probably some dogs that didn't make it across the pond.

I got the biggest quahog I ever found in that pond. It weighed two and a half pounds. I showed it around, and some people wanted me to open it up to see how much purple was on the shell, but I figured if it had lived long enough to get so big, it should die of old age and threw it back into the pond.

One day, I was fishing with a young guy who wasn't very healthy. We were fishing in pea-soup fog, and through the fog came a bolt of lightning. I'd never seen lightning through the fog before, and it was really spooky. I said we should get out of there in a hurry. I left, but the other guy stayed, yelling over to me that he'd rather get struck by lightning. I saw another bolt hit the pond after I left, but he escaped. I guess it just wasn't his time.

Weir fishing in Nantucket Sound

Tiggie weir fishing

Tiggie and Boris at Quanset Harbor

Tiggie and Gerry Quigley scallop fishing in Pleasant Bay, *photo by Barry Donahue*

Tiggie and Willie Sehls at Quanset with striped bass

Willie Sehls and Tiggie striped-bass fishing in Pleasant Bay

Tiggie bass fishing

Tiggie bass fishing in the 1980s

Tiggie bass fishing in the 1980s with umbrella rig

Tiggie bass fishing off Monomoy

Tiggie in the 1980s and early 90s quahogging

Tiggie pickerel fishing in Harwich at the reservoir

Tiggie smallmouth bass fishing in Sheep Pond

Tiggie with 8.5 pound brown trout
from Cliff Pond in 1970s

Tiggie in WWII, Walken, Germany
holding Gralien fish

Trout after fishing during WWII

Chapter Forty-Six
Bay Scalloping and Bobby Our

Bobby Our had grown from a boy of ten or twelve right into a man. He had left school rather young—he was more interested in hanging around the dock and on fishing boats and would skip school to make trips. By the time he was fifteen, he was a full-fledged fisherman. He was always there, and he was big, over six feet tall and over two hundred pounds. He stayed at the fishing game for ten years or so. He eventually became a very successful contractor, digging cesspools, pumping them, and doing various other types of digging. He used to say he was in one of the few businesses where he took everybody's crap and made money from it.

Bobby and I had done various jobs together: cutting brush, painting, even fishing together for brief intervals. We had worked well together, and we liked the same things: girls, drinking, and flashy red convertibles.

I was sitting on the dock one day, and Bobby approached me, told me that there was an indication that there were a lot of bay scallops in Pleasant Bay, and asked if I would be interested in going with him in the fall, when the season opened on the first of October. I said that I would think about it, but we had no equipment whatsoever. He said that he thought he could get a skiff, if I could locate an outboard motor, which I did. We had to scrape up nearly $100 between us for the drags, rope, and other miscellaneous equipment. We also managed to pick up a second-hand trailer, which we needed to carry the scallops.

Bay scalloping was a very erratic enterprise. The average life of the bay scallop was approximately twenty to twenty-two months, and the supply was very uncertain. Pleasant Bay would be full of them one year, and fifty or sixty fishermen could make a good living, but the next year, you couldn't get enough of them to eat, or you might get three good years in a row or six or eight bad ones. And the price was just as erratic. The year before we went, the price was $1 a pound. This year, the opening day price was a big disappointment—seventy-two cents a pound—but it was to get much worse. Most of the time, from then on, it was forty-eight to fifty-five cents a pound—the worst price that any of the fishermen could remember in recent years. It was so bad that Bobby and I had to work about eighty to ninety hours a week to make about $90, providing we didn't have a breakdown with our motor; it seemed that something went wrong with it every other day.

Anyway, opening day of the season officially started at sunrise. There were about fifty skiffs and boats going from Harwich and Chatham of all types of descriptions and varying in size from twelve feet to forty feet. It seemed that everyone took their two-week vacation in the first two weeks of October so that they could go scalloping; painters, carpenters, plumbers, and people from any other occupation you could think of. Consequently, instead of fifteen fishermen living for three months at scalloping, it sometimes only lasted a month because of the influx of all these other people. This created a bad feeling between the fishermen and these sometimes fishermen. Full-time fishermen felt that we didn't build houses or compete with these other people in their field of endeavor, so why the hell should they compete with us?

Besides, some of these vacation fishermen doubled their legal limit by bringing their wives along, who usually just sat in the bow and went along for the ride. They were able to take two legal limits, and we, the full-time commercial fishermen, could not. We were allowed the five bushels per person, and they got ten. This was a constant sore spot between the single and the married fellows. The wardens kept telling us that we didn't own the scallops; these other guys had a right to take them, too, but that didn't make it any better—we didn't want those guys horning in on our action.

That first morning, as we came out of the harbor, we saw two fellows that neither of us knew. They had a very nice boat and rig. Bobby said that they looked like a couple of the vacation fishermen, and every scallop they got was one less we fishermen had a chance at. About a half an hour later, I noticed the boat going by us again, but there was only one man in it, standing in the bow, culling the scallops (keeping the live ones and throwing back the immature small ones, or as they say, seed). When he looked up, he noticed his partner was gone. There was a lot of shouting and searching, but the guy must have gone overboard and drowned.

For about a week, we didn't start fishing until the Coast Guard helicopter flew over the area seeing if they could spot the body, holding us up for an hour each day. They eventually offered a $500 reward to whoever found the body, but it wasn't found till months later. A couple of people walking along the beach found it rolled up in dried eelgrass up on the high-water mark.

The bay's really not that big, and it was hard to find a good spot to fish in the fierce competition. With all these boats fishing and scallops being more numerous in one spot than another, whenever one found a good spot, he would put a little marker on it and just because he found it, he would think it was his exclusively. And if you fished around his spot with him, even if he was a good friend of yours, before the day was over, you were not speaking to each other. There were usually threats and counter-threats. But as Bobby was my partner, I didn't have much to fear, as you didn't argue with Bobby too long before you got hit in the puss. We were like a sort of Mutt-and-Jeff team.

You were allowed five bushels per man, and this was supposed to consist of four ten-quart pails filled to overflowing, and believe me, you would try to put as many as you could possibly get in the pails. But Bobby would put in an extra bucket for good measure, because if you didn't and took your exact limit, it would be meager pickings due to the poor prices. Most fishermen tried to push the envelope. Naturally, all the fishermen were scared that you might steal just one more than they, and they always claimed that you were taking over your limit. I always found that the ones that shouted the loudest were the biggest crooks.

As nobody would tell Bobby to his face that he was a crook or anything like that, they put in an anonymous call to our shellfish warden, Roger Munsey. We got along with him pretty well, but he would have to check us out on the complaint. One afternoon, as we approached the landing, we anticipated or sensed something was just not right. The warden was looking in our direction, and there was a group of fishermen standing around when they would ordinarily have loaded their scallops on their trucks and hurried home to open them.

As the boat hit the beach, Roger Munsey said that he had had a complaint and that he was going to check us out.

He looked at the size of the bags and hefted a few and said, "I guess you will have to measure them, Tiggie, and see if you can get them into four buckets."

I wished that I was someplace else. I was also trying to figure out how I could possibly get what was in one bag into the four buckets. I dumped the bag onto the calling board, and the pile looked so huge that I knew it was going to be impossible.

The bottom of the boat had about four inches of muddy water and I started to get a glimmer of an idea. Every time Munsey turned his head, or wasn't looking directly at me, I kept pushing some of them into the muddy water until I finally got the four buckets properly filled.

Munsey looked at me and said, "I see it, but I don't believe it."

He never looked inside the boat. When Bobby looked up at the crowd as Munsey got out of earshot, he made the announcement that if he ever found out who it was that had complained, he was going to break his arm off and jam it down his throat. That was the end of the complaints. And the warden never bothered us the rest of that scalloping season.

While dragging for scallops, various things came up in the drag such as spider crabs or once in a while, a blue crab. Quite often, we'd see toadfish, a small fish very rarely longer than a foot, with a large head, big stomach, and hardly any tail at all that was very slimy and slippery. And it had a bite like a bulldog. You got numerous bites from them when you were probing in the pile of scallops and seaweed, etc. If they did bite a finger or a thumb, you just had to sit there until they decided to let go. One day, I pushed both hands into a pile of this stuff and came up with a toadfish on each thumb. I figured you had to be real lucky to do this. Bobby looked at them and laughed like hell. I sat there for five minutes before they let go.

Dragging scallops was the easiest part of the deal. We would usually get through at noontime, load the ten bushels of scallops onto our trailer, drive down to Wychmere Harbor, unload them into a fishing shack we had there, and open them. Scallops ran very small this year, and we would work as late as ten o'clock at night sometimes. The empty shells had to be carried out and dumped in a pile and the fishing shack cleaned out. Then there was nothing to look forward to but getting up at 6:00 a.m. in the morning and doing the stupid thing all over again.

The season started October first, and the weather was fairly mild in October on the Cape. For the first two or three weeks, you worked with bare hands or light gloves. Then came a light frost, and each successive day seemed to grow colder and colder until finally, the winter regulations went back into effect, which stated: "No scalloping when the temperature is below thirty degrees." The reason for this was that cold would kill the seed scallops that you caught along with the adults. But when the temperature went up later in the morning, you had another go at it. Then, about December, you would get days when the temperature didn't go above thirty degrees. Finally, you found that you only got two or three days a week that you could fish. Then, pretty soon, everything froze over, the harbor, the bay, and all. Then you started to panic, trying to figure how the hell you were going to make a buck.

This particular winter, the scalloping was over. We had sold the skiff and the drags; we were running out of stuff to sell and eventually, had to sell the trailer.

Bobby said, "I guess that is it."

About the only thing we had left were our cars. Bobby and I were sitting in the car one morning looking at this huge pile of scallop shells and wondering if it was possible that we had opened all of them this year. We had also received word from the selectmen's office to get them out of there. We were trying to figure how we were going to do it without the trailer when a fellow drove up in a big truck, got out, walked over to the pile of shells, walked around it, looked over at us, and said, "Do you know who these shells belong to?"

Bobby said, "Yes, we do."

Then the man said, "Tell him I'll give him $50 for them."

Bobby said, "Sold." After we had sealed the deal, the guy kind of chuckled and said he would have been willing to pay $75 for them.

Bay scallop shells had two uses on the Cape. One was for driveways. You threw them in the driveway and let the car grind them all up until they were all eventually small, small pieces, and you had sort of a "salty" crushed-stone effect. The other use was to catch oyster spat. The shells were spread on the oyster beds, and the spat swam around and eventually settled to the bottom and adhered to the shells. The reason they used the scallop shells was that as the oyster grew, you could break him off the shell since the shell was quite fragile. Then, you set him back on the bed as an individual oyster. If you used a quahog shell, you would be unable to do this, as the shell was too hard to break without damaging most of the oysters. Our shells were going to be used for oyster spat, and we were kind of happy about that as a bonus to the money.

When I read the story of bay scalloping with Bobby Our and Tiggie trying to fit all the scallops from one bag into a bushel basket, I laughed out loud. The quick thinking and devious behavior brought back a flood of memories of when I was sent to check the catch of the commercial fishermen. I could see Tiggie standing there at the culling board, looking at what he was doing but out of the corner of his eye, not moving his head, keeping watch on the warden. I could see his deliberate actions and sleight of hand—into the basket or into the muddy water on the boat's deck. I could see Bobby Our distracting the warden every chance he got so he wouldn't watch Tiggie too closely. Maybe this was where the term "shell game" came from. From my perspective, it was very comical and accurate.

The story reminded me of my run-in with Tiggie decades ago at Quanset Pond when I was sent to check the fishermen as they came in with their catch of scallops. The end of that story is that the fishermen were "allowed" to take the large illegal seed scallops until after Christmas that year. Gardy and I and the selectmen did have the meeting, and all the fishermen showed up along with the state biologist. The result, after a rancorous assault on both Gardy and me that a newspaper reporter who was there still remembers to this day, was that the selectmen closed the bay to scalloping by the end of the first week in January, ending the income stream for the winter.

In return for closing the scallop season, the selectmen made it very clear that I was to research the problem and answer a whole lot of questions about the scallops in Pleasant Bay. The fishermen were shut out from making a living on these scallops, and if they could have hung me by my thumbs, they would have. Tiggie was one of the loudest in the bunch, but no one was happy that I even existed.

My research confirmed that the large scallops the fishermen had harvested were, in fact, immature seed scallops. Tracking scallops that remained in the bay, we found that the vast majority did survive to spawn and survived until the following fall to be harvested as adults.

I had the evidence from my research, but the report was greeted with skepticism at best. For a while, the size of scallops once again made no difference—they had to have a raised ring.

In the fall of 1983, two years after the bay had been closed to scalloping, Pleasant Bay experienced the most productive year in the recorded history of the town. I couldn't help but think that saving some of the large seed a couple of years earlier made a huge difference. But scallops had been transplanted from the Nauset system to Pleasant Bay as well. The bonanza of 1983 was probably a result of both saving the seed and transplanting scallops and Mother Nature smiling down on us that year. Whatever the positive events were, it was the last time scallops were prolific in the bay to date.

While researching the large seed, we also found a small percentage of scallops that had a small ring at the hinge. We called them "quirks." They were the result of a late set, unable to grow much before winter set in. The following year, they grew well, but only forty percent of them spawned that summer. They lived through the winter and put on a tremendous growth spurt the following spring and summer, added a regular-type ring on the shell, and spawned in the summer. That meant they had two growth rings—one at the hinge and a normal one further up on the shell. Unfortunately, most of them died before harvest, creating yet another management dilemma.

We concluded that if they are harvested the first fall when they have a ring at the hinge, they will be legal because they have a ring, in accordance with the state statute but they will be biologically immature. At least half of them will not have spawned the previous summer. If they are left in the water to spawn naturally, most won't live to be harvested, but they can contribute to future crops because they were allowed to spawn. The same phenomenon has been reported on Nantucket, where they call them "nubs," but on that island, Nantucket officials have prohibited harvesting them, a decision not without controversy. Even in the new millennium, the battle continues over harvesting these odd ring-at-the-hinge scallops.

I went to the fish market in November 2005 and bay scallops were selling for $22.95 a pound! What an extreme example of supply and demand! *Wouldn't Tiggie have loved to have gotten some scallops worth that much*, I thought as I munched on a snack of raw "pure gold" scallops.

Chapter Forty-Seven
Small Skiff Armadas

"Do you remember the year there were scallops in Cape Cod Bay?" I asked one morning.

"Yeah, that was really something. Word traveled pretty quick that Cape Cod Bay had a set of scallops, a huge set," Tiggie answered.

The season opened in October, and within two days, there was an armada of boats out there.

"I think the number of boats rivaled the Normandy invasion," Tiggie said with his usual touch of hyperbole.

Everybody who was able got a commercial license that year and went out in anything that could float. Boats that were used in Pleasant Bay or the Town Cove, protected bodies of water, that shouldn't be used in heavy water, were out there, and it was a miracle nobody was drowned.

Cape Cod Bay is deceptive for small boats. Sand flats extend a mile or more from shore, but they are covered with a ten-foot tide at high tide, and it is a wide-open bay. You have two choices: fish for a relatively short time over the high tide (four hours for a large boat and maybe five for a small one), or you fish over the low water and are out there for eight hours or so. The weather can turn nasty very quickly, especially at that time of year, and the seas can build remarkably fast, so you have to be extremely careful. Most of the smart people in small boats were only fishing over high tide.

"The first couple of weeks were great," Tiggie said. "The warden was pretty lax. We were allowed ten bushels each, but we were using anything we could get our hands on. I saw some guys using grain bags. We couldn't get them fast enough. Most of us didn't open them ourselves, like we usually did. There were too many of them, so we hired people to open them, and we just went out and got more. We all knew, though, that the bay could freeze up at any time and that would be the end of it."

"Gardy knew that, too, and that's why he let you guys take whatever you could get," I responded.

"I remember we were out one day, and all the skiffs were working real hard, getting as many scallops as they could fit in the boat. It was a real pain in the ass with the weekend bastards that don't know what they're doing. Most commercial fishermen know how to drag for scallops without cutting someone else off, but those other characters that took a couple of weeks off to go scalloping didn't know the etiquette—is that a good word?"

"Great one," I answered. I loved it when he used a word and asked me if it was a good one to use. He was always so pleased with himself that his vocabulary was more extensive than he let on to most people.

"... the etiquette of scallop dragging, and there was a lot of swearing going on. The sky got more and more gray, and the winds picked up over the tide. The boats got loaded down with scallops, and it was getting more and more dangerous, but no one wanted to be the first chicken to head in. Finally, one boat with two big guys aboard—neither were commercial fishermen—headed for the harbor. A parade of boats followed them in. No one stayed out as long as they could have that day, and it was a good thing—some boats had only inches of freeboard as they made their way to shore."

"I remember that day, too. Bruce was telling me that he and his friend George were the ones that decided to be the first ones to leave. Bruce always had a sixth sense about danger, and he said he didn't care what anyone else was doing—they were heading in."

"I didn't know who it was."

"It was also the day Gardy put up a sign that said from then on, it would have to be regular bushels and that they would be measured," I added.

"We found out that some bastard had complained to the warden that they weren't getting their fair share because of the hanky-panky going on with the limits. Our one great opportunity to actually make some decent money, and some crazy bastard ruined it for everyone. It didn't do any good to bitch to Gardy—he didn't change his mind."

"He didn't have a choice."

"I bet he didn't know how creative some of the fellas got," Tiggie said. "They were hiding bushels on board to be picked up at night when no one was around."

"That doesn't surprise me. There was just too much money out there in those scallops," I said. "There hasn't been a bonanza of scallops in Cape Cod Bay since that fall. Too bad."

"It was a long time ago," Tiggie ventured.

"It was 1976," I said.

"There was another year when scallops were everywhere in Pleasant Bay, and we thought we had learned our lesson," Tiggie remembered. "When the scallops were in Cape Cod Bay that year, everyone, including the part-time guys, or those who took a vacation just to go scalloping, got a license as soon as they heard about the scallops. That ruined it for us, the guys who made a living out there. After that, we got the regulation changed that said you had to get a license in the winter, before you knew if there was going to be scallops. We figured that would keep the carpenters and plumbers ashore and leave us alone."

"I remember. That was another of those meetings that was not fun."

"But the selectmen screwed us. They changed the rules of the game and let everyone get a license so we lost out again. We got a lot of scallops anyway, but it didn't last as long as it would have without the fly-by-nighters."

"There was a ton of scallops out there. Do you think you guys could have gotten them all before the dead of winter?" I asked.

"Sure, if it was only us. But them bastard fishermen from Chatham were coming over and stealing our scallops. We kept complaining to the warden, and he said he never saw anybody. Of course not. They were out at night and in the fog. We knew it, they knew it, but the warden either didn't believe us or never could catch them."

"It wasn't that he didn't believe you," I countered. "He never heard any boats, and he lived nearby."

"But that was the last good year for scallops. There were a few after that, but nothing like the bonanza that year."

"I know. I wish things were different out there, and we could have scallops again," I said ruefully.

Chapter Forty-Eight
Striped Bass

Tiggie became as well-known and respected for his skills as a bass fisherman in the latter part of his life as he was for his skills at offshore fishing in the earlier part. So I was surprised when I read the next chapter to his stories.

I think of all the fish that I have caught commercially, the one that I disliked the most early in my fishing career was undoubtedly the striped bass. For saying this, I imagine that I will invoke the wrath of many of the so-called striped-bass fishermen that call themselves true sportsmen. But I can truly say that I feel that they don't fit into that category. I classified myself as a true sportsman when it came to trout fishing, because I very rarely kept a trout unless it was five pounds or better, releasing all the others. But I had yet to see any so-called striped-bass fishermen turning back any of their catches. Most of them could not get down to the fish buyers and sell their fish fast enough, for the few bucks they got out of it. Most of the time, they accepted a cheaper price than we commercial fishermen would.

I think the biggest reason I sort of have a grudge against Mr. Bass is because of a beautiful dark-eyed waitress I once knew, by the name of Rhoda. She used to work in the Rexford Restaurant in Harwichport. During the slack periods, she would sit down with me and have coffee, and she got to know that I was a commercial fisherman. I could see that she was quite interested in fishing, and this would be my wedge in the doorway. She said that she had read and heard a lot about striped-bass fishing on Cape Cod and asked if I was very good at it. Naturally, I lied and said that I was, looking ahead and visualizing the two of us lying on a blanket at Nauset Beach, waiting for a bass to start to bite, which, as far as I was concerned, could be not at all. Boy, was I ever wrong! I had picked a girl who was bound and determined that she was going to catch a bass in the surf, if it killed the both of us. I took her fishing every night for about two weeks in a row. Naturally, all the boys and the waitresses at the restaurant, with their knowing grins, would say, "Going fishing again tonight?" And so we did—just fish, fish, fish. At this stage of the game, I was getting a little bit discouraged, but with much perseverance and charm on my part, plus the fact that she finally caught a bass, I finally got to kiss her goodnight and goodbye at the same time. This dampened my enthusiasm for night surf fishing.

At various times, when commercial fishing was poor, you filled in with striped-bass fishing. One of the fellows who used to do quite well was Charlie Matthews; Al Hanson also did quite well. They used to troll with sea worms from a small skiff. The biggest problem was getting the large-size sea worms, which cost seventy-five cents a dozen, and if you had a bad night, the price of worms far exceeded the money you would get from the bass. But you would always keep hoping that you would get that big load. Al came up with an idea that we should try our sea worms at Nauset Beach. Anyone who had ever been to Nauset Beach knew how bad the surf was there. We used to launch these light plywood skiffs into the surf and row like hell away from the beach, quite often ending up in the surf capsized.

Al and I fished about one week at this and were doing quite well, almost breaking even. One night, the bass were biting quite well. We had about thirty fish or about three hundred pounds. We were so engrossed in fishing that we hadn't noticed that the wind was picking up from the east, and at Nauset, that was the worst possible direction—seas built up fast.

We finally realized that if we were ever going to get ashore, we had to make a try immediately. We approached the shore several times, and the surf was roaring. Finally, we worked up the courage, and on the crest of a big one, we made a perfect landing on the beach—upside down.

We lost most of the tackle and only saved a half dozen bass that washed ashore. That was the end of that type of foolishness.

Al and I had had numerous big trips of bass (of over a thousand pounds) at various times off Monomoy Point. It seemed that if you deliberately set out to look for bass, you very rarely located any. So we used to make it a policy to always have gear, and if we saw any bass, we would fish for them, and if not, we would go after cod and haddock. Usually, Al would run the boat, and I would work the four lines, two over the stern and two outriggers.

On one day, they were biting fast and furious. The four lines were usually tight with fish. For about two hours, I would go from line to line, haul one, drop the lure back, go to the next one, and there would be another fish on the line I had just dropped back. I had maybe twenty fish lying on the deck and was hauling a particularly large fellow of about fifty pounds when Al came to the stern to gaff it for me. One of the bass got in his way, and he kicked it. Half a dozen of the dorsal fin spines penetrated his boot and broke off, parts of the fin in the boot and in his foot. We had an awful time trying to get the boot off his foot. From then on, neither of us kicked much bass—kicked about them verbally, though, from then on.

Chapter Forty-Nine
Insane Seining

There had been a lot of seining going on for bass, which was definitely illegal and even frowned upon in some circles. But most of the commercial fishermen had no qualms about it whatsoever as striped bass were seined and netted relentlessly all the way up from Chesapeake Bay. So we figured that we were entitled to our share. About the only way this could be done was by a large group of men, usually comprised of the combined crews of four or five boats. The group in Chatham had been doing fantastically well, averaging twenty thousand pounds a set. They were quite proficient in their seining, since they had been doing it for four or five summers. Naturally, when one group did well in fishing, there was always another group that horned in, and then neither one did very well thereafter. The world record on striped bass caught on a line was about seventy-two or seventy-three pounds—some of the fish they caught one year approached ninety pounds. But nobody had the guts to say that they caught it on a line and enter it in a contest.

The boys in Harwichport thought that it was about time that they got into the act. Attics and cellars were searched for nets, lead lines, rope, and various other paraphernalia, which would be required for our new venture. When we got all of the equipment ready, all hands agreed that it was undoubtedly the biggest pile of crap ever assembled in one particular area. It was finally agreed that some money would have to be spent to procure something a little better than this—not brand-new gear, but maybe some fairly decent second-hand equipment. We finally mustered enough pieces and sections of seine to make up eight hundred feet, but we needed two or three hundred feet more. Johnnie Costa went through the pile of old stuff that he had discarded and came up with a section that he said would be okay. We sort of fancied him as more or less of an expert at this, because of his Provincetown dragging and seining experiences. He was able to knit and mend the nets in an expert fashion. And so we were set for our big venture.

As seining for bass was against the law, most of it was done in the dark, with the exception of foggy mornings. This particular try was at night, and Johnnie was on the bow. There were several men in a big boat, three or four in the dory with the twine, and a couple of men holding one end on the beach. Johnnie spotted a huge school of bass. It was a perfect set. We encircled them; the two men holding the end on the beach and the dory completed the circle coming to shore further up the beach. From then on, it was back-breaking work, pulling the net up on the beach, the circle getting smaller and smaller and the fish closer and closer. As the fish panicked, they started charging the net, splashing, and trying to jump over the cork lines. We had a tremendous school, estimated at fifteen to twenty thousand pounds, and just as we almost had them on the beach, that lousy rotten piece of old gear that Johnnie Costa said would be okay parted, and we lost the whole damn school. Needless to say, on the way home that night, Johnnie was a little unpopular.

At about this stage of the game, I was beginning to feel like a sort of pirate, doing something illegal, and yet, it was not as if I was stealing anything in particular from any individual or group, but looking back at it now, I realize that it was pilfering a resource that belongs to all of us.

Like many of my fishing pursuits, this was turning out to be par for the course—the element of risk and hard work—a week's maximum effort for nothing. But the other fellows talked me into trying one more time, which was my last pursuit of bass with square hooks, which means a net.

This particular set would have to be worked rapidly—the tide was right just before daylight. But we had fog and figured that it would not burn off till a couple of hours after daylight. We made the set, but missed the biggest portion of the school and only managed to get three or four thousand pounds. However, while we were working, daylight came on, and the fog lifted immediately. There we were, like a bunch of nudes stuck out in the middle of the road.

Just about then, a jeep-load of Coast Guardsmen came into view. I looked at Al and said, "What the hell do we do now?"

He said, "There is nothing you can do, unless you want to try to swim to Harwichport, eight miles away."

I thought we had had it. But the Coast Guard boys came running down to the beach and asked if they could help us pull the net in. We said, "Sure." We gave them a fish each, and they were as happy as pigs in a cabbage patch. This was too close for me, and I got out of this business.

"I read the stories about bass fishing on the beach—trying to impress a woman and the seining," I said one morning steering the conversation to fishing. "You said you hated bass fishing back then, and then you go and switch gears later on and become one of the best bass fishermen around. What happened to change your mind?"

"I never liked fishing off the beach," he answered. "I know a lot of guys like that, but I really didn't like fishing at night."

"You're kidding," I said. "You fished half your life offshore at night."

"That was different. You had lights on the boat, so at least you could see what you were doing. Out on the beach, that's not the case. I just didn't like it."

"What happened to the woman you taught to fish?"

"I never saw her again. That's all she wanted was to learn how to fish," he lamented.

Chapter Fifty
Commercial Rod-and-Reel
Bass Fishing

Our conversation about bass fishing left a perfect opening for me to ask Tiggie questions about bass fishing in the estuaries around Orleans. His reputation as a bass fisherman was unmatched. Everyone I talked to said something about how they tried to compete with him but never came close. I wanted to know more about this part of his life.

"How did you get started in the bass-fishing business?" I asked.

"After my close call with the Coast Guard seining for bass on the beach, fishing for striped bass didn't have much allure for me. Bass gave me a bad taste in my mouth, but eventually, I changed my opinion and became very good at bass fishing from a boat.

"I started fishing for them commercially," he continued. "They were worth a fair amount if you could get enough of them, and like everything else, I had to learn new ways of doing things. But I soon mastered the technique and became very good at it. Some of the guys were using hoochies, but I wasn't having much luck with them— couldn't quite get the hang of it."

Hoochies are a plastic lure with a hook hidden in a plastic skirt that sort of looks like a hula grass skirt.

"Hoochies come in all different colors. They come with a single hook. One day, I was talking to Joey Davis who suggested I use a treble hook and throw the other one away. I caught four or five fish, certainly

259

nothing to write home about or pay the bills. Then I cut off one of the hooks and added pork rinds to the other two hooks. Bingo. Up to forty fish."

"You love that number forty," I teased. "Every time you talk about the number of fish, it's forty. Are you telling me the truth?"

"I wouldn't lie," he said with his best poker expression.

"What made you switch from hoochies to tube and worm?" Tiggie was the acknowledged master at the tube-and-worm approach for bass fishing. Many people copied him, but few were as successful.

"I met up with Fred Bennett who had a tackle store," he began. "He was a good fisherman, too. They were using clear plastic tubes with hooks to catch bass, and one day, they got a shipment of tubing that was the wrong kind—it was opaque. I asked if they would make me up some tubes with the new stuff, and to everyone's surprise, it worked extremely well.

"I fooled around with the idea and added a few details. I tried wire to get the line down but didn't like it, so I switched to lead core line. It gets the line down to the bottom fast and is much easier to use. I put a seaworm on the end, but it has to be a nice, big, healthy seaworm. Some of the junk they pass off as good worms isn't worth a damn, so you've got to be careful in what you buy, especially at the highway robbery price these days.

"Then I added teaser hooks with worms—what a deadly combination. The fish had become wary of just the tube and worm, but with the teasers, it was one right after the other. Now, everybody tries to copy me, and they say I was the one who perfected the method, and I guess I did. Some people call it a 'Tig rig.'"

"That's a great name for it," I said. "I hadn't heard that one before."

"But how you hold the rod or how much line you let out are just as important as what you have on the end," he added. "When you let out the line is important, too. It's probably why I caught so many fish while all the boats around me weren't doing as well."

"You talk about fishing with or around Bob Gardner in Cape Cod Bay, too. I didn't know you fished over there."

"I was the first one to fish off the flats, and I was doing really good for a while."

"How many years did you fish Cape Cod Bay?"

"I fished in Cape Cod Bay for about four years. All the party boats were fishing way offshore off Billingsgate Shoals, but I went looking one day closer to shore and found a couple of decent holes off the Brewster flats. No one fished there, so I got some hoochies and some umbrella rigs—the gear everyone else was using—and I tried my tube and worm, too. I located some ranges, lining up two radio towers and a house with a Brewster landmark and began to fish. The holes were good. Bass were lying in them just as they had in other places I had fished. The fish have to get out of there before low tide or they will be trapped for the six long hours before the tide floods again.

"I was doing real well on the flats for quite a while and had the place all to myself. But sure enough, someone came over to see what I was doing, and when they saw I was catching fish, they tried it, too. It was such a nice place for small boats, but more and more boats showed up. I was getting crowded out. By the fourth year, I was getting so pissed off that the assholes in the other boats were cutting my lines off so often that I had to give it up. The only time I could have some peace out there was at night, and I didn't trust Cape Cod Bay at night in a small boat.

"I used to see a guy named Sherrill Smith out over the flats of Cape Cod Bay a lot," he continued. "He was a good fisherman, worked for the state fisheries people, and he also wrote a column for the local newspaper."

"Yeah, I talked to Sherrill. I read a lot of the articles he wrote about you."

"He wrote about me every once in a while saying that even though I shared what I was doing, it wasn't enough. I was still getting more fish than anyone out there. I'm not sure why I caught more fish, but I learned to think like a fish even though that sounds crazy.

"I guess I just made whatever I was throwing at them seem more enticing than the next guy," he said.

"Sherrill said it was embarrassing and better to just pretend you weren't there or pretend you had your own little honey hole," I said.

"That was fine by me," he responded.

Chapter Fifty-One
Pleasant Bay Bass

"From Cape Cod Bay, you switched to Pleasant Bay?" I asked another day.

"Fishing the flats in Cape Cod Bay was good most of the time, but I also enjoyed fishing in Pleasant Bay. I got to know every shallow and hole where fish would be, especially the bass. I loved getting the schoolies. I was fishing commercially, but I also liked what I was doing, and I got a lot of fish.

"I used to get pissed off at the tackle store guys. Your husband was one of the worst. People would come in and ask him where to go to find fish, and he'd say, 'You know the back side of Strong Island? Just follow the guy in the red tin skiff. He'll yell and scream at you to get out of his way, but he catches the most fish of anybody around.' So, I'd be out in Pleasant Bay, behind Strong Island, and all these boats would be following me all around the place."

I smiled at his remark, wondering how many people had been told to follow that little red tin skiff.

"I never liked to show anyone what I was doing exactly," he continued. "If someone came near the boat, I'd keep the rod in the water so they couldn't see what I was using. My brother-in-law came by one day and wanted to know what I was using. I wouldn't tell him. If someone wants to show you, okay, but if they don't, you just have try and see from a distance. He had the nerve to come up beside the boat to see for himself. I wasn't ready to let out the line again, but I put the rod over the side so he wouldn't see. The bastard lifted the rod

262

out of the water to see what I had on. I never spoke a civil word to him again.

"People were always trying to copy me," he went on. "They'd go where I went and used what I used, but they could never get the same number of fish. Sometimes, I'd even take people and teach them the basics, but they still couldn't get as many fish as I could. They'd follow me around like obedient puppies, and I had to find new hiding places to catch my fish. The bays around here are too small for all the people trying to catch fish."

"How long have you used that red tin skiff?" I asked.

"I had a couple of different boats, but I used a tin skiff in the later years in Pleasant Bay," he said, not really answering the question. "One of my favorite places was behind Strong Island. The sand shifts creating shallows and deeper holes, and each year, I had to learn the bottom all over again, but it didn't take me long to find the fish. I knew their habits, and I knew where they would be at certain times of the tide and at certain times of the day. I knew if bluefish were around, if the herring were in the bay or not, what other types of bait were available, and if they were swimming in the eelgrass or on top of the shoals. I knew how much lead core to let out and how to play the rod, whether to add a teaser and what kind to add. I knew how to catch fish, and I caught a lot of them. I had a mental road map of the bay and could go anywhere at any time and not get into trouble. It was my world.

"Strong Island was my favorite place, but there was another hole closer to Broad Creek that not that many people knew about. It was small but deep, maybe fifteen feet deep. Bass liked that hole on the ebbing tide, probably just waiting for things to come by as the tide was dropping, so I'd make a pass about one hundred feet north of the hole, and when I got to the hole, I'd make a sharp turn east or west. The worm would drop in the hole, and I'd snag a fish. I watched the guys following me around the bay, and they'd start their run way up-tide. By the time the worm hit the hole, it would be all weeded up and useless."

"What do you mean?" I asked.

Tiggie used his hand and arm to explain his technique.

"Here's the hole. There's grass leading up to the hole. I make a run way up-tide from the hole. The tide is dropping, so I'm going with the tide. But I don't let out the line until I'm about one hundred feet from the hole, just over one color on the lead core. Just as I hit the hole, I make a sharp turn either east or west, it really doesn't matter. By the time I make the turn, the line has just gotten to the edge of the hole, and wham, I've got another fish on."

"The people watching you must think that you've let your line out way up-tide and the fish are on the shallows," I ventured.

"If they do, they don't know the habits of bass. You have to work the edge.

"I watched the other people fishing around me, and their rods were seldom bent over—with their long rods, it was pretty easy to tell. I stuck to short boat rods and got the fish off the hook so fast it was hard to tell that I had caught another fish. I could hear the swearing on the other boats when they figured out that I was outfishing them and just chuckled to myself. If they had spent as much time on the water as I had, maybe the story would be different.

"I taught a few people some of my secrets and some of my favorite spots, but then I'd want to fish there again, and they'd be crowding me out. There were some guys that were pretty good, and I had to watch out for them, and everyone wanted in on the action of selling a few fish.

"Some people just struck me right, and I took them fishing," he added.

"I met a guy who told me you took him with you," I said. "He's from Vermont. He told me about a time when you took him and a friend fishing one day. He said you made sure that he sat facing you so he could see exactly what you were doing and you told him, 'I'm going to teach you how to fish.' He said you told him to let out two colors of the lead-core line. You were busy with your own rod, but when you looked at his, he had let out two-and-a-half colors. He said you calmly explained, using a few colorful expressions, that when you said two colors, you meant two colors. He said he reeled in half a color and hooked a fish. He caught on pretty fast and says he still comes to the Cape to go fishing but switched to the Cove."

Then I asked, "Did you use tube and worm exclusively out in Pleasant Bay?"

"No. It was effective lots of the time, but I used other things, too. Like hoochies at dawn. That's when they worked the best. I might switch to mini-umbrellas."

"You used those damned things, too? I hate those," I stated emphatically.

"So do I, but they are effective at certain times. Sometimes, I'd use them instead of hoochies at dawn. I'd spray them silver to simulate sand eels, then switch to black and red just after daylight and then switch to all black during the day."

"No wonder people always wondered what you used."

"It's why I didn't show many people. But they would have had to figure out when I was using the colors, too," he said knowingly.

"Did that hole you were talking about fill in after the inlet broke through in 1987?" I asked, realizing the vast changes in Pleasant Bay after 1987.

"No, it never did. There was another hole near some rocks that was hard to fish, at the bottom of the tide; sometimes, it was the only place, though. You needed to let out one-and-a-half colors to get to the edge of the grass where the fish could come up out of the grass to get the worm.

"My world came crashing down when they established a size limit that was twice the size of the fish I was catching, but eventually, I learned how to get the big ones, too."

Tiggie was talking about the change in regulations that raised the size limit. He was no longer able to fish for schoolies or small bass. According to Paul Caruso, sportfishing expert with the Massachusetts Division of Marine Fisheries, sixteen inches was the size limit for bass beginning in the 1940s. By the seventies, stocks were low, and in 1984, the federal bass act was passed. Most Atlantic states closed the bass fishery entirely, and it remained closed for several years. By 1989, Massachusetts was the only state to have a commercial fishery. But the size limit had been raised in 1981 to twenty-four inches then to thirty inches and higher still to thirty-six inches in 1989. Closing the fishery along the entire range was credited with bringing bass stocks back to historic levels and has been widely touted as a fishery management success story. The current commercial size limit is thirty-four inches. Harvesting tender, sweet, but young schoolie striped bass appears to be yet another memory, but fishing for them and releasing them is widely practiced. Local fishermen begin to salivate in the spring waiting for the first sign of bass in the bays.

"Now, the rage is flyfishing for bass." I continued with our discussion of bass fishing.

"I did that long before anyone else," Tiggie said.

Surprised by this revelation, I said, "I thought you were strictly rod and reel."

"I caught most of my bass with rod and reel, but I did a lot of flyfishing, too."

"For sport or commercial?"

"Both. But I mostly sold whatever I caught. Flyfishing for bass has become very popular. I did it years before anyone else around here even thought of using a fly rod."

"I can't believe you actually used a fly rod commercially." It seemed an inefficient way to catch fish commercially to me.

"Why not?" Tiggie asked. "Sometimes, it's the only way to catch them. I had a contest with young Dan Marino one time. The bets were on the first fish and the largest fish. I caught the first fish, first cast, and it was a beauty—about thirty pounds, but he caught the biggest one later. This was behind Strong Island."

"It still seems hard to believe for me," I said.

"Like any other fishing, it can be tricky. You never let the fly touch the water on the back swing or a bass may hit it and you'd go over backwards. The best fly has some gold. Silver or aluminum are good, too, but they work best if you take a fingernail and make a single crease down the center to make it twist in the water. Under the right conditions, you can do pretty well with a fly rod for bass. Most of the guide services are now using fly rods and they seem to be doing okay.

"I guess there's one positive thing to come out of the bass size restrictions and flyfishing. It means there's more 'catch and release.' I did that all the time for freshwater fish but took almost anything I caught in the saltwater. Now the fish has to be pretty big, twenty-eight inches, to be taken—those nice, tender, young smaller schoolies have to remain in the water so they can get big and grow up, and I guess that's not such a bad idea with so many more people out there fishing for them."

"Twenty-eight inches is for recreational fishing, isn't it?" I asked. "I thought the commercial size limit was thirty-four."

"Yeah, I guess you're right. That's a big fish."

"I know," I responded.

"Actually, my 'killer instinct' that I had when I started fishing is just about gone now, and I don't want to kill anything. I remember one day, I had a bass on that was about forty pounds."

"There you go with the forty again," I chided.

"It was about forty pounds, and back then," he continued, ignoring my comment, "it was worth about one dollar a pound, a real nice fish. A second fish about the same size came up alongside the first one and actually rubbed against it. I'm holding the first fish by the lower jaw, in the water, before I get it into the boat, but the second fish is actually touching it. I figured they belonged to the same school and had probably been together all these years, so I let my fish go and watched them both swim off together. It was probably a stupid Guinea thing to do because someone else was sure to get one or both of them. But I felt good letting it go and watching it swim off with the other fish."

"So you're just a big softie, huh?"

"Yeah, but don't tell anyone. It will ruin my reputation."

"Do you still let things go?" I asked.

"Yeah, more than ever. I still love watching everything in and on the water. I was going by Strong Island one time and saw a fox on the shore. She followed me along the shore for quite a while, both of us looking at the other. I didn't think much about it until the next day, and she was there again. She followed me day after day for over a month. One day, as I passed her, she ignored me. She was intent on something in front of her. I stopped the engine and drifted, watching. Finally, I saw what she had seen—a field mouse in the grass had moved to the shore. Now, the mouse had no cover, and it scurried as quick as it could to the water. The fox chased after it but for some reason, did not go in the water. The mouse was swimming, and I found myself cheering for the mouse that had outwitted the fox. Just as I thought the mouse was in the clear, a big bass swam along the boat and headed toward the mouse. Before I could get a rod in the water to try to get the bass, it got the mouse. I would never have believed it if I hadn't seen it myself. I knew no one else would believe it either."

"I do," I said earnestly.

Chapter Fifty-Two
My Best Friends

"You've always had dogs around, haven't you? At least for as long as I've known you, you've had dogs. Did you always have Huskies?"

"No, I started out with Weimaraners. One thing about fishing close to home was that I could bring my dogs with me wherever I went. I had always loved animals and had cats and dogs whenever I could. I started out with Weimaraners and then switched to Huskies. I liked both kinds, because they had some spirit. At one time, I had sixteen of each breed, and I didn't have a kennel.

"When I went into the Army, we had a dog named Peter, a spitz. I didn't have too much to do with him when he was young, but he still favored me over my sisters. As I walked out the door to go to Europe, my five sisters had a lottery to see who would get my room if I died.

"Anyway, I didn't die, but my sister tried to move into my room anyway after I left. Peter wouldn't let her in the room," Tiggie explained. "He just protected my room. Whether Peter was the reason or not, I don't know, but she left the house and joined a water follies team for five years that mostly toured in New Zealand.

"I got home, and after four years, Peter went crazy when he saw me. I couldn't believe it. I hadn't been home in all that time, and he still knew me."

"Of course he knew you," I said. "Dogs don't forget people."

"I let him on my bed, and he was getting pretty old. One day, I woke up and felt a paw on my thigh. I looked over, and he was dead. Shortly after that, I left for the Cape."

"That must've been hard to wake up and find that he had died in his sleep."

"It was, but to have his paw on me when he died was pretty special."

"When I was in Harwich," Tiggie said as he began a new story, "I was driving to the pier, and when I got there, some of the fishermen said that there was a brush fire near my shack, and they were afraid my shack was burning. I raced back home and found my dog running down the road. I was so glad to see he was okay. I stopped and picked him up and headed back to the dock. I figured if the house was on fire, the fire department was there already, and there was nothing I could do anyway but get depressed. And it was really just a shack. But when I got to the dock, some of the fellas asked me where my wife and daughter were. I was so happy to have found my dog that I had forgotten they were at home."

"You can't be serious."

"Yeah," he said sort of sheepishly. "I raced back there, and the police wouldn't let me through. They said my family was fine, but the house was gone. My wife wouldn't speak to me for a month."

"I can't say that I blame her."

"One of my dogs, Suzy, was a great water dog." Clearly, this was a day to talk about dogs. "Weimaraners aren't known for swimming ability like labs, but they are retrievers, and so they have a certain amount of retrieving instinct. Suzy retrieved things even if they were underwater. My friend, Bill Monroe, was down the Cape one time, and we were at one of the ponds fishing or swimming or both. I dropped something, I don't remember what it was now, in about twenty feet of water and told Suzy to go get it, never thinking she'd actually dive down. But dive she did, and after an eternity, she came back up with the treasure in her mouth. We called her a wonder dog after that, and whenever we went under, she would, too. Bill and I loved to snorkel in the ponds, and Suzy would come with us, diving and surfacing and keeping up with us, always by our side.

"For the last twenty-five years I fished around the shores, I had Boris and then Boris's daughter, Nina, with me. They were Huskies and loved being on the boat. I told Sherrill Smith a story once about how Boris actually knew when there were bass around. I was ready to leave the area I was at, and Boris went crazy, barking and howling. He could detect a swirl beneath the boat and could probably sniff the smell of fish feeding before I could. It smells sort of like watermelon. Over the years, I had learned to pay attention when he acted up that way, so I stayed and caught eight more fish. He really did know.

"Sherrill wrote about another time with the dog and bass," he continued. "The dog jumped or fell out of the boat, and just as I reached for him, a goddamn bass hit the line. With one hand holding Boris and the other on the rod, it was a real commotion. I was trying to keep tension on the line so the fish didn't get away and get Boris back in the boat at the same time. I thought for sure I had lost the fish but after a while, I actually landed them both.

"Boris went with me for about twelve years. One winter, I was going out every day I could, figuring the temperature would get above freezing sometime mid-morning. For days, the weather didn't break, and it was frigid. One day, Boris refused to go. I called him everything in the book, but he just wouldn't get up and go with me. I had to admit it was pretty foolish to try to get out again and finally let him have his way. We didn't go out that day.

"His daughter, Nina, took his place in the boat when he got too old to go with me. She had a mind of her own, just like any woman. I was digging clams in the Town Cove finding a lee where I could get out of the wind. Nina went on her travels, looking for a soft touch somewhere along the Cove where she could get a treat. Back then, lots of people liked dogs, and they could roam a bit looking for handouts. I would whistle for her when I wanted to leave, and she'd come running back.

"One day, she didn't come. I called and called and whistled for half an hour and was so goddamned mad that I left. The next day, I was digging worms closer to Nauset Harbor at one of my favorite flats."

"That's a couple of miles from where you were the day before, isn't it?" I asked when I thought I might be able to get a word in.

"Yeah, it was closed to taking clams, and the warden caught me there, but I showed him that I was only digging worms so he let me continue. So there I was, about two miles away from where I had been the day before, and I looked up, and there was Nina, standing on the shore just looking at me with a sly dog-smile.

270

"All my dogs are gone now, and I'm too old to get another, but I sure do miss them. Boris came back to visit one day. I was sitting in my living room, and I saw him. He was lying by the rocking chair. He put his paw on the rocker, crossed his paws, and then he got up, walked across the room, and was gone. People don't believe that one either, but I swear it's true. I could see him. Nina and the cats all perked up, too—they sensed he was there. It didn't scare me to see him. Actually, it was a comfort. I never saw him again, but he sure was a good buddy to me. When he died, I wrapped him in a blanket to bury him. I couldn't throw dirt in his face—it didn't seem right, and he was my friend. They were all my friends."

"Did I ever tell you about the time," Tiggie started on another day, "that Charlie was with me in Pleasant Bay, and we saw the swarm of bees?"

"You mean your nephew, Charlie Anastasia?"

"Yeah. You see some funny things on the water. I was out quahogging with my nephew Charlie one summer day when I saw a black cloud heading across the bay. I watched it for a while and realized that it was a swarm of bees heading right for our boat. I told Boris to lie down and told Charlie to jump in the water. We both went overboard just in time as this huge swarm flew right over us. I could never figure out why they fly over water, but it had happened before out there, so I knew what it was. It was very strange, but luckily, Boris did what I told him and stayed down so he didn't get stung and neither did we."

"That's pretty weird."

"Charlie has a business in Canada now. He wanted me to work for him one time, but the guy I'd be working with had just told another guy to kill a Husky because she had a sore paw. I couldn't work for anyone like that. I know they have a different idea of what dogs are for, but to kill a beautiful dog just because it had a sore paw was not something I could do. I told Charlie no."

PART V – FRESHWATER FISHING

Chapter Fifty-Three
Trout Fishing

"We've talked a lot about saltwater fishing, but I know that you have done a lot of freshwater fishing, too. Is that what you did for fun?"

"When did you ever know me to do anything for fun?" he shot back.

"Well, you can't sell them so why else would you fish for them?" *For fun,* I thought.

"I never lost my love of freshwater fishing. I started fishing with Pa all those years ago in the North Shore rivers, and now I've fished pretty nearly all the lakes and ponds from Dennis to Truro. That's a lot of them. I probably like trout fishing the best, but I've fished for all the species found around here.

"I always liked watching the habits of fish whenever I could. I started doing that with my old friend Bill Monroe back in Foxboro where we went swimming together. We used to fool around with diving in the ponds up there, and I continued when I got to Cape Cod. Bill would come for a visit, and we would snorkel in many of the ponds on the Cape. I could hold my breath for a really long time, so I'd dive down, stay still, and watch fish, especially trout, and learn their habits underwater. Bill and I went in Seymour's Pond one time and saw twenty-three different kinds of fish in that one pond. I wonder how many are there now."

"You counted twenty-three different species?" I asked, amazed.

"Yeah," Tiggie said. "Just in that one pond. Bill went on to be an expert SCUBA diver. You ever heard of Truk?"

"The island in the Pacific?" I asked.

"Oh, you've heard about that."

"You trying to catch me on something that I don't know?" I teased, knowing this was one of his favorite games.

"No, I just didn't know if you knew about this. It was important in World War II. Bill dove there and found all the Jap planes that went down."

"I didn't know about the planes that went down," I said.

"There were a lot of them. Bill was a famous nuclear physicist. He came to see me last year, but he wasn't too good. His daughter had to drive him down."

"You had some interesting friends."

"Yeah, it's funny how they put up with a dummy like me."

"You're no dummy. That's for sure. You just don't have much formal education, but that has nothing to do with smarts. Look at all the things you've researched on your own just because you wanted to know about something."

"If I saw something I hadn't seen before, I found out about it."

"I know," I responded.

"Did I tell you about the baby quail in my yard?" he asked.

"Yeah, you mentioned it." Repeating conversations was part of this morning ritual. "I heard one myself this year. I haven't heard that sound in a long time. What do you think happened to them?"

"Maybe foxes. Or coyotes," he suggested.

"Coyotes weren't around here when the quail disappeared. I'd buy foxes, though. There're a lot of them around. I like watching them."

"I like watching them, too. They're death on squirrels."

"Well, that's probably why there's a fox—good eating with the number of squirrels."

Conversations about wild animals were not uncommon. Tiggie was quite observant of the world around him, and I enjoyed the subject myself.

We didn't talk much about freshwater fishing. Tiggie gave me a couple of articles he wrote that his daughter indicated were published in sporting magazines many years ago. They are vintage Tiggie, talking like someone who, as he said himself, learned to think like a fish.

Chapter Fifty-Four
Guaranteed Limits

In the 1960s, I got the only freshwater fishing guide license in Massachusetts and began a fishing guide service. I got some business cards made up that said: "BOAT, BAIT, GEAR. GET YOUR LIMIT OF TROUT OR IT COSTS YOU NOTHING." I added my phone number and let it go at that. I never thought to have a company name like they do now—I just put enough information on the card to attract interest in fishing.

I was a professional guide during trout season, which lasted from the third Saturday in April through mid-October for the reclaimed ponds and from April through February for the unclaimed ponds. Trout fishing had "hot spells" and slack periods. Some places were good early in the season or late in the season, but on the Cape, we had good trout fishing from beginning to end, even in the hottest weather in mid-summer. Most people didn't fish for trout in mid-summer, though, because the fish were hard to catch then. But I found a way.

I had started trout fishing the usual way, with a lot of ties I tied myself, primarily streamers, nymphs, and wet flies. I met the Harwich police chief, Isaiah Kelly, who taught me to use grass shrimp as bait. I had trouble, though, both finding enough grass shrimp and keeping them alive.

I found shrimp around old docks and in marsh creeks including salt marsh creeks. I settled on a foam ice chest half filled with ice and burlap on top to keep the shrimp cool so they'd last about three days. I made some screen trays to hold the shrimp so they weren't directly on the burlap. The fresh shrimp attracted the larger trout, but I also had to use two-pound test leaders because the heavier leaders didn't work.

I thought that I wouldn't get any fish when summer arrived, but Isaiah told me that I had to fish in early daylight and sunset hours and only in the deepest parts of the lakes. I got depth charts from the state and found the deepest holes.

One day, I just couldn't find any bait. I remembered reading an article about someone using kernels of corn successfully in California, so I gave it a try. It worked like a charm. It was cheaper and so much easier than getting the grass shrimp that I switched to corn exclusively and found that the fish loved it. I used corn to chum for fish. I was getting as many trout as I wanted almost whenever and wherever I wanted and decided that I could do it and make myself some money, too, so I got a guiding license.

All my parties got their limit or there was no charge. We usually ended up with thirty or more fish every trip. The editors of *Outdoor Life* were skeptical of this claim and sent their field editor, Ted Janes, down to check out the story. I was the first one to try corn as bait for trout in this area, and I could catch trout morning or afternoon in almost any lake that had trout. We spent a lot of time together, and when he left, I guess he had enough material to write something because then he wrote a five-page article, "Cornball Trout," (*Outdoor Life*, July 1968) about fishing with me. We had fished in mornings and afternoons and early evening and always caught fish, so he was able to set the record straight that I wasn't lying about catching fish any time I wanted to in any pond that had trout.

We became fast friends, and my last trip of the season was usually with him.

Chapter Fifty-Five
Change of Pace

One of the last times I went with Ted, it was late fall, and we fished under the most adverse conditions—bright and sunny, with southwest winds of forty miles per hour. I was very much against going, because it was almost impossible to keep the boat anchored steady, but Ted insisted on going. The trip was not a complete disaster, and in fact, it worked out rather well—we managed to get thirty trout of twelve to sixteen inches. While fishing, Ted asked me what I did when the trout season ended. I told him that was when I really enjoyed fishing because that's when I went for pickerel and smallmouth bass which were almost completely ignored by most fishermen on Cape Cod.

I loved to fish for trout, but sometimes, I wanted a change. Most of the time, there was no camera around when you caught the really big fish, but I was lucky one day and had someone with me when I caught a beauty of a smallmouth bass. It had to have been near the state record for that year, but I never entered it. Fishermen always say that, but I have the picture to prove it.

I met a fellow named Joe Connors who used to fish from the shore of a nearby lake. I'd drive by and see him fishing, weekend after weekend, with his friend Larry Larsen. Joe and I hit it off pretty well. He had the potential of being a good fisherman, and I told him about beautiful browns that were in this particular pond. Up until this point, Joe was a "one-method" fisherman—fishing from shore with a sliding sinker and live herring for bait which could be caught in this particular pond. It became a ritual every weekend, talking with Joe and Larry and watching them fish.

One day, we were discussing the leaders he was using. Joe was using two rods, each with six-pound test. So far, the catch had been one rainbow. I asked him if he'd mind if I rigged a spinning rod with two-pound test leader to see if it would make a difference. I rigged my rod my way, and we fished side by side. I caught seven fish including three beautiful brownies, each over two pounds each. That convinced Joe that two-pound test leader was about the only thing to fool the brownies. He fished that pond right up until it froze over, landing about twenty-five brownies, over three pounds each.

That winter, Joe would often visit me, and we'd talk over what we were going to do in the spring. I told him some of the best fishing was from a boat. He was a shore fisherman and doubted what I was saying. He was difficult to convince. When spring came, I got him out on the boat, and he had his best trout season ever, landing his best trout—a six-pound brownie.

Trout over eight pounds on the Cape were the "uncatchable" class. The larger trout in the reclaimed ponds fed on the small trout, and you were not allowed to use fish for bait. These large fish were strictly "meat-eaters." Over the years, I'd had a dozen or so of these big fish grab a small trout from my line. I managed to land two of them, just under eight pounds each.

Chapter Fifty-Six
Sleuthing

In the fall, I tried to pick two or three ponds that I had never fished before. Using the maps and charts, I showed Joe and Larry where some good spots were. I can remember driving by some of these ponds, and, with the exception of trout ponds, I'd never seen anyone fishing them at all. It was like a game for me to try to figure which ones would be good for pickerel and smallmouth bass, and half the time, I came up with something real good. If that happened, I ended up fishing one or two ponds each fall. I doubted if I'd ever hit all of them!

One year, I told Larry and Joe that we'd cover more ground if we split up into teams—they'd pick a couple of ponds, and my cousin, Guy, and I would check a couple. If we didn't find any new good ponds, we could always go back to our old reliable ones. Joe and Larry picked two ponds in Harwich, and Guy and I picked two ponds in Chatham. We agreed to meet that night and discuss the results of the day's fishing. As we approached our first pond, it looked like a typical pickerel pond, very weedy and lots of lily pads, but the trip was a complete "skunk." There were plenty of shoestring pickerel of ten to twelve inches long but nothing of any size.

A few years ago, we used artificial lures and plugs with treble hooks, but these injured the fish too badly, so now we used perch bellies on a single (number four) hook. Pickerel have vicious teeth and usually bite through a six-pound leader, so I made a leader of about ten inches long or twenty-pound monofilament. I preferred this rig over a wire leader, because the wire leader didn't give as good an action, especially if the pond you were fishing was weedy. Wire leaders would carry the perch belly too deep, and you didn't see the strike on the surface. For me, the best part of pickerel fishing was that big "surface smack."

Our second pond was beautiful. As we approached it, we saw a little stream running from the pond above. The stream was full of herring on their way to the sea. Our spinning rods were already rigged. I made my first cast while Guy mumbled, "I don't know what kind of fish we're gonna find here."

I said, "From the looks of this place, I think just pickerel. It's not sandy, and I doubt if there are any smallmouth bass here."

On my second cast, I got a terrific strike, but a complete miss. I cast back again—another beautiful strike. This time, the fish was on solid. All at once, the fish came up. I was thinking I'd gotten a pickerel. What a surprise—a five-pound largemouth bass! I had never come across largemouth bass on Cape Cod. I landed him and looked him over, a beautiful full-bodied fish—it was apparent that they were feeding on herring—then I released him. We fished another hour. Guy got a bigger bass, which he lost after the second jump. We landed a dozen pickerel, too. The top fish for the day was five pounds.

On the way home, we were elated about discovering the largemouths. I mentioned the fact that a perch belly was hardly the best bait for largemouths—I had always considered golden shiners the best overall bait, but we had a problem. We had to find a source of golden shiners.

Guy said, "I know that you'll come up with something, Tiggie."

I assured him that the next time we fished together, I would have scouted a pond that had golden shiners.

Later that evening, Joe and Larry stopped by, and we compared notes on the day's fishing. Their two ponds were full of small pickerel and yellow and white perch. Guy and I told them about our experience with the bass. Joe was anxious to go with me and give "my pond" a try. Since Guy was going home the next morning, Joe, Larry, and I planned to take my johnboat to try to get some live herring. We tried one brook and only got six herring, but we used the ones we had. Larry fished from shore, and Joe and I were in the boat. We went across the pond to get out of the wind. Joe had left his camera in the car.

I said, "What if you get a large bass? Who'll believe you without a picture?"

He said, "Come to think of it, I don't think I've ever caught a largemouth bass in my life."

I looked in the bait pail at the six lonely herring. I was going to use perch bellies and fish for pickerel and let Joe use the herring to try for a bass. Joe was using a spinning rod with four-pound monofilament, plastic float, and a number-six hook. The reason for the smaller hook was that a larger hook would kill the herring, but with the smaller hook, the herring would live for at least a half hour.

I was casting toward the shore with my old favorite perch belly. I was having good pickerel fishing, landing four fish from two to four pounds, releasing them all. Joe's herring was swimming on top of the water. Characteristically, they do this when they weaken. Suddenly, there was a tremendous smash on the surface! Joe gave the fish half a minute or so and set the hook. He was fast onto a beauty. He landed him fifteen minutes later, using four-pound test monofilament.

Since we never carried a landing net of any kind, I had the honor of grabbing the fish by the lower jaw and lifting him out of the water and removing the hook. Joe handed me the scale so we could weigh him—seven pounds, three ounces. I looked at Joe.

"What do we do? Release him and maybe catch him next year, or keep him?"

He said, "Just let me heft him."

Then he gently placed him back in the water.

I said sarcastically, "We got a beautiful picture of him, didn't we?"

"We never have the camera when we get a good fish," he mumbled, "and probably will never get another one like that the rest of my life." It sure was some fish for his first largemouth.

We moved the boat about one hundred feet down shore. I was still having good pickerel fishing, but Joe was being bothered by large white perch and by now was down to three herring. Suddenly, there was another big smash! He was onto another big bass, and this one weighed out at seven pounds one ounce. He released it.

By now, Joe had the shakes. I was still riding him about forgetting the camera. I told him if he got another big bass, we'd have to go ashore and get the camera. I realized the odds were unlikely that he'd get another big one. There were only two herring left in the bucket. When he hooked his last bait on, he hooked it too deep and just about killed it. A few minutes later—he had another hit.

He said, "I think it's a yellow perch. It feels as big as those two bass."

The fish didn't break water. In the process of landing it, we discovered another bigger fish following behind it.

I said, "This one we keep for a picture."

It weighed seven and one half pounds.

Joe said, "Do you realize that I landed three largemouth bass today for a total of almost twenty-two pounds?"

In the meantime, Larry was still fishing from shore. When we came in, he looked the bass over and said, "I thought I had a big surprise for you boys—I got a big pickerel."

His fish was on a stringer tied to a bush, and it sure was a beauty, just a shade over six pounds. We released his fish, too.

Chapter Fifty-Seven
Smallmouths

Joe wondered if there were smallmouth bass in the pond. I told him I'd fish it during the week and let him know. I fished four days that week from shore with poor bait—all I could find were some chubs. I landed nine bass, mostly four- to five-pounders and one little fella of about two pounds. I think I missed getting larger fish because they like large bait, and I couldn't give them that.

The next weekend, we gave up on the largemouths because of the bait situation and turned to some of my favorite ponds for smallmouth-bass fishing. Joe wasn't too keen on it as he fished for smallmouths in New Hampshire, which was considered one of the top smallmouth-bass states.

I said, "Don't knock Cape Cod. We've got some pretty fine smallmouth-bass fishing here."

In a lot of the smallmouth bass ponds, you were unaware the fish were there because they rarely came to the surface and they rarely took an artificial lure. In fact, you couldn't get them to show on a fish Lo-K-Tor (electronic depth recorder and fish-finder). The fish hugged the bottom so close that they blended right in with the reading of the fish Lo-K-Tor, but I found that the smallmouths are not the least bit leery of a boat. Largemouths won't do that. The best depth for smallmouths is ten to fifteen feet. Grass shrimp work well if there are not too many perch around, but crayfish are the ultimate bait. Smallmouth bass will take crayfish even when they're gorged with bait fish. [Lo-K-Tor was the first portable, transistorized electronic sonar unit used for sport fishing, also called the little green box. The company designed the unit in 1957 to be "portable, compact, lightweight, contain its own batteries and be relatively inexpensive" (Lowrance County Website)].

I usually use a fly rod, a twelve-foot leader of four-pound test and a number eight hook. Fish it straight up and down, right beside the boat. You don't need a sinker. Keep the crayfish about a foot off the bottom. Hook the crayfish through the tail, gently so as not to kill him and never use crayfish longer than one inch. Put the large "breeders" back as they are useless as bait. There are numerous ponds where you can get crayfish with a dip net or small sweep seine. All the local tackle shops will advise you where you can get the crayfish—the people in the shops are most cooperative. If you don't get a bass within fifteen minutes, you'd better move and try another spot. If you get one, you'll probably get half a dozen hits in that spot. If the action slows down for more than half an hour, move to another spot.

Joe, Larry, and I fished a large pond, by Cape Cod standards, over seven hundred acres, but one of the problems with the large lakes in the fall was windy conditions eight out of ten days. As luck would have it, this day was a perfectly calm, sunny fall day. It was cold, about thirty-five degrees, but we were dressed warmly, and without the wind, it was quite pleasant. I reminded Joe to bring the camera, but he wasn't going anywhere without it. We had a batch of beautiful crayfish, and everything seemed about perfect. The first spot we tried—nothing! This spot had been very good in the past. We tried three other places with the same results. Larry was giving me funny looks over the top of his glasses. Joe was silent except for an occasional comment about the good smallmouth-bass fishing in New Hampshire. I wasn't discouraged yet—I just had to find the right spot. We moved, and this time, I had two hits and lost the fish. I swore they were bass, but Larry thought they were perch. Another hit! This time, I landed a three-pound bass. I told Joe and Larry to be alert; there was probably a pod of bass under us. I was right—we caught five and lost about an equal number right there. We moved twice more and ended up with fifteen bass, from two to five pounds, for the day. It took some doing, but I made a believer out of Joe about smallmouth bass on Cape Cod.

Chapter Fifty-Eight
One Last Story

Tiggie and I had been sharing breakfasts for over one and a half years. Most stories had been repeated many times, but once in a while, he uttered a new tidbit of information that surprised me.

He had loaned me a photo album of his fishing days, so that I could have some pictures for the book. I took a few out of their pages to copy and looked at some of the early pictures in the album. I had passed by them on my first glance at the album, but this time, I stopped and looked more closely. They showed Tiggie in his Army uniform with fish displayed on the ground in front of him.

"Tiggie," I asked one morning, "what are those pictures all about that show you in your Army uniform with fish displayed? You weren't fishing during the war, were you?"

"Yeah, I fished then," he answered matter-of-factly. "What are you so surprised at?" he asked, looking at my expression.

"How'd you pull that off?"

"I had my rod, and I fished."

"You mean to tell me you packed a fishing rod when you went overseas to Europe during World War II?" I asked incredulously.

"Yeah. My mother cut a rod down into seven pieces for me, so I packed that and a couple of flies. I kept it in my sack."

"I can see you now—a rod on one shoulder and rifle on the other."

"I don't see that as so odd."

"Well, I sure do."

"I was a mess sergeant and had a colonel who happened to love trout. The rivers were full of them over there. We'd be in a convoy, and I'd jump out of the truck when we went by a good-looking river and go fishing. If I wasn't back by a reasonable amount of time, the colonel would send a jeep out after me. I fed a whole battalion of 120 men on the fish I caught."

"I can't believe you fished the rivers of Europe during the war."

"The river banks are quite steep over there on some of the rivers," he continued. "Sometimes, I'd be fishing, and there'd be salvos going over my head—one army on one side of the river and the other army on the other side."

"And you calmly fishing below. What a mental image."

"One time, I walked around a corner, put my rifle on the ground, and cast out in the river. Then I glanced upriver and saw a German soldier sitting on the bank soaking his feet in the river. His rifle was on the ground next to him. I thought, *I'm a goner now.* But he just nodded to me. Then he put his socks and boots on, got up, and said whatever they say in German that means 'goodbye,' I guess, and off he went."

"And you're still fishing, I suppose, this whole time."

"Yeah. He just walked off."

Tiggie didn't like talking about his time in the war. I didn't push him for more.

Epilogue

Tiggie's fishing days are over. He passed away in February, 2008 after many health-related set-backs. In his last couple of years, he couldn't get into his little red tin skiff by himself, but kept it in the yard just in case someone offered to go with him. He didn't even carry a rod in the truck and that said a lot.

The last time he tried to scratch a few quahogs, he fell and nearly drowned. It was a cold day, and as he lay face down, he said he remembered the days when he trained himself to swim underwater by holding his breath for a long time. The training may have saved his life. He somehow struggled to his feet, got to his truck with his bushel-basket of quahogs, and headed for the market to sell his catch. In his wet clothes, hypothermia was beginning to set in, but he had to sell his catch before he could head home and get warm. It was what he had done all his life, and this day was no different.

When he was able, he spent his days going from coffee shop to coffee shop, looking at all the pretty girls and talking to the "boys". The guys told him what was going on and he told them what it was like when he was fishing. Then he got some bread and went down to the fish pier in Chatham and feed the gulls. He had to keep up with what was going on at the pier, knowing he'd become the old-timer who used to fish, the character others watched now just as he watched the characters in Harwichport and Chatham.

In June 2003, his daughters threw him a party for his eightieth birthday. He was very surprised and touched by the people who came—his sisters; his cousin, Arthur, from North Carolina; and Charlie Sheldon, who fished with Sten and Tiggie, came from Seattle. Even his doctors came, the ones who saved his life. His nephew, Charlie, brought lobsters and snow crabs for the gang and helped out in lots of other ways, too. And there was a raw bar with littlenecks and oysters, of course.

Tiggie was hung up on a waitress named Mary at the time. She showed up, and he was so glad she came that he didn't spend as much time with some of the guests as he probably should have. Later, he realized that had been a mistake, but spending time with a pretty girl was part of who he was. He saw people he hadn't seen in years—people who were offshore fishermen or inshore bass fishermen or shellfishermen or freshwater addicts. He had done all those types of fishing. The fishermen came to acknowledge and honor his place in the fishing community, and he was visibly touched. The people assembled there roasted him, too, and that was only fitting, for the man had certainly given grief to many in his life.

Fishing is a hard way to make a living. The work is dangerous and exhausting, and the money, especially in the early days, was barely enough to get by. But Tiggie said that if water is in your veins instead of blood, there's really no better place to spend your life than on the water. He felt he was lucky. He learned that early and stuck with it.

One of his favorite sayings was, "Things are not so bad that they can't get worse," and he believed it. But he had another saying, a more positive one, that I think sums it up better. "Have an idea, and see it through; you'll be amazed at what you can do." He lived by his wits and by hard work. Along the way, he became very good at what he did.

At age 84, he was still telling his stories about a life on the water. There was something compelling about them. Maybe it was that they were timely in reminding us that the fishing industry is not what it once was, timeless about the human condition and nostalgic in the face of tumultuous changes over the course of his life, all at the same time.

We have Tiggie to thank for giving us a glimpse into his world, a world so often closed to those on the outside. He fished offshore at an important time, long gone now, when you needed more than machines to tell you what to do and when to do it. You needed hands-on experience, and you needed courage as well as a love of the sea to get you to where the fish were and safely home again loaded with your fresh catch. By sharing his written stories, he has succeeded in keeping that type of fishing alive for us.

He was a good fisherman. Almost anyone who knows him will say the same thing. He fished when fish were abundant, and he saw the decline in all types of fish stocks. Whether or not fishing survives is a debatable topic, and it will depend on what humans do both onshore and offshore. Tiggie knew that he needed to make a living from harvesting the sea, but he also knew that the sea was finite in its ability to produce. He applauded efforts to curb bad habits or bad practices. He was not perfect, and he sometimes got carried away. But he tried to be a good fisherman in all that that statement implies.

This book was first published in 2005. I asked the owners of the Hole in One if we could do a book signing there and they heartily agreed. It seemed the appropriate venue for the first signing as it was where all the conversations had taken place. They set up a table for us and we did a bit of advertising but most of the 100 or so people who showed up had heard about the event through the grapevine. Tiggie was in his glory, basking in all the attention and showing off his outrageous side. Our next event was at the Yellow Umbrella Bookstore in Chatham and it was a resounding success. He saw people he hadn't seen in years and it was obvious that seeing his stories in print meant a lot to him. It was a joyous occasion. I was glad I had been able to pull it off and get the book published while he was still with us and he loved the admiration it garnered. He attended other events but as attendance dwindled, he couldn't just sit and act nice to people who walked by and didn't buy the book and I finally told him he didn't have to go if he didn't want to – I'd handle it, but it was another sign that he was failing.

I got the message that he had passed just as I was preparing to leave for a trip to Oregon to attend the annual Fisher Poets Gathering where I was to do a couple of readings from the book. The first passage I chose was from the chapter called "Crossing the Bar" and I said that he had just made his final crossing of the bar. The audience knew what I meant. By attending the gathering, I was able to bring his stories to the West Coast and thought he'd be pleased about that.

Spring was coming and that meant that a new breed of fishermen/ farmers would be engaged in aquaculture. They would be setting out their plastic mesh cages or would be anchoring plastic netting on the bottom to protect tiny seed shellfish, purchased from commercial hatcheries, from being consumed by predators. Shellfish aquaculture, mostly for oysters, conducted by the towns in public waters and on privately leased "shellfish grants," has mushroomed on the Cape in recent years, a practice rarely seen in Tiggie's day.

And with any luck, the bass would be back, the schoolies scuttling along the shallow water of Pleasant Bay or on the flats of Cape Cod Bay followed by their mothers and fathers. They would arrive from the Chesapeake and Hudson Rivers to spend the summer as they have done for generations.

Fishermen, commercial and recreational, would try their luck in boats and on the beach, armed with the latest gear, hoping to gain an edge over the guy in the next boat. Many of the recreational fishermen would go to a tackle shop and ask for a tube-and-worm set-up, and someone may say, "Oh, you want a Tig-rig," and the man behind the counter would have to explain what it is, how to use it, and where to go. Maybe he'd even explain where the name of the tackle came from. And then, the generations of fishermen that take Tiggie's place on the water will discover the joy and exasperation of fishing, their experiences becoming the stories of the future. They will be working the edge.

Tiggie told me that he couldn't end his story without thanking me for the work involved in writing this book. In reality, though, it is I who must thank him for allowing me the privilege of telling the tale of an extraordinary fisherman who fished in extraordinary times and who wanted to share his experiences. To me, the stories he told succeeded in preserving the culture of an era along the New England coast.

About the Authors

Tiggie Peluso arrived on Cape Cod in 1946 after serving in the Army in World War II to begin a career in commercial fishing. He became proficient in four separate types of fishing—longlining for cod, haddock, and halibut; shellfishing for scallops, quahogs, and clams; rod-and-reel and fly-fishing for striped bass; and freshwater fishing—an unusual achievement. He was one of the founding members and president of the Chatham Seafood Co-op, the second largest fisherman's cooperative in New England. After twenty-five years of fishing, he dictated stories of his experiences to a secretary who transcribed them. Forty years later, he decided to work with Sandy Macfarlane, a local author, with whom he had shared shellfish experiences—on opposite sides of the law—in the 1970s and '80s.

Sandy Macfarlane spent summers on Cape Cod, moving there permanently after graduation from the University of Massachusetts. She later earned a master's degree in resource management and administration from Antioch New England Graduate School. She became the first municipal shellfish biologist in Massachusetts working in Orleans and the first conservation administrator for the town of Orleans. As a shellfish officer, she enforced shellfish regulations, often butting heads with commercial fishermen like Tiggie. Her first book, *Rowing Forward, Looking Back: Shellfish and the Tides of Change on Cape*

Cod, earned her high praise for her ability to infuse "...personality with science and to demystify the complex biological processes that unfold in the marine environment." She is past president of the New England Estuarine Research Society and a member of the National Shellfisheries Association. After retirement from the town, she founded a consulting company, Coastal Resource Specialists, dealing with shellfish issues. Her collaboration with Tiggie proved to be an ironic twist of fate.

CPSIA information can be obtained at www.ICGtesting.com
Printed in the USA
LVOW061615090212

267951LV00003B/1/P